MALVERN IN 50 BUILDINGS

PAUL HARRIS

AMBERLEY

First published 2025

Amberley Publishing, The Hill, Stroud
Gloucestershire GL5 4EP

www.amberley-books.com

British Library Cataloguing in Publication Data.
A catalogue record for this book is available from the British Library.

ISBN 978 1 3981 2305 2 (print)
ISBN 978 1 3981 2306 9 (ebook)

Typesetting by SJmagic DESIGN SERVICES, India.
Printed in Great Britain.

Appointed GPSR EU Representative: Easy
Access System Europe Oü, 16879218
Address: Mustamäe tee 50, 10621, Tallinn, Estonia
Contact Details: gpsr.requests@easproject.com,
+358 40 500 3575

Contents

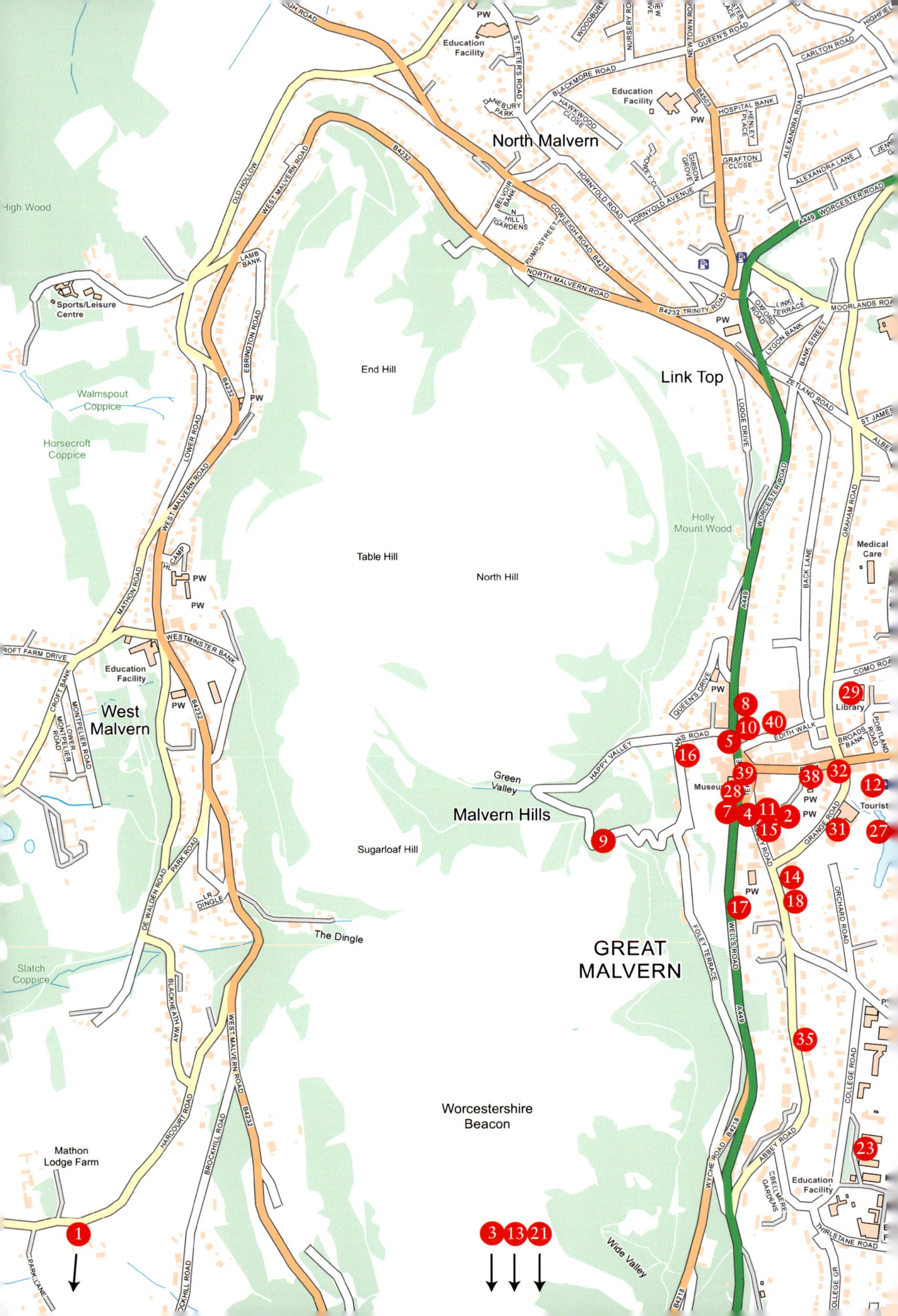

North Malvern
Link Top
West Malvern
GREAT MALVERN
Malvern Hills
End Hill
Table Hill
North Hill
Sugarloaf Hill
Worcestershire Beacon
Green Valley
The Dingle
Wide Valley
High Wood
Walmspout Coppice
Horsecroft Coppice
Slatch Coppice
Holly Mount Wood
Mathon Lodge Farm
Sports/Leisure Centre
Education Facility
Medical Care
Library
Museum
Tourist
PW
West Malvern Road
North Malvern Road
Worcester Road
Wells Road
Wyche Road
Abbey Road
Graham Road
Back Lane
Lodge Drive
Queen's Drive
Happy Valley
Edith Walk
Grange Road
College Road
Orchard Road
Foley Terrace
Bellmere Gardens
Thirlstane Road
Harcourt Road
Brockhill Road
De Walden Road
Blackheath Way
Park Road
Park Lane
Mathon Road
Lower Road
Old Hollow
Lamb Bank
Ebrington Road
Westminster Bank
Croft Bank
Montpelier Road
Lower Montpelier Road
Croft Farm Drive
Cowleigh Road
Pump Street
Belvoir Bank
N Hill Gardens
Hornyold Road
Hornyold Avenue
Gibson Grove
Grafton Close
Hospital Bank
Henley Place
Alexandra Road
Alexandra Lane
Newtown Road
Queen's Road
Carlton Road
Blackmore Road
Hawkwood Close
Danebury Park
St Peter's Road
Nursery Road
Trinity Road
Oxford Road
Link Terrace
Lygon Bank
Bank Street
Moorlands Road
Zetland Road
Como Road
Broads Bank
Portland Road
B4232
B4219
B4503
B4218
A449
1
2
3
4
5
7
8
9
10
11
12
13
14
15
16
17
18
21
23
27
28
29
31
32
35
38
39
40

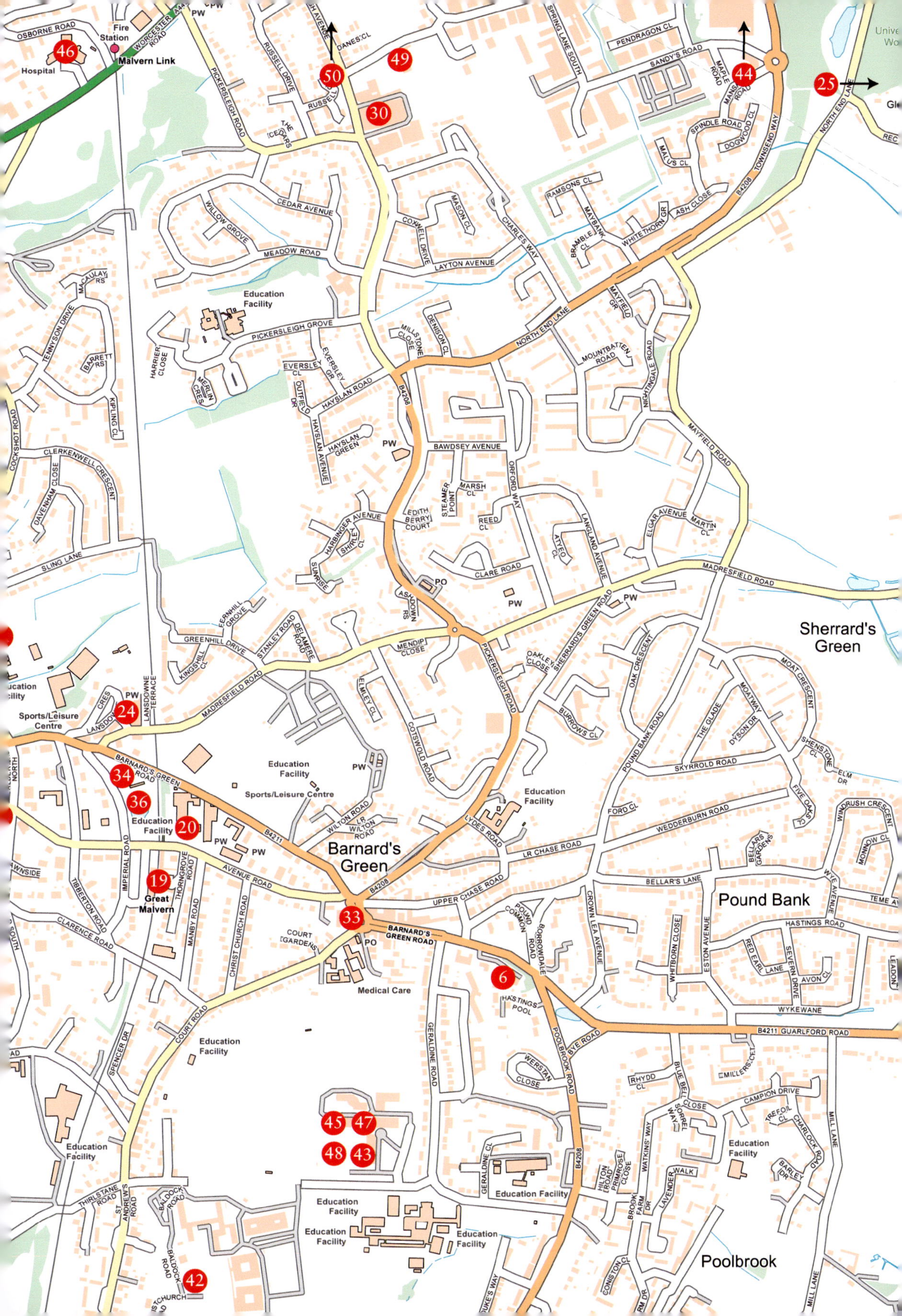

OSBORNE ROAD
46
Hospital
Fire Station
WORCESTER ROAD
Malvern Link
PW
PICKERSLEIGH ROAD
RUSSELL DRIVE
DANES CL
49
50
RUSSELL
30
THE CEDARS
SPRING LANE SOUTH
PENDRAGON CL
SANDY'S ROAD
MAPLE ROAD
44
25
MANOR ROAD
SPINDLE ROAD
DOGWOOD CL
MALUS CL
NORTH END LANE
TOWNSEND WAY
B4208
CEDAR AVENUE
WILLOW GROVE
MEADOW ROAD
COXWELL DRIVE
MASON CL
CHARLES WAY
RAMSONS CL
MAYBANK
BRAMBLE CL
WHITETHORN GR
ASH CLOSE
LAYTON AVENUE
MACAULAY RS
Education Facility
TENNYSON DRIVE
BARRETT RS
KIPLING CL
HARRIER CLOSE
MERLIN CRES
PICKERSLEIGH GROVE
EVERSLEY CL
EVERSLEY GR
OUTFIELD DR
HAYSLAN ROAD
HAYSLAN AVENUE
HAYSLAN GREEN
MILLSTONE CLOSE
DENISON CL
MAYFIELD GR
MOUNTBATTEN ROAD
NIGHTINGALE ROAD
MAYFIELD ROAD
COCKSHOT ROAD
CLERKENWELL CRESCENT
DAVENHAM CLOSE
BAWDSEY AVENUE
STEAMER POINT
MARSH CL
ORFORD WAY
REED CL
EDITH BERRY COURT
HARBINGER AVENUE
SHIRLEY CL
SUNRISE
ATYEO CL
LANGLAND AVENUE
ELGAR AVENUE
MARTIN CL
CLARE ROAD
PO
SLING LANE
MADRESFIELD ROAD
Sherrard's Green
ASHDOWN RS
FERNHILL GROVE
GREENHILL DRIVE
KINGSHILL CL
STANLEY ROAD
DELAMERE ROAD
MENDIP CLOSE
OAKLEY CLOSE
SHERRARD'S GREEN ROAD
OAK CRESCENT
MOAT CRESCENT
MOATWAY
THE GLADE
DYSON DR
SHENSTONE CL
ELM DR
Sports/Leisure Centre
24
LANSDOWNE TERRACE
LANSDOWNE CRES
ELMLEY CL
COTSWOLD ROAD
BURROWS CL
POUND BANK ROAD
SKYRROLD ROAD
FIVE OAKS CL
WINDRUSH CRESCENT
BARNARD'S GREEN ROAD
34
36
20
NORTH
Education Facility
Sports/Leisure Centre
WILTON ROAD
LR WILTON ROAD
LYDES ROAD
FORD CL
WEDDERBURN ROAD
LR CHASE ROAD
BELLARS GARDENS
MONNOW CL
B4211
Barnard's Green
AVENUE ROAD
IMPERIAL ROAD
THORNGROVE ROAD
LAWNSIDE
19
Great Malvern
TIBBERTON ROAD
CLARENCE ROAD
MANBY ROAD
CHRIST CHURCH ROAD
33
UPPER CHASE ROAD
POUND COMMON ROAD
BORROWDALE
CROWN LEA AVENUE
BELLAR'S LANE
Pound Bank
WYE AVENUE
TEME AV
HASTINGS ROAD
WHITBORN CLOSE
ESTON AVENUE
RED EARL LANE
SEVERN DRIVE
AVON CL
LEADON
COURT GARDENS
Medical Care
6
HASTINGS POOL
WYKEWANE
GERALDINE ROAD
POOLBROOK ROAD
BYE ROAD
B4211 GUARLFORD ROAD
COURT ROAD
SPENCER DR
WERSTAN CLOSE
RHYDD CL
BLUE BELL CLOSE
SORREL WAY
MILLERS CT
CAMPION DRIVE
TREFOIL CL
CHARLOCK ROAD
MILL LANE
45
47
48
43
WATKINS' WAY
GERALDINE CL
HILTON ROAD
PRIMROSE CLOSE
LAVENDER WALK
BARLEY DR
THIRLSTANE ROAD
ST. ANDREW'S ROAD
BALDOCK ROAD
BROOK FARM DR
CONISTON CL
Poolbrook
42
DUKE'S WAY

Key

1. British Camp
2. Great Malvern Priory
3. Little Malvern Priory and Court
4. The Priory Gatehouse
5. The Unicorn
6. Hastings House
7. The Mount Pleasant Hotel
8. The Foley Arms Hotel
9. St Ann's Well
10. Royal Library and Assembly Rooms (former)
11. No. 23 Abbey Road
12. The Coach House Theatre
13. Holy Well
14. Park View
15. The Abbey Hotel
16. Aldwyn Tower
17. Tudor House
18. Malvern House
19. Great Malvern Station
20. Malvern St. James Girls School
21. St Wulstan's Church
22. Elmslie House
23. Malvern College
24. Wesleyan Methodist Church
25. Madresfield Court
26. The Council House
27. The Bandstand
28. Lloyds Bank
29. Malvern Public Library
30. Morgan Motor Company
31. Malvern Theatres
32. The Water Cure
33. War Memorial Bus Shelter
34. Hatfield House
35. Hardwicke House
36. The Edinburgh Dome
37. Malvern Splash
38. The Lyttelton Well
39. Belle Vue Island
40. The Theatre of Small Convenience
41. Malvern Cube Community and Arts Centre
42. Malvern Technology Centre/QinetiQ
43. Malvern Hills Science Park, Phases One and Two
44. The Malvern
45. Malvern Hills Science Park, Phase Three
46. Malvern Community Hospital
47. Malvern Hills Science Park, Phase Four
48. Malvern Hills Science Park, Phase Five
49. Morgan Experience Centre
50. The Community Hub

Introduction

The name 'Malvern' comes from the Welsh *moel* meaning 'bare' and *'bryn'* meaning 'hill'. '*Moelbryn*' had by the time of the Domesday Book gradually changed to become Malferna and of course subsequently to 'Malvern'. Those 'bare hills' made excellent sites for hill forts and settlements and beacons, hence the signs of early occupation upon their slopes and summits. The hills also spouted a great many springs of clear pure water, which encouraged settlement on the lower slopes. A scattering of villages around the Malvern Hills were encouraged in their growth from the medieval period onwards by a substantial ecclesiastical presence, notably in the form of Great Malvern and Little Malvern priories. It was in the eighteenth and nineteenth centuries, however, that the town we see today developed, largely as a result of the quality of its pure drinking water.

By the mid-nineteenth century Malvern was a 'boom' town as a result of the setting up of a large number of 'water cure' establishments that provided courses of treatment mostly involving the drinking of and frequent immersion in the cold spring water coming from the hills. The 'water cure' fell out of fashion by the early twentieth century but the town had become quite a well-to-do place as a result of its spa status and hosted many quality educational establishments and cultural events. Many famous names are associated with Malvern from this time, most notably the composer Sir Edward Elgar, authors C. S. Lewis and J. R. R. Tolkien, and artist Dame Laura Knight. Malvern has a history of scientific and technological innovation, from the introduction of the astrolabe in the medieval period to the creation of the first British motor car, the Santler, and subsequent development of the world-famous Morgan range of cars from the early twentieth century and still going strong today.

The Second World War brought a wave of scientific and technological experts to work and live in Malvern, whose endeavours led initially to the development of radar, radio astronomy and, more recently, touchscreens and LED displays among many other innovations. The scientific and particularly IT and cyber security

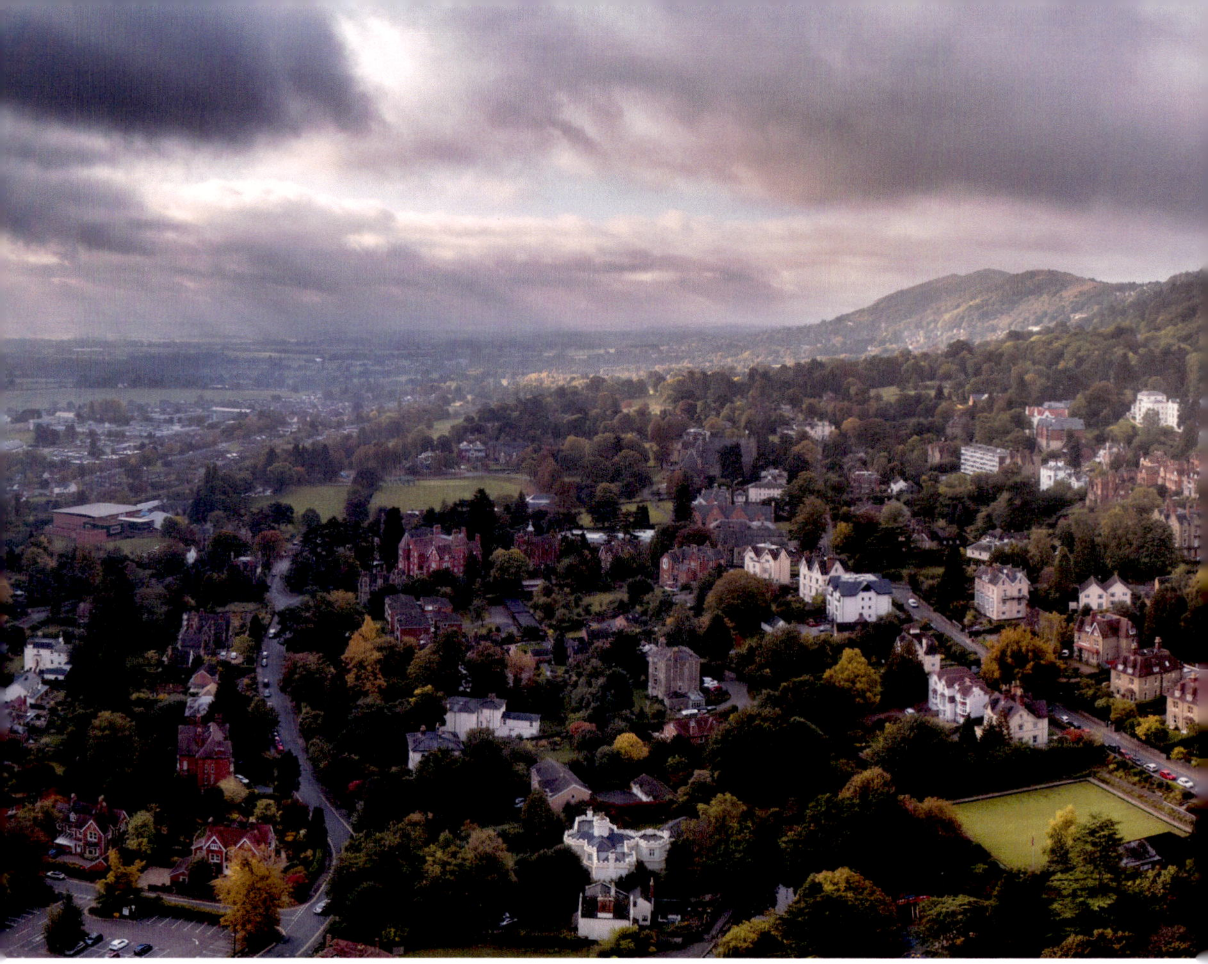

Great Malvern from the air. (© Jan Sedlacek @Digitlight)

fields have become increasingly important for the town, which seems to have successfully evolved with changing times.

I first visited Malvern back in 1975 with my father, who was using a family holiday to revisit Malvern where he had previously been during the Second World War. I have since learned this was probably at HMS Duke. I remember the steep walk up Happy Valley and the hike over the majestic hills that was 'rudely' interrupted by the close flyover of a number of Royal Air Force jets, no doubt on a training exercise.

It was many years later when I returned, this time with my partner, Candida. We were breaking a journey to Wales with a stopover in Malvern overnight, having decided to stay here after reading an article about the town in the *People's Friend* magazine. To say I was impressed would be an understatement. The cluster of historic buildings around the Abbey Hotel where we stayed, the hike up to St Ann's Well, the views across the town and the Vale of Evesham, Belle Vue Island with its Malvhina spout, and the town's connections with so many notable and creative people all served to inspire me to make this the subject of my next book. Having just had published

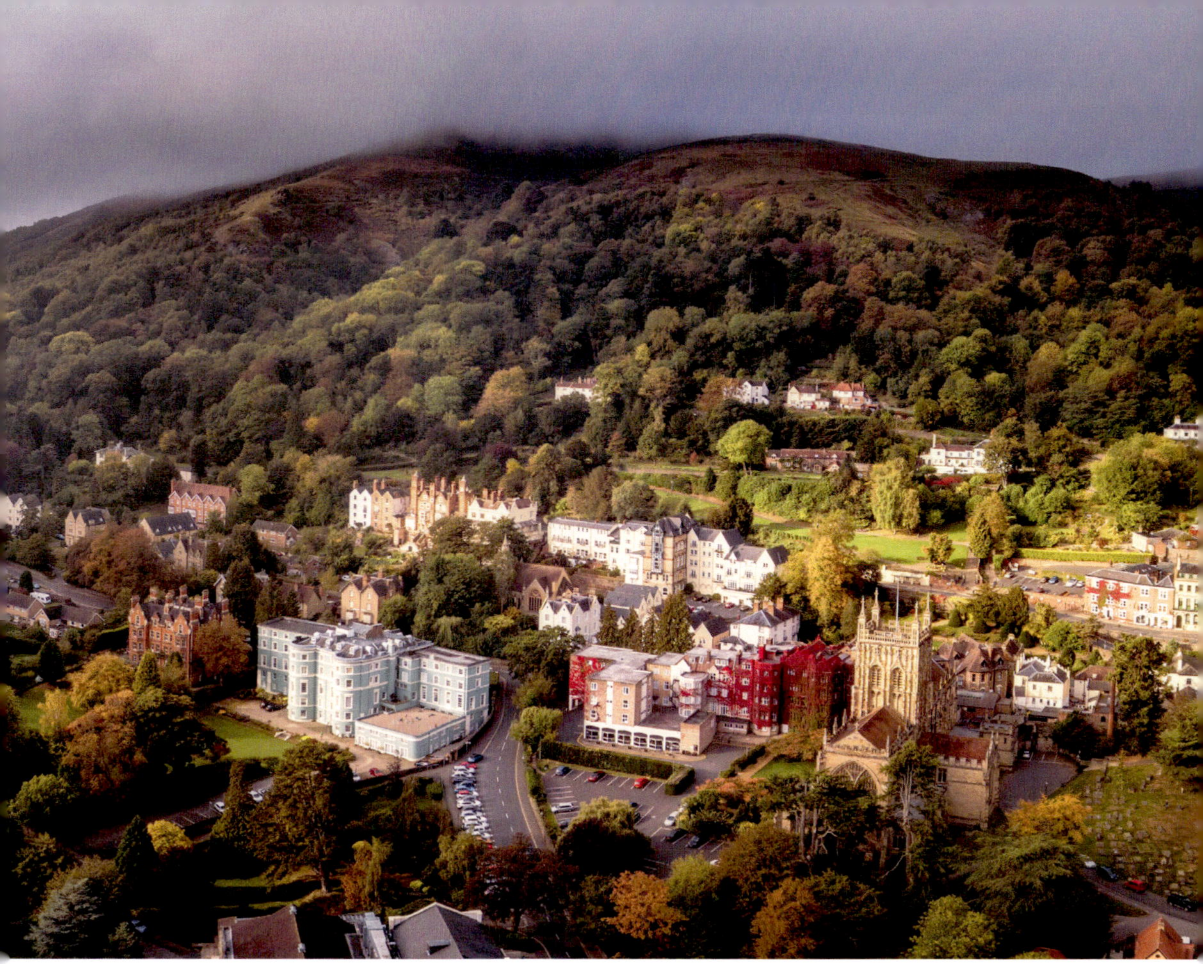

Dover in 50 Buildings the previous month it seemed Malvern would make an excellent next project in the series, and a good excuse to return on subsequent occasions and explore further.

The various stages of Malvern's history have each left a rich legacy of interesting buildings from an Iron Age hill fort, through the medieval period evidenced by the priories, to the hydropathic establishments and educational, cultural and commercial buildings of more recent times.

I hope my choice of fifty buildings proves interesting to readers – each has its own story. Some of the buildings chosen may have historical importance, some are particularly architecturally significant or have literary, cultural, commercial or scientific dimensions to their heritage.

With any compilation of this sort, facts and details are sometimes disputed and unintentional mistakes made. If you notice any errors or omissions, please contact the author or publisher and we will endeavour to put things right in a future edition. So, without further ado, let's embark on our journey through Malvern's history as visible through its current built environment.

Paul Harris

The 50 Buildings

1. British Camp (*c.* 200 BC), Herefordshire Beacon, Accessible from Malvern Hills Hotel, Jubilee Drive, Wynds Point, Great Malvern, WR13 6DW

Probably one of the finest examples of an Iron Age hill fort in England, British Camp dominates the skyline of the hill known as the Herefordshire Beacon.

The fort covers some 32 acres and consists of a number of embankments and ditches surrounding an area that once enclosed a large number of both rectangular and round hut dwellings, estimated to have housed around 2,000 people.

Archaeological investigations and surveys have been carried out from time to time, most notably in 1869, 1879 and in 2000, the latter undertaken by English Heritage. It is not yet clear whether British Camp was occupied on a long-term

British Camp. (© Jan Sedlacek @Digitlight)

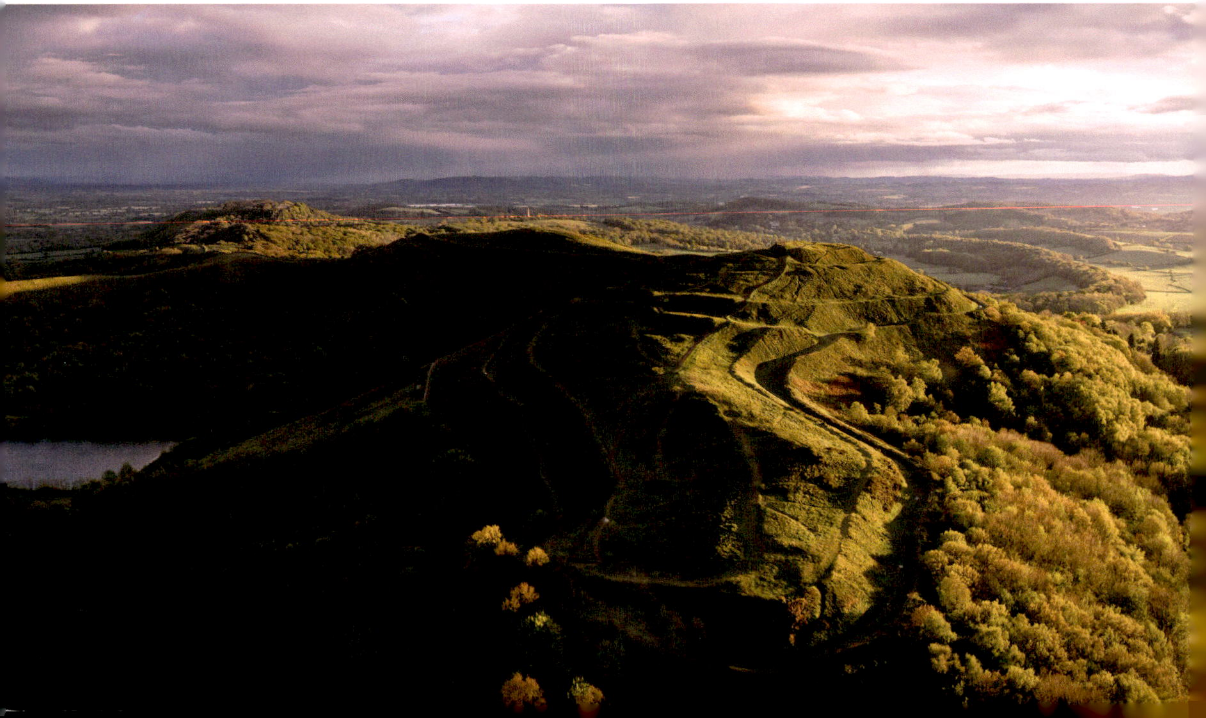

basis as a viable settlement or just temporarily, perhaps during seasonal festivals or as a refuge in times of trouble. It is believed by some that this hill fort was one of the last of such British bastions to hold out against the Romans during Caesar's initial invasions of 55 and 54 BC. Local legend has this as where King Caractacus made his last stand against the Romans, though as far as I know no evidence of this has been forthcoming.

During the medieval period a Norman ring and bailey fort was built within the hill fort defences. This was relatively short-lived and destroyed apparently by Henry II in 1155.

In more recent times a hotel was established nearby, now known as the Malvern Hills Hotel. This was famously inhabited by war artist Laura Knight (the first female member of the Royal Academy) between 1940 and 1944. Today the British Camp site is recognised as a Scheduled Ancient Monument and is owned and maintained by the Malvern Hills Conservators.

2. Great Malvern Priory (1085 to Mid-fifteenth Century), Church Street, Great Malvern, WR14 2AY

The priory was founded by a Worcester monk named Aldwin, who had been directed and supported by Wulstan, the then Bishop of Worcester, in 1085. With a group of about thirty monks Aldwin set about building the original priory, which would have been a much simpler affair than that which we see today, and functioned as a Benedictine monastery under the directorship of Westminster Abbey. In 1120 a new prior named Walcher was installed. He came from Lorrain, which is now in France but was at the time an independent kingdom. Walcher was a learned man and introduced the Arabic system of numerals to this country, as well as the use of degrees to describe geometric angles. He died in 1135 and the inscription on his tomb describes him as a 'Philosopher, and able Astrologer, a Geometrician and Mathematician, a pious Christian and humble monk'.

Great Malvern Priory functioned well for over 450 years as a centre for religious observance but also as an important pastoral centre for the local population, providing medical treatment and back up food supplies, as well as accommodation for the passing traveller. The period from 1430 to 1502 saw major improvements and additions to the priory both inside and out. Rebuilding included the use of coloured sandstone blocks, which are particularly evident in the Perpendicular-style towers.

Misericords were installed to ease the discomfort of the monks having to stand at prayer for long periods. These have all been decorated with fine wood carvings showing a variety of mythological creatures, domestic scenes and the labours of the monks. One particular carving is believed to be the earliest depiction of urinoscopy (diagnosis by urine sample). There is also a large collection of

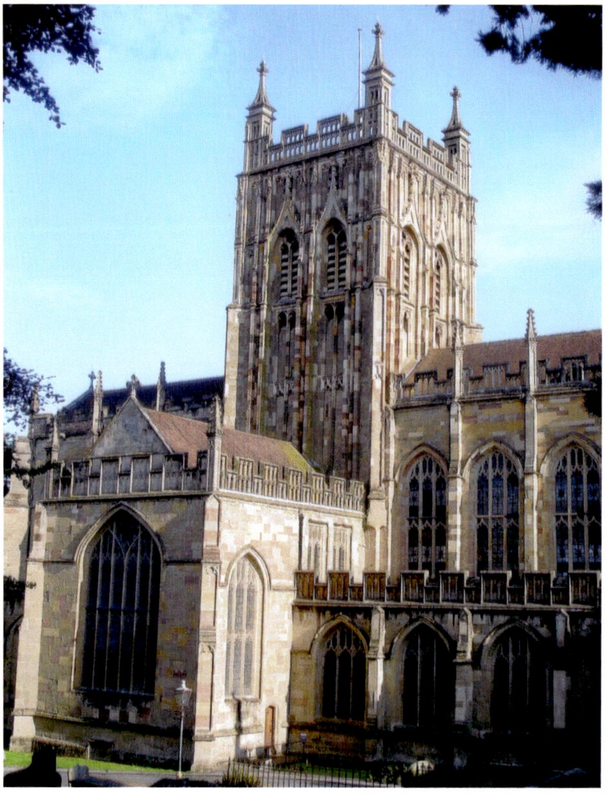

Left: Great Malvern Priory.

Below: Priory Tower showing coloured sandstone blocks.

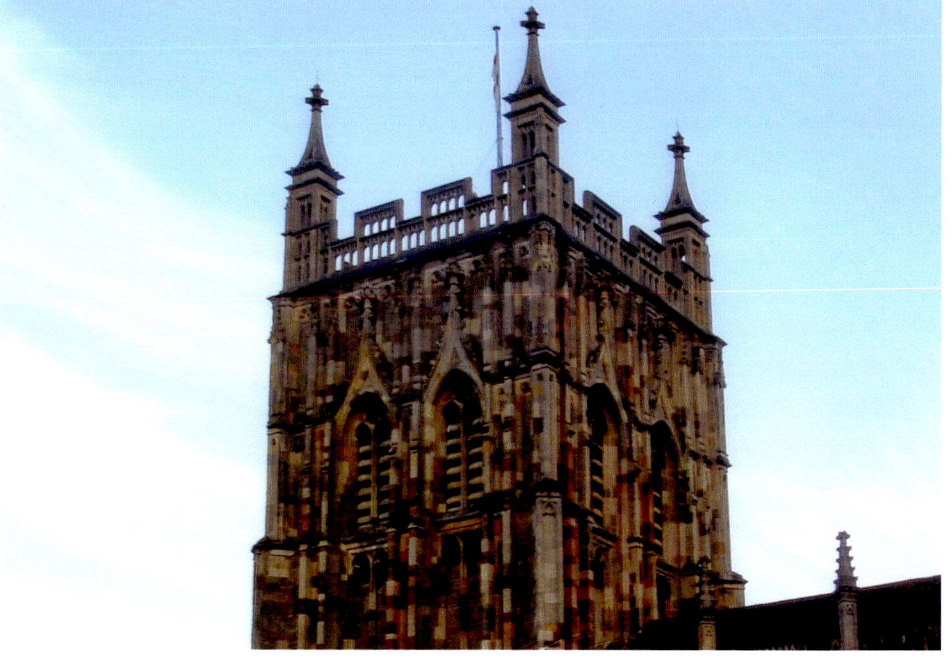

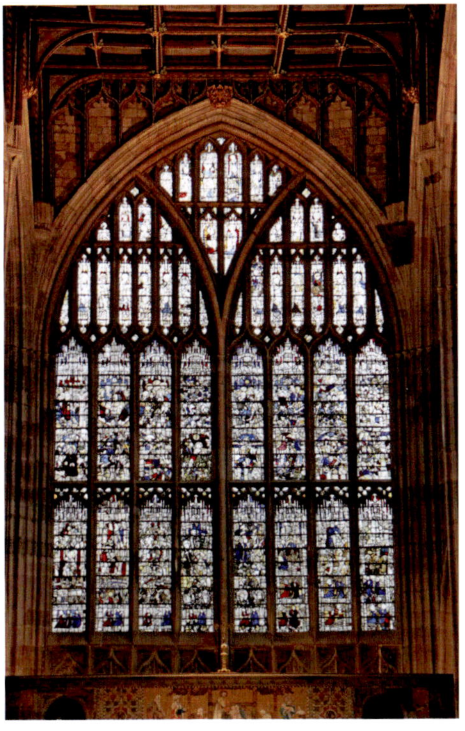

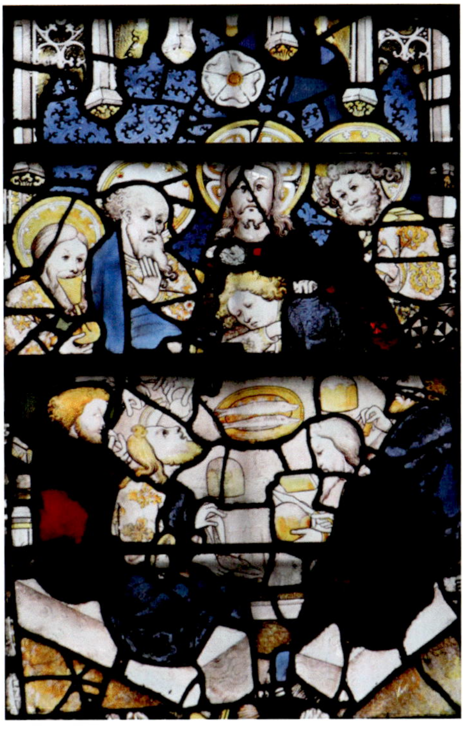

Above left: East window, Malvern Priory. (© Katherine Little)

Above right: The Last Supper (detail from east window). (© Katherine Little)

Right: Magnificat Window, Malvern Priory. (© Katherine Little)

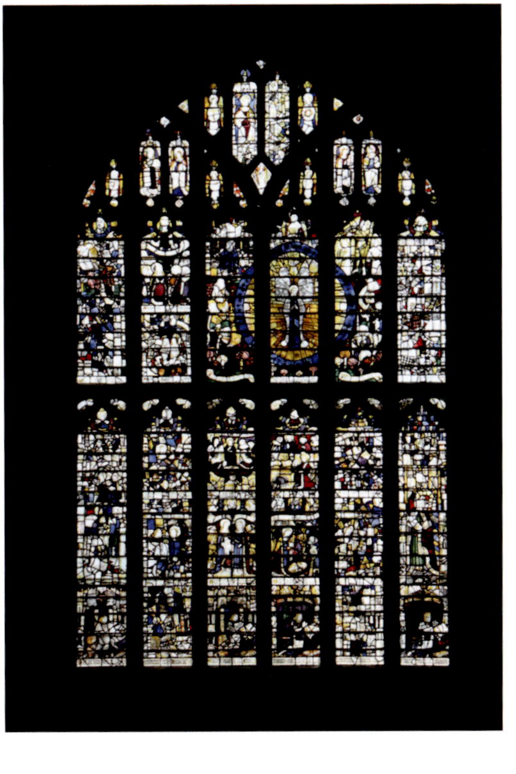

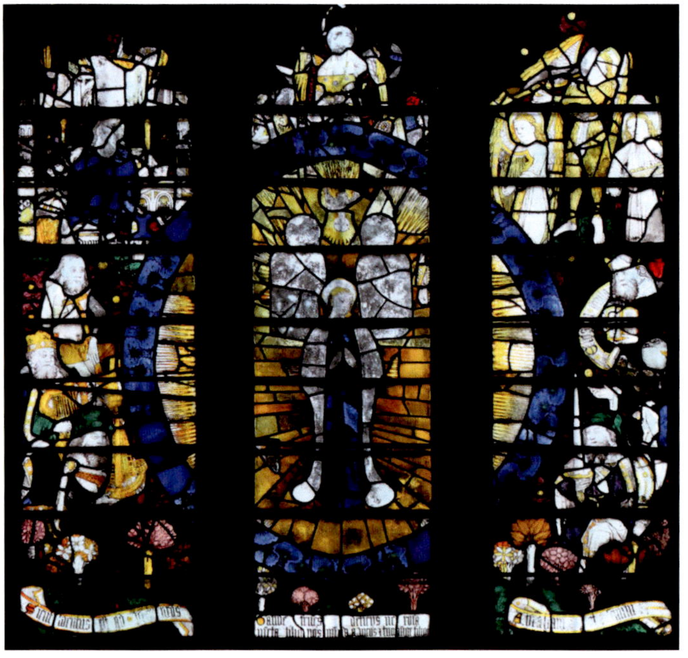

The Coronation of Mary (details from Magnificat Window). (© Katherine Little)

locally made fifteenth-century tiles to be seen in the church. The most impressive example of fifteenth-century restoration work though is perhaps the priory's stained glass. Malvern Priory contains the most complete and extensive examples of fifteenth-century stained glass of any English parish church. The great east window is particularly impressive as is the Magnificat window, which was given to the priory by Henry VII in 1502.

The Benedictine Priory of Great Malvern was forced to close in 1539 as part of Henry VIII's Dissolution of the Monasteries. The priory church, however, survived because the local villagers managed to raise £20 to buy the church so that it could continue as a place of worship. Since then, the church has functioned as the parish church for Malvern and had further much needed restoration work carried out, most notably by Gilbert Scott in the 1860s. More recent additions to the priory church include the two Millennium windows, modern stained glass by Thomas Denny, installed in 2004, and an astrolabe inspired candlestand by artist Mathew Galpin installed in the north aisle in 2007. An astrolabe is an ancient astronomical instrument used in navigation and time telling and first introduced to the western world by Malvern's second prior, Walcher, in 1092 or earlier.

The priory churchyard contains the grave of Charles Darwin's daughter Annie, who came to Malvern for the 'water cure' but sadly died of tuberculosis. The churchyard is also graced with a number of impressive trees including yews, cedars and a very tall Wellingtonia or Sequoia gigantea. Above the entrance to the priory church is a fine statue of S. Mary with the baby Jesus.

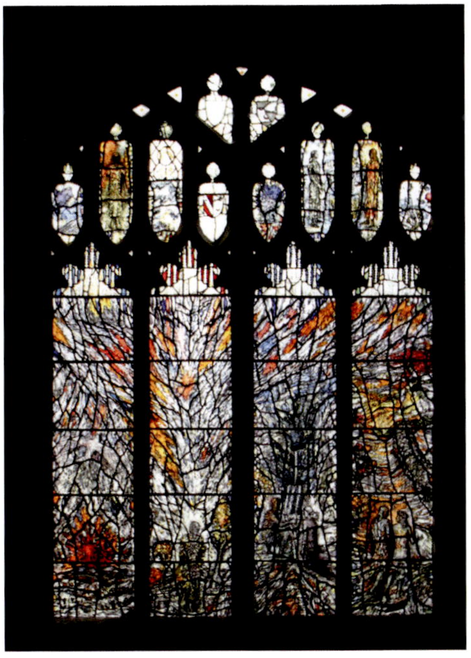

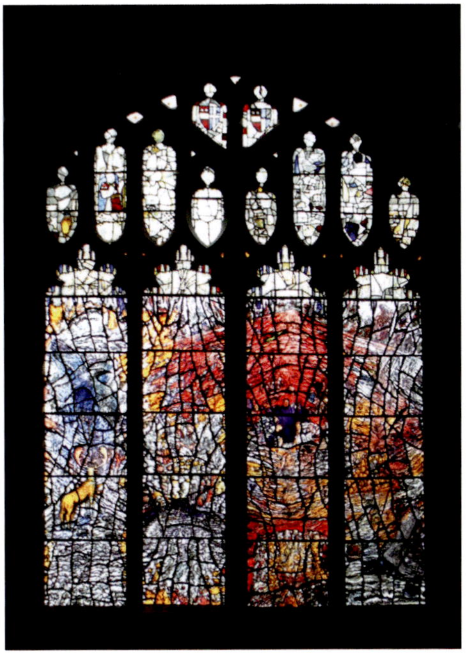

Above left and above right: The Millennium Windows, Malvern Priory. (© Katherine Little)

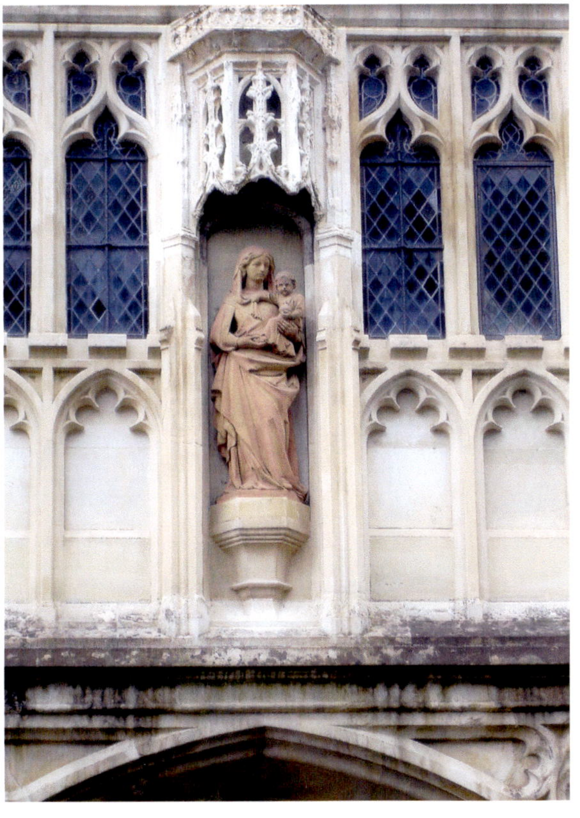

Right: Statue of St Mary and baby Jesus above main entrance, Malvern Priory.

3. Little Malvern Priory and Court (1171), No. 45 Wye Way, Little Malvern, Malvern, WR14 4JN

Little Malvern Priory was founded as a Benedictine community by monks from Worcester Cathedral around 1171, though it is possible it may have existed a little earlier. The former priory has a literary claim to fame in that it is widely believed that the poet William Langland was probably educated here in the mid-fourteenth century. Later when he returned to London, he wrote the monumental work *The Vision of Piers Plowman*, in which his main character Will, out walking in the Malvern Hills one spring morning, becomes weary and, resting by a stream, experiences a dream vision encompassing a range of theological, political and satirical issues, which he commits to a poem of extraordinary length and complexity – it's not a light read!

The late fifteenth century saw the rebuilding of the twelfth-century church and the development of the Priors' Hall and its associated rooms and cells. Then a few decades later the monastery was closed and some of its buildings demolished on the orders of Henry VIII as part of his Dissolution process.

The Berrington family purchased what was left of the monastic buildings and created the manor house of Little Malvern Court created from the Prior's Hall and cloisters. The monastic grounds became the gardens for the new court.

Little Malvern Priory. (By kind permission of Sue Johnson and Alison Hunka)

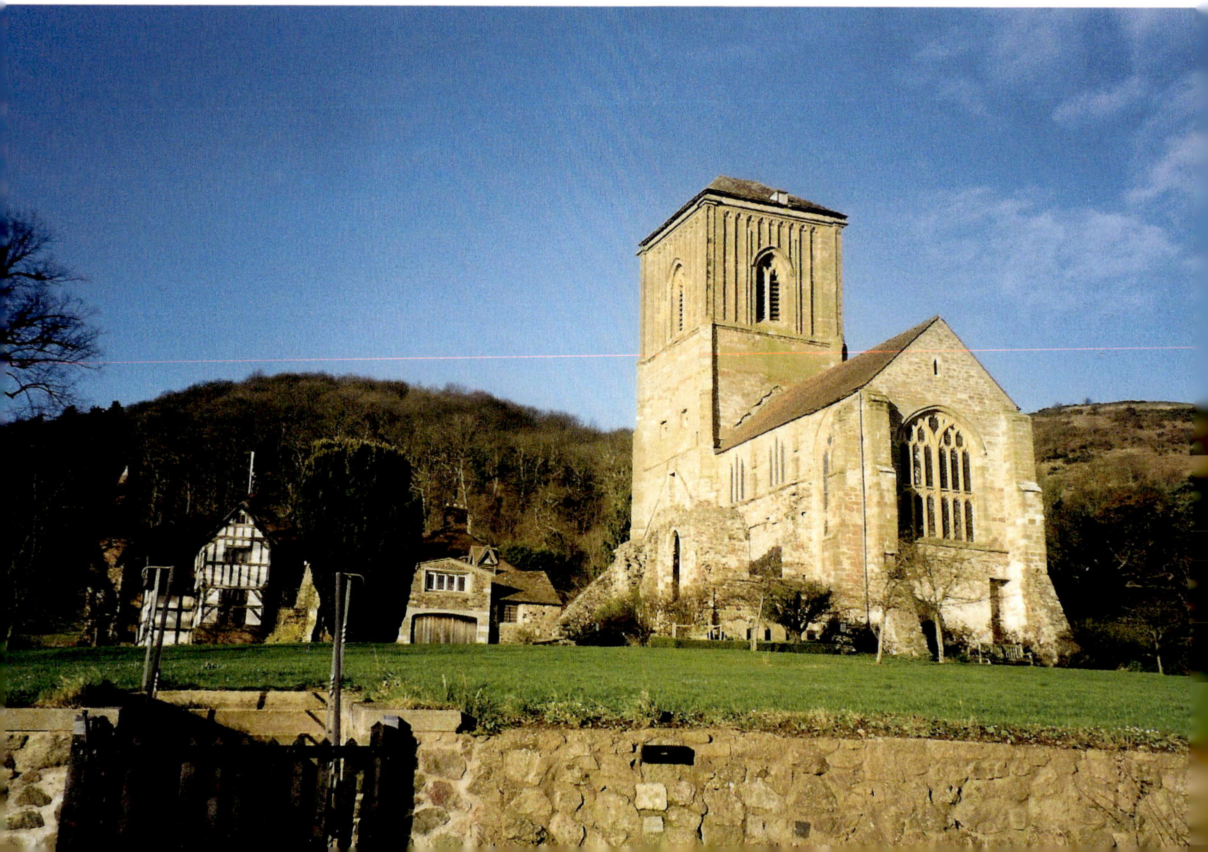

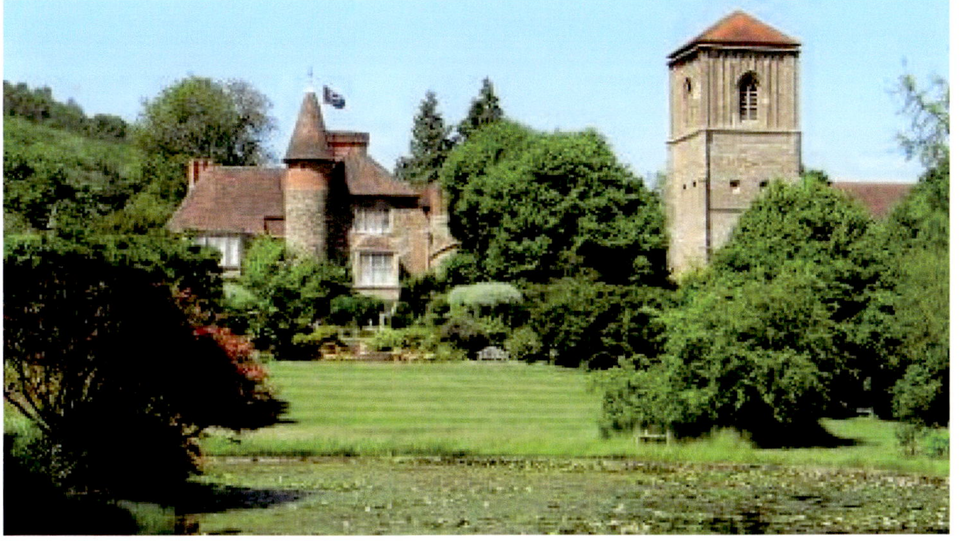

Little Malvern Court. (Photo by David Adams)

Some Victorian restoration was carried out including the topping of the little tower in the court, which contains a spiral staircase, with a conical roof giving it a Gothic feel.

Today the Priory Church of St Giles and the more recently developed Little Malvern Court are all that remain of the former priory. Restoration of the buildings was carried out by the Berrington family in the 1960s and the gardens fully restored in the early 1980s. Both the St Giles' Church tower and Little Malvern Court are Grade I listed buildings and are open to the public to a limited extent, though the attractive gardens are open most days. It's best to check the relevant website for details of opening days and times.

4. The Priory Gatehouse (1480), Abbey Road, Great Malvern, WR14 3ES

The gatehouse was the original entrance to the Great Malvern Benedictine monastery. Following the Dissolution of the Monasteries by Henry VIII in 1539 the gatehouse was sold to the Mason family. In around 1560 some restoration was carried out, and the red-brick south-facing wall of the gatehouse dates to this time. Since then the building has had many uses including as a magistrates' court, a fruit, veg and game shop, an estate agent and architects' office. For a time, the nearby Abbey Hotel used the gatehouse as accommodation for some of its staff.

The artist J. M. W. Turner produced a watercolour called *Great Malvern Priory and Gatehouse* in around 1830. In 1891 the north side of the gatehouse was restored, elaborately panelled and refaced by Nevinson and Newton. This is the north face we see today.

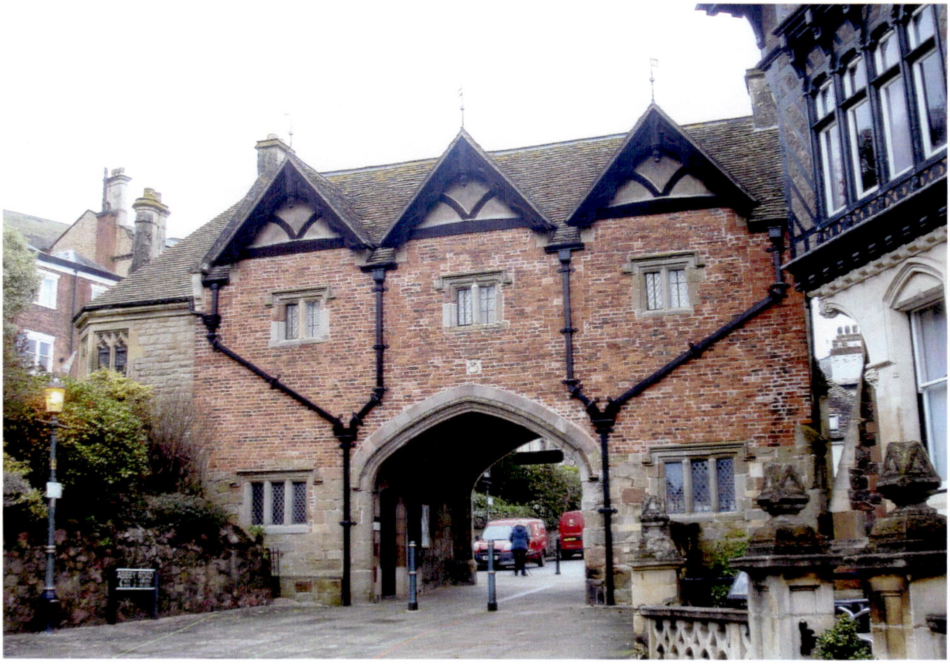

The Priory Gatehouse from the south.

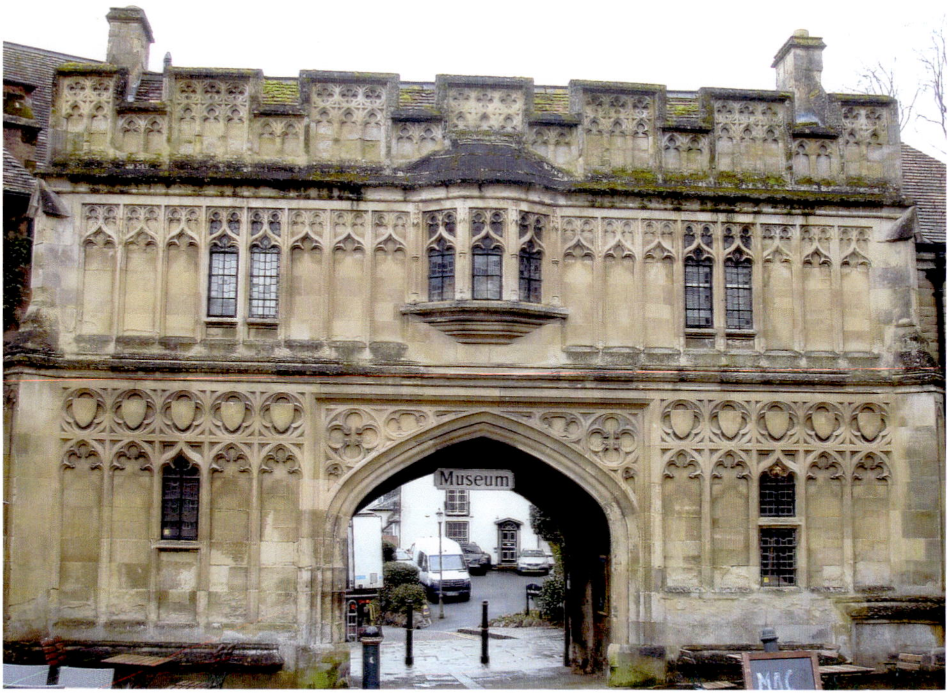

The Priory Gatehouse from the north.

For many years traffic flowed freely along Abbey Road and through the narrow archway of the gatehouse until one day in 1979 an ice cream van got stuck, causing damage to the arch in the process. After this the road under the archway was closed to traffic and the building was occupied from 1980 onwards by the Malvern Museum of Local History. Still going strong after more than four decades, this excellent facility can tell you entertainingly all about Malvern's geology, archaeology, Benedictine Priory, 'water cure', Victorian development, Sir Edward Elgar, the development of radar, the steam-driven Santler car and its Morgan successors and much else – it is highly recommended! The museum is open from April to October. The Priory Gatehouse is currently a Grade II* listed building.

5. The Unicorn (*c.* 1500s), No. 2 Belle Vue Terrace, Great Malvern, WR14 4PZ

One of the oldest buildings in Malvern and the third oldest in Great Malvern (after the priory church and gatehouse). This was once a staging post on the Ledbury to Worcester Road. By *c.* 1550 it was already marked as 'Le Taverne' on village maps and has continued in that use ever since.

The Unicorn's particular claim to fame is that it was used regularly by author C. S. Lewis, who would meet his friends here, perhaps before or after their walks up the steep road into the Malvern Hills. C. S. Lewis is best known for his series of children's books on Narnia, an imaginary land entered initially by the children in the story by way of the back of a wardrobe. *The Lion, the Witch and the Wardrobe* was the first in the Narnia series of books and has since been made into both a television series and more recently a big screen cinema production. In the

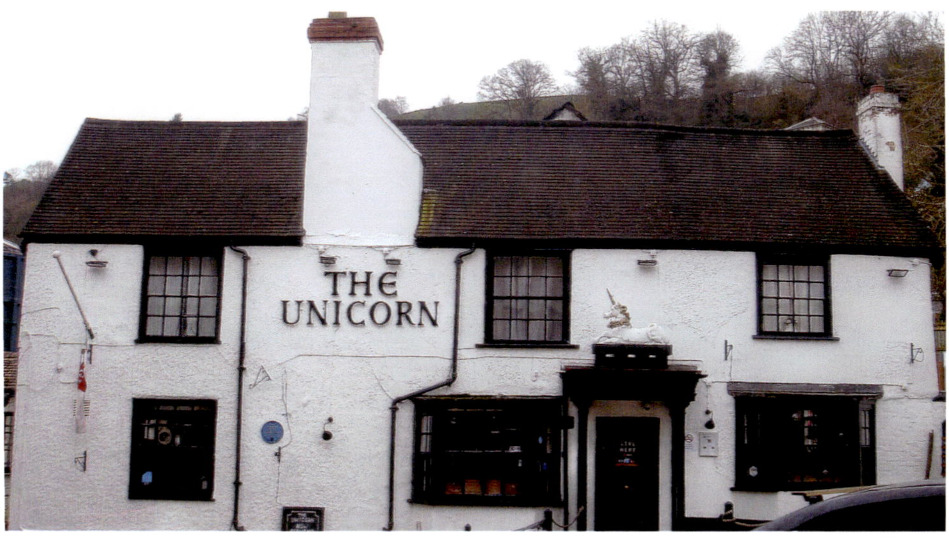

The Unicorn public house in Great Malvern.

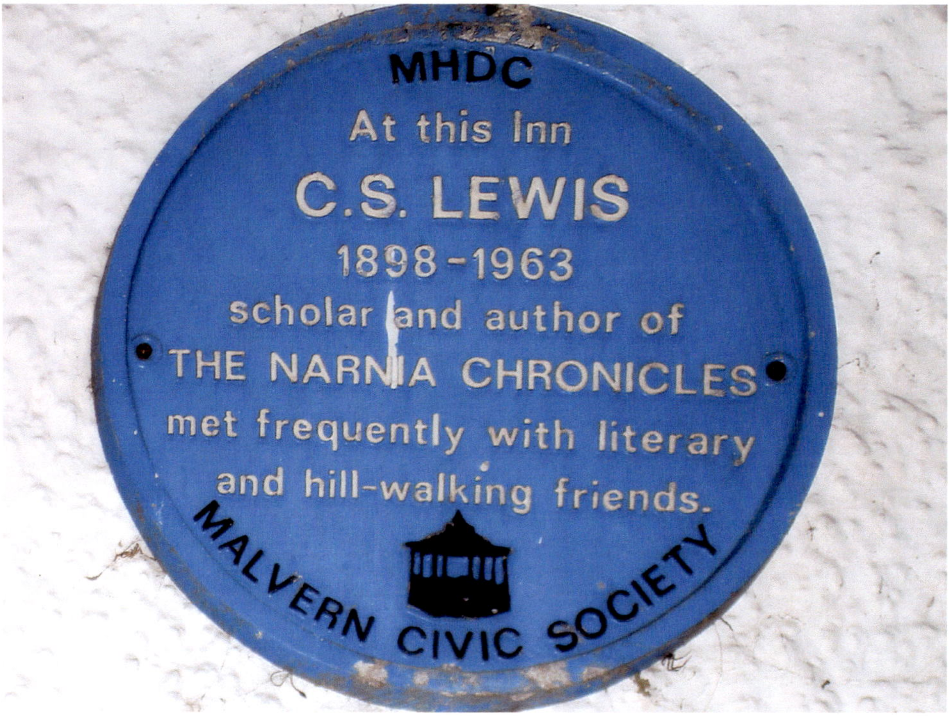

Blue plaque for C. S. Lewis at The Unicorn Inn.

stories an old-style gas lamp features at the entrance to Narnia. As Malvern has numerous such lamps, many still working, it has been assumed that they inspired the use of one in his stories, but apparently this was not so, at least not consciously.

C. S. Lewis is remembered as a children's author but did write for an adult audience as well, *The Screwtape Letters* and *That Hideous Strength* being examples. I was most impressed by his interplanetary adventures *Out of the Silent Planet* and *Voyage to Venus*, which seemed to me more imaginative and wonderful than many more modern science fiction novels.

The Unicorn was the venue for Lewis' meetings with his close friends, George Sayer, who lived in Malvern, and J. R. R. Tolkien, who travelled from Oxford. Some of Tolkien's locations in his books on Middle Earth; *The Hobbit* and *Lord of the Rings* are thought to have been inspired by the three friends walking expeditions in the Malvern Hills. Certainly, Tolkien was reminded of some of the scenes from his books during his walks in the Malverns but the original inspiration for his locations were various places elsewhere including the Swiss Alps, according to local author Peter Smith, who has discussed this issue with George Sayer in the past. Apart from its literary connections The Unicorn is interesting because of the age of the building and of course its convenient location at the bottom of the steep road that leads up into the Malvern Hills, a good starting or stopping point for welcome refreshment. The Unicorn is a Grade II listed building.

6. Hastings House (1635), No. 10 Poolbrook Road, Malvern, WR14 3NQ

This is one of the oldest houses in Malvern dating from a time when the current town was just a collection of villages. This beautiful house with stuccoed exterior, three wide bays and a pedimented Tuscan porch is believed to date from 1635.

On the outside wall is a blue plaque noting that a one-time resident of the property was Sir Charles Hastings, the medical surgeon who founded the British

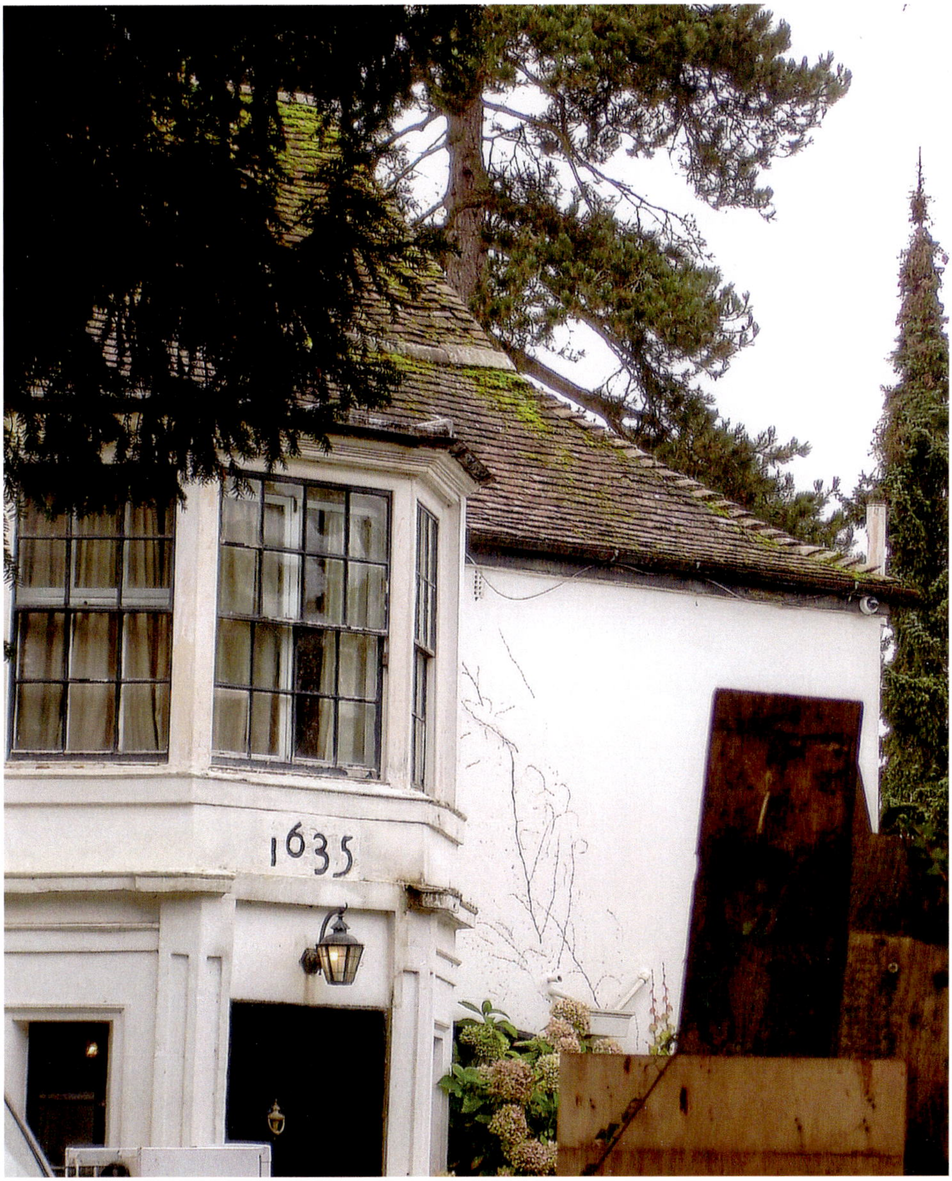

Hastings House, Barnards Green.

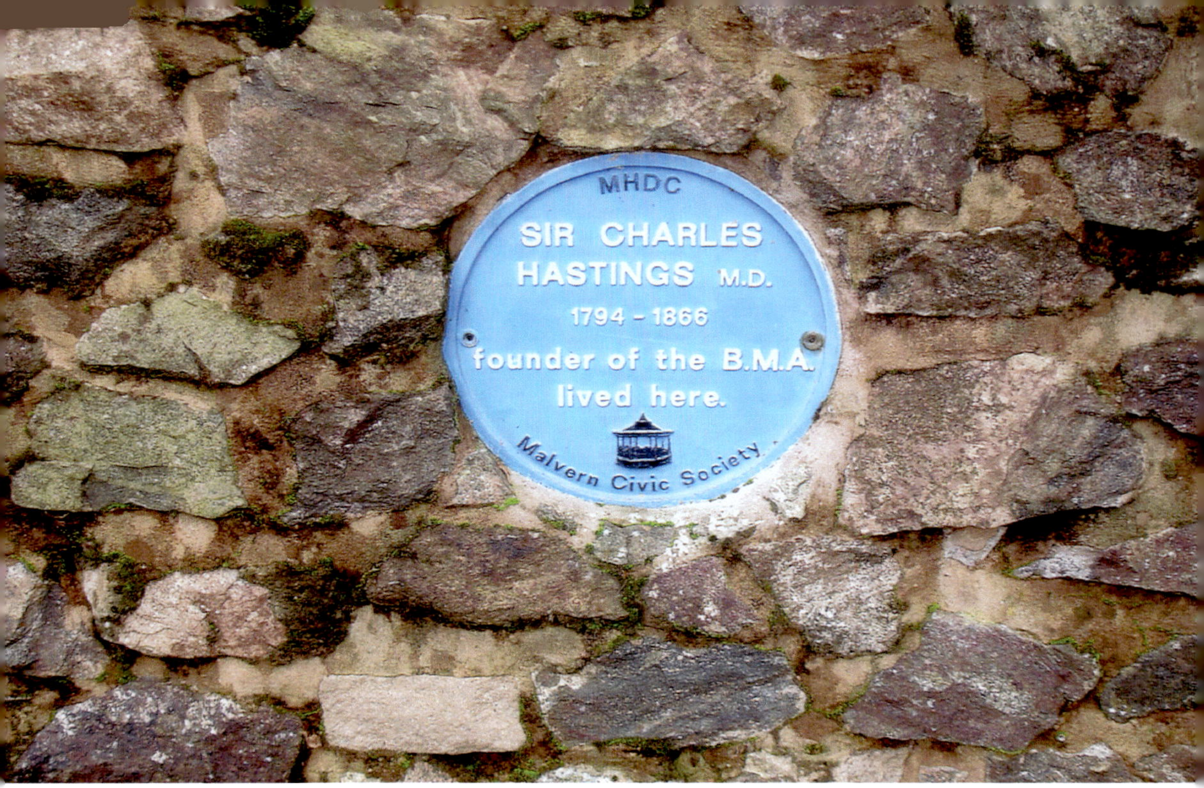

Blue plaque commemorating Sir Charles Hastings.

Medical Association and spent his final years at Barnards Green House. Sir Charles long advocated a partnership between the state and medical services and might have been heartened by the establishment of the National Health Service some eighty years after his death in 1866 at the age of seventy-two. He also founded Worcester Museum of Natural History and was knighted by Queen Victoria in 1850. Hastings House is a Grade II listed property.

7. The Mount Pleasant Hotel (1790), No. 50 Belle Vue Terrace, Great Malvern, WR14 4PZ

This fine Georgian building is variously dated; Pevsner thinks around 1790, while Historic England estimates around 1816. The summerhouse and orangery date to 1816 it seems. The spout and basin build into the garden wall at the side of the Mount Pleasant Hotel were installed here in 1892, having previously been situated at St Ann's Well, up the hill behind Great Malvern.

A blue plaque at the Mount Pleasant Hotel commemorates the presence here of Dame Laura Knight, one of the most distinguished female artists of the twentieth century. She moved to Malvern from London at the start of the Second World War and initially stayed at the Mount Pleasant Hotel, producing some notable works whilst there. These *included Love Lane* (a view of Happy Valley), *Holiday Time* (a view from the hotel window showing people enjoying

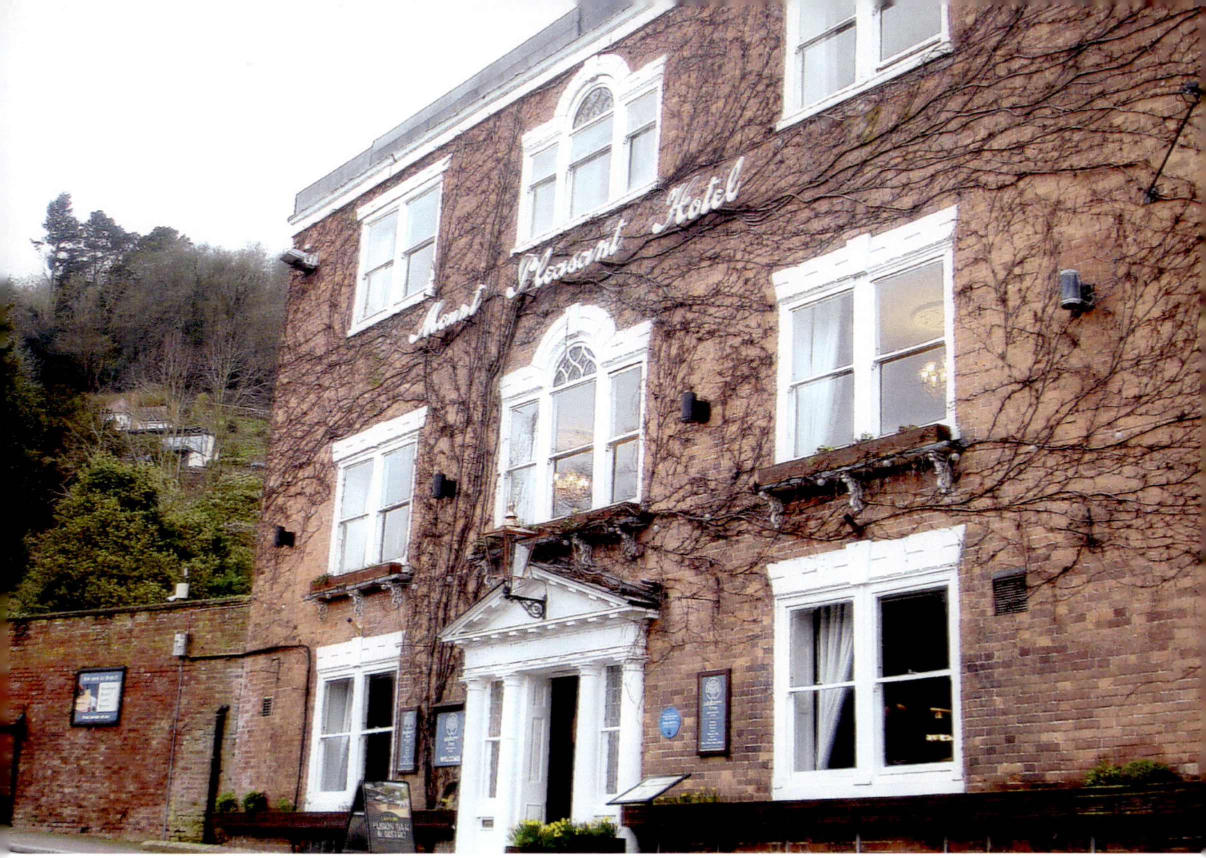

Mount Pleasant Hotel.

tea, and a local bus being boarded at the nearby bus stop) and a number of pictures depicting gypsies hop picking in the nearby countryside. By this time she had already been made a dame and was the first woman to be elected to full membership of the Royal Academy.

Today the Mount Pleasant Hotel has acquired Grade II listing status and as well as being a popular hotel, it also has The Lantern, a restaurant serving 'Asian fusion' dishes for brunch, lunch and dinner from Tuesday to Saturday (at the time of writing).

8. The Foley Arms Hotel (1810), No. 14 Worcester Road, Great Malvern, WR14 4QS

Following an increasing interest in the pure waters emerging from the Malvern Hills a boom in the town's fortunes developed, transforming the collection of Malvern villages into a thriving town. Hotels for the many visitors coming to take the waters were needed and this was one of the first. Originally named the Down's Hotel after its owner it was renamed The Foley Arms after the lord of the manor, Edward Foley. The building was designed by Samuel Deykes and opened as a coaching inn.

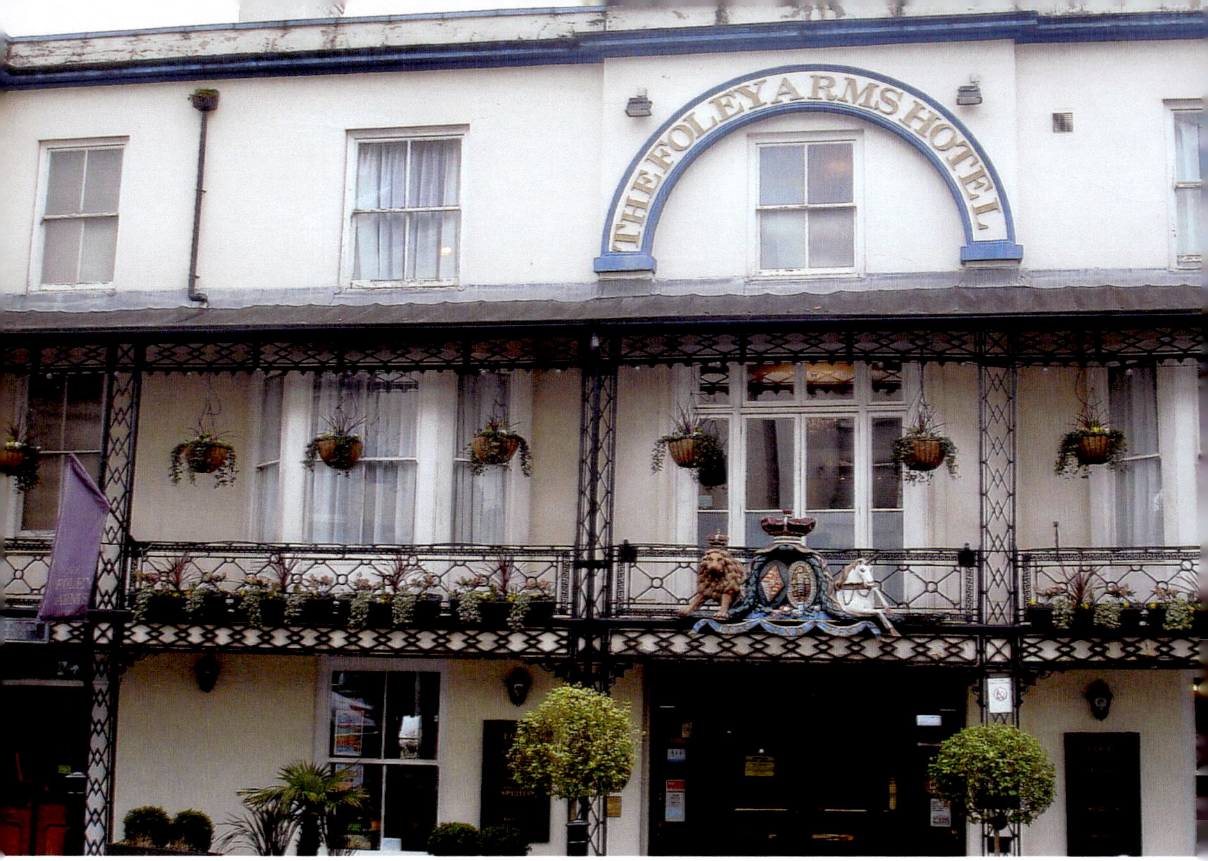

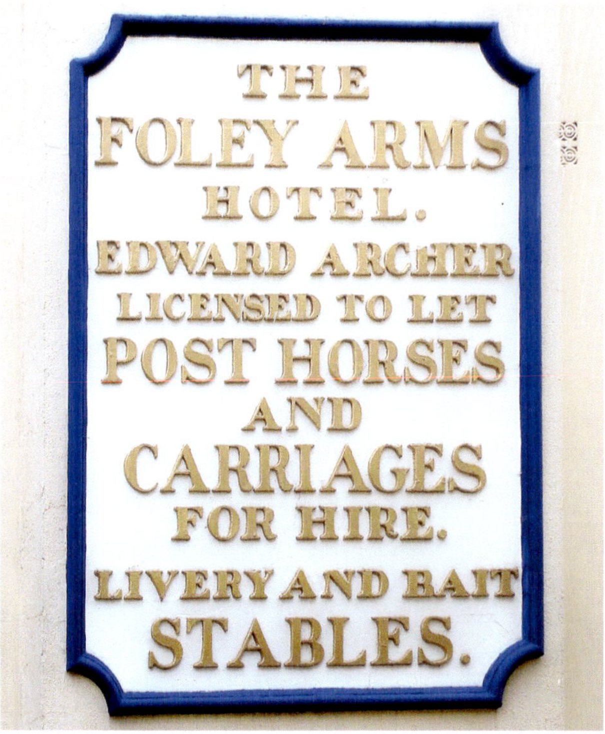

Above and left: The Foley Arms Hotel.

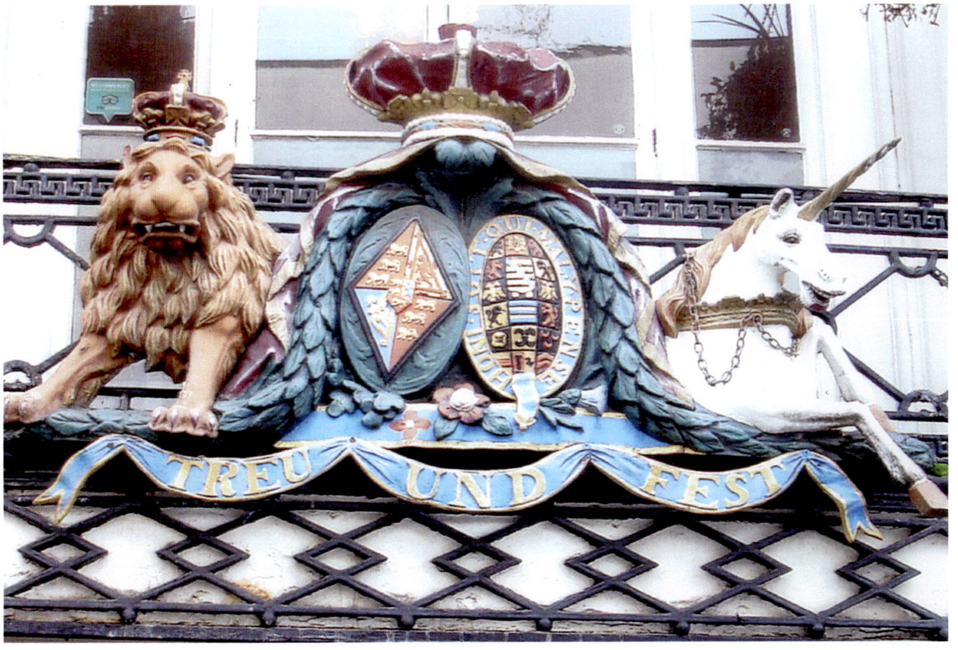

Family crest of Princess Mary of Teck above the entrance to the Foley Arms Hotel.

The hotel was very successful, particularly so when a pump room, the Coburg Baths, also designed by Samuel Deykes, opened just down the road in 1823. The former Coburg Baths building is now occupied by the Nationwide Building Society but is still recognisable by the classical Doric columns flanking the entrance.

In 1891 Princess Mary of Teck, who later became Queen Mary, the royal consort of George V stayed at The Foley Arms for six weeks and presented the hotel with the family coat of arms featuring a lion and a unicorn, which sits above the entrance.

Since then, The Foley Arms has had various owners and closed for a while until 2010 when the JD Wetherspoon chain took it over. They have since refurbished the interior of the building in their own style, which preserves and enhances the best of the original and has information on display concerning the history of the building and area.

9. St Ann's Well (1813), St Ann's Road, Great Malvern, WR14 4RF

At over 820 feet above sea level, the spring here is perhaps the highest in the Malvern Hills. It is also the earliest of the celebrated springs, being used perhaps by the monk Werstan in the eleventh century, and certainly marked on a map of the Foley Estate dated 1744.

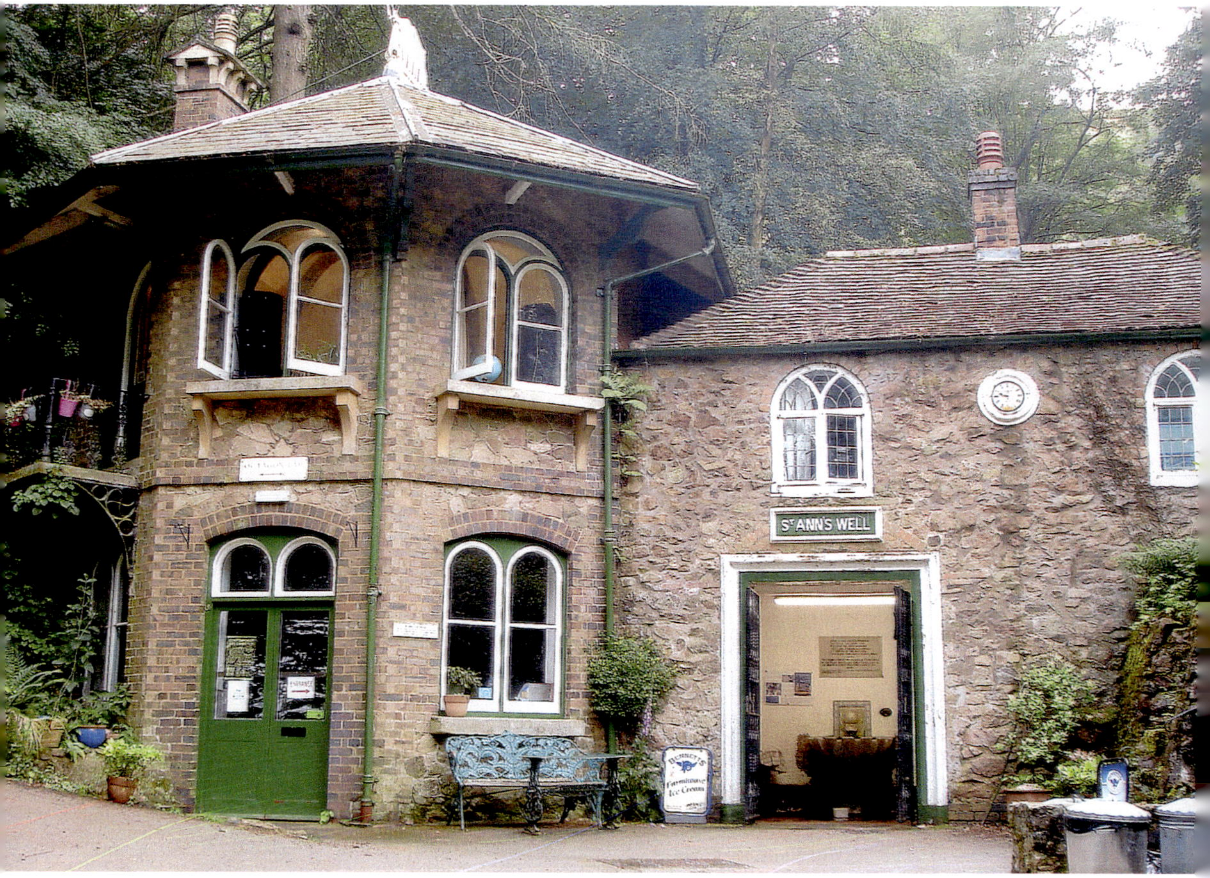

St Ann's Well, Great Malvern.

The building we see at the well today was constructed in two main phases. The small cottage, constructed from Malvern stone in 1813, is known as Well Cottage. The picturesque octagonal section was added in 1844 and is today a popular vegetarian/vegan café.

Visitors to Malvern, attracted by its growing reputation as a health spa on account of its pure water, would flock to Well House or Cottage to be given glasses of spring water to drink and if required be given assistance to apply the well water directly to any part of the body requiring healing. The waters here, along with all the others in Malvern (excepting the Chalybeate Spring near Priory Park), are completely free of any minerals or impurities. As the 'water cure' craze swept Malvern in the mid-nineteenth century hot and cold baths were available at the premises. The marble dolphin head spout and basin in Well House were donated by Lady Emily Foley in 1892.

The popularity of St Ann's Well declined during the twentieth century and over time Well House and its octagonal wing deteriorated. By 1960 demolition was being considered. Eventually though the buildings were refurbished and brought

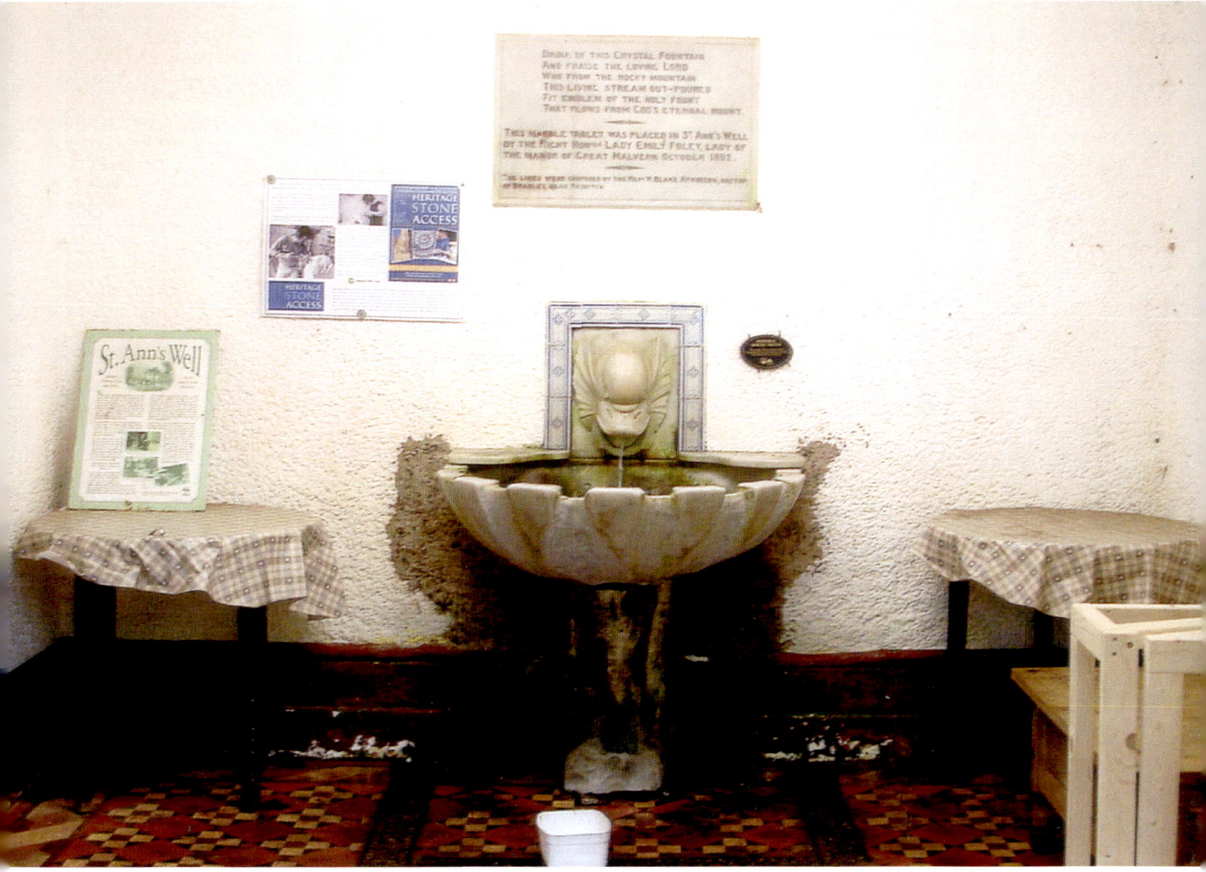

St Ann's Well, Great Malvern. The interior of Well House with spout and basin.

back into use. In 2005 the pond garden feature was added, with the help of the Heritage Lottery Fund and local sculptor Rose Garrard. St Ann's Well is today a Grade II listed building.

10. Royal Library and Assembly Rooms (1818), No. 2 Worcester Road, Great Malvern, WR14 4QW

Designed by architect John Deykes in 1818, this beautiful building was completed in 1821 and intended as a place for the increasing number of visitors to Malvern hoping to spend time in genteel and educational surroundings. The new building was only a hundred yards or so down the road from the then newly opened Down's Hotel (later to become The Foley Arms Hotel).

The former Royal Library and Assembly Rooms building is particularly distinctive for its south-facing Regency bow front and Ionic columns. The prefix

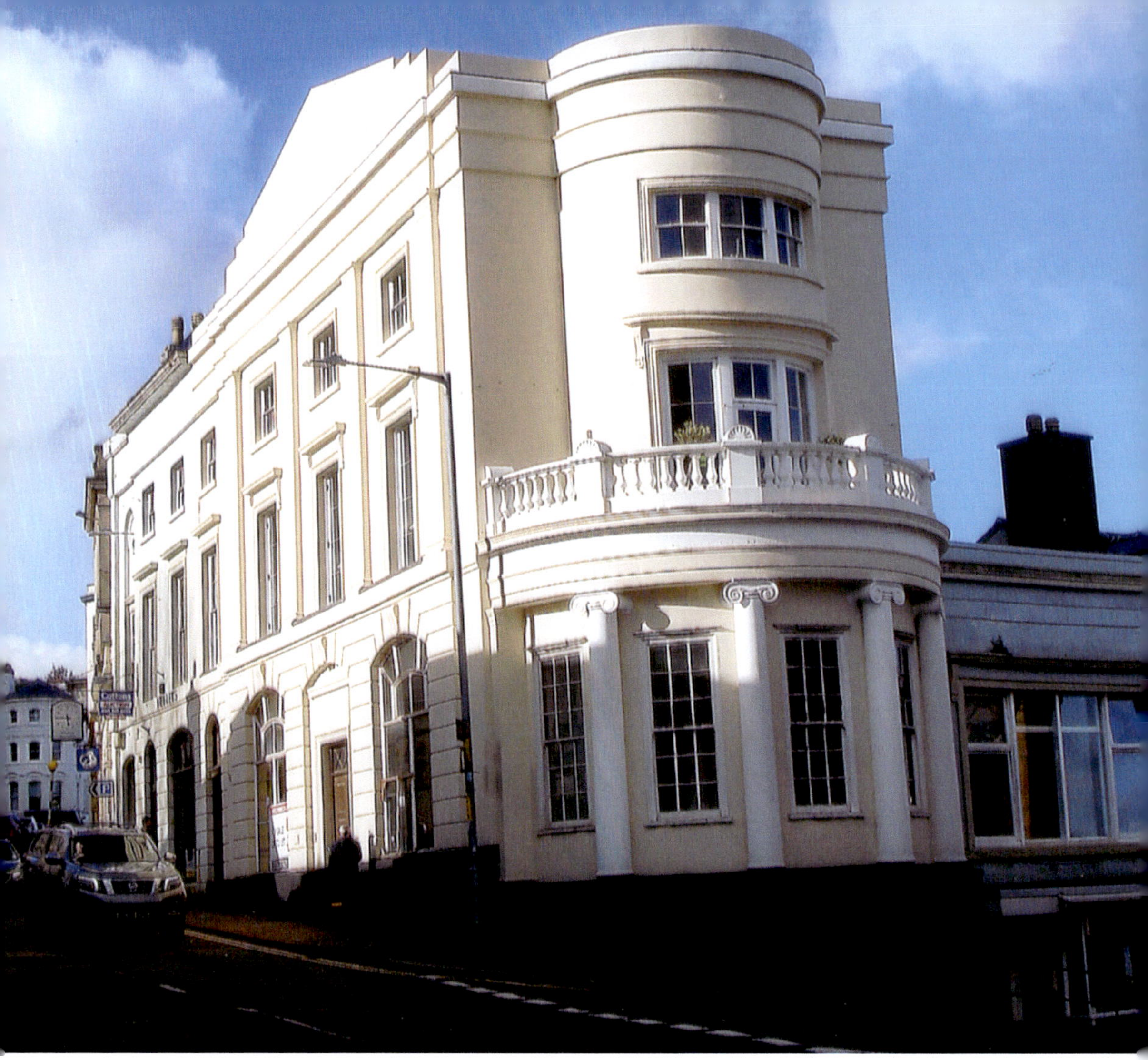

Above: The former Royal Library and Assembly Rooms.

Opposite: No. 23 Abbey Road, Great Malvern, currently Mac and Jac's café.

'Royal' was added following a prolonged visit to Malvern in 1830 by Princess Victoria with her mother the Duchess of Kent.

In 1930 Guy Pemberton adapted the building for Barclays bank, who subsequently operated a branch here until its controversial closure in August 2021 due to 'low footfall'. This justification was challenged by both customers and the local Member of Parliament since the previous eighteen months had been marked by the Covid pandemic, which had caused 'low footfall' everywhere.

Following the closure this fine building stood empty for a while but in April 2024 it was put up for auction for a guide price of £275,000. This is undoubtedly one of Malvern's iconic buildings and is Grade II listed. Let's see what the future holds.

11. No. 23 Abbey Road (1830), Great Malvern, WR14 3ES

This building is a good example of Regency Gothic architecture with its light-coloured exterior, battlemented gables and pinnacles, a style popular around this time with other examples elsewhere in Malvern and around the country.

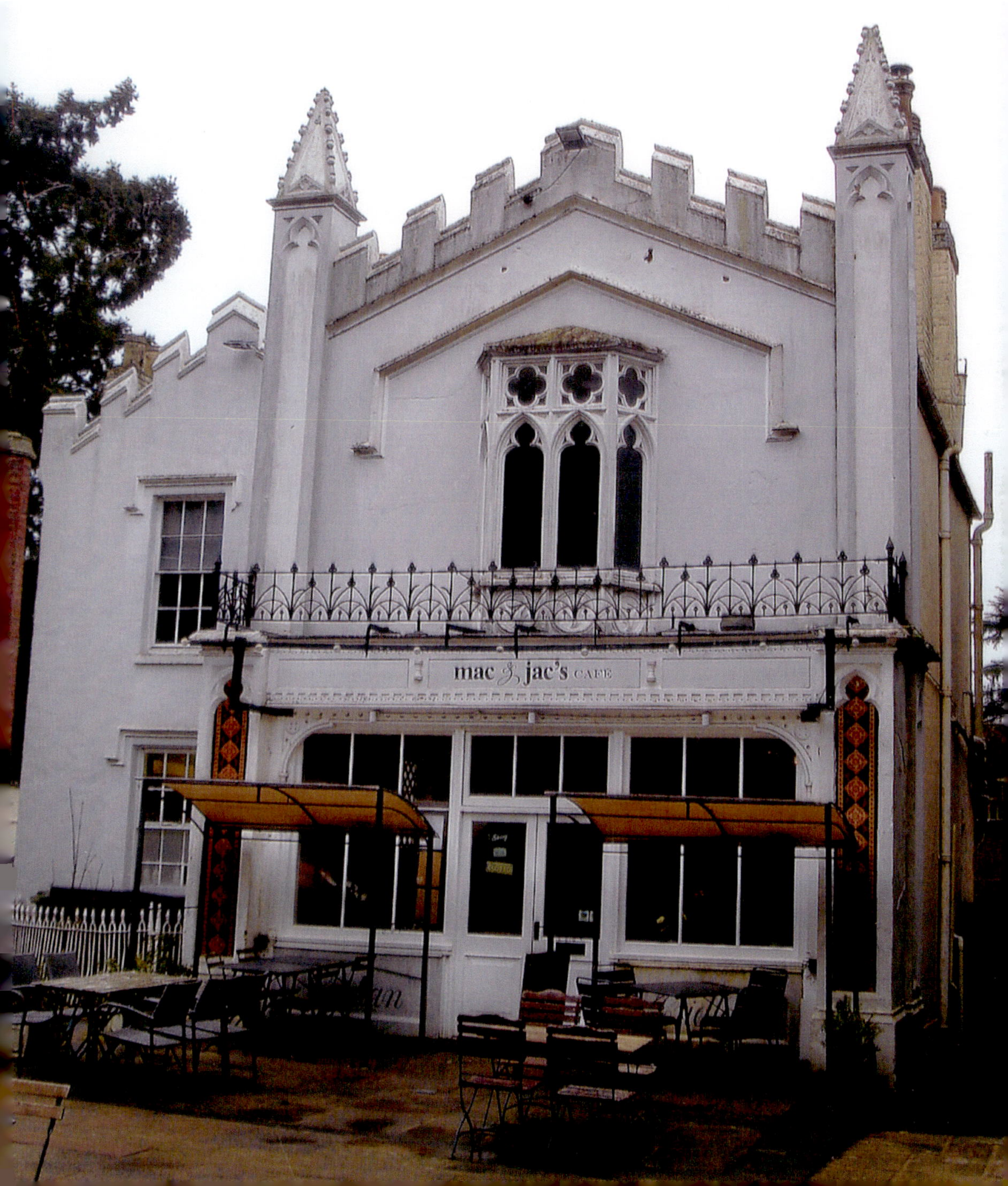

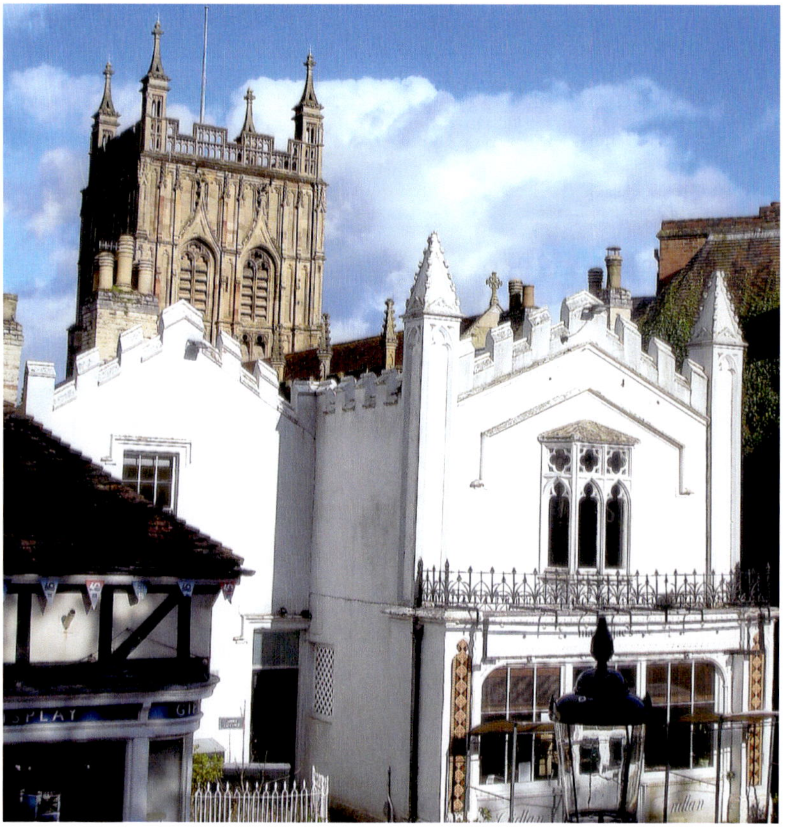

No. 23 Abbey Road, Great Malvern, with the priory church tower behind.

It complements well the variety of architectural styles densely packed in this part of Great Malvern. Formerly the building was used as a butcher's shop, then later a restaurant called Pepper and Oz. Today it is Mac and Jac's café offering coffees, breakfasts, lunches and Holywell Spring water. The business was opened here in 2012 having previously been situated in Worcester.

12. The Coach House Theatre (1833), Grange Road, Great Malvern, WR14 3HA

Originally this was the coach house and stabling for the Grange, a large house after which Grange Road is named. Since then this now Grade II listed property has been used as a store for the local council and a scenery store for the Malvern Theatres next door. The building gradually deteriorated and was due for demolition but saved in 1984. In 1997 the building was extended and workshop facilities included. In 2004–05 the premises were developed as a theatre by The Malvern Theatre Players. The 110-seat theatre has subsequently been developed as a community arts venue and opened in May 2006 with a production of *Billy Liar.* The theatre's small size and intimate layout has proven particularly suitable for

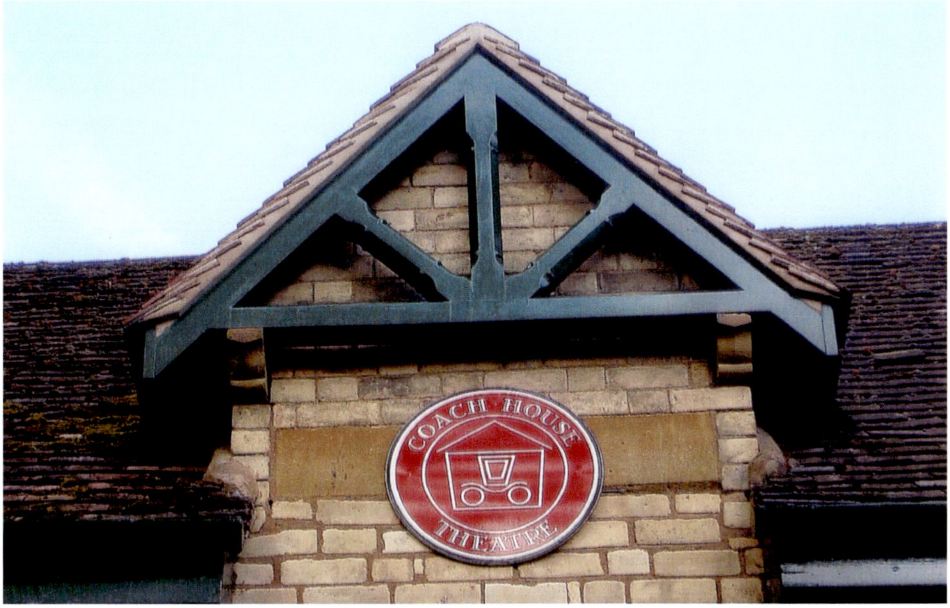

Above and right: Coach House Theatre.

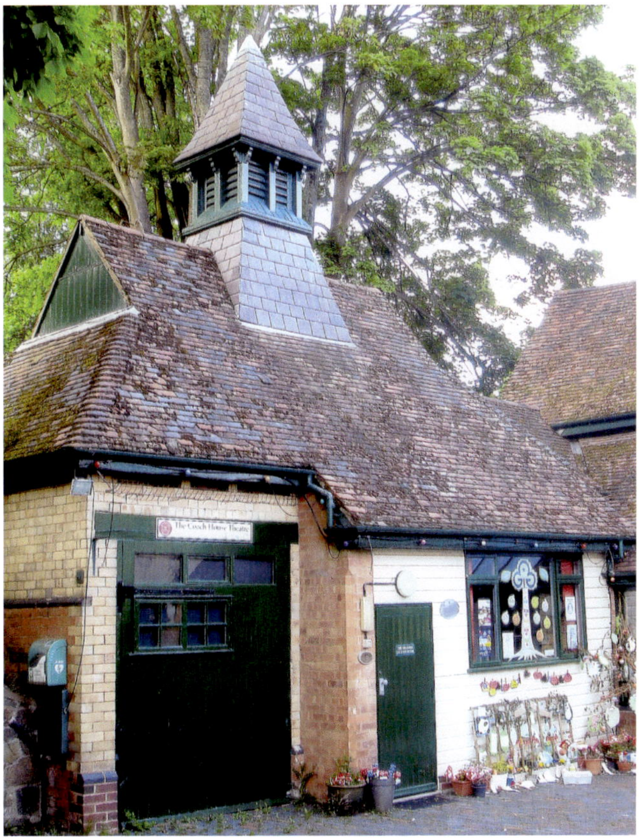

small-scale productions, children's performances and novice players. A particular speciality of this venue is the screening of French films.

In 2014 the district council sold the building to the Coach House Theatre, a registered charity set up specifically to own and manage this important cultural asset.

13. Holy Well (1843), off Holy Well Road, Malvern Wells, WR14 4LE

In legend the spring at Holy Well was first mentioned as having been revealed to a hermit monk by St Oswald. In history the first record of this spring, in whom Queen Elizabeth I granted it and the surrounding land to lord of the manor, John Hornyold, was in 1558. In 1612 a crippled man is recorded as having travelled to this very spring from Leicester to relieve his terrible gout.

It was really Dr John Wall from Worcester who set the ball rolling in a big way following his scientific analyses of the water from what we now know

Opposite: Spout and basin at Holy Well. (Photo by Nathan Adams)

Below: Holy Well House. (Photo by Nathan Adams)

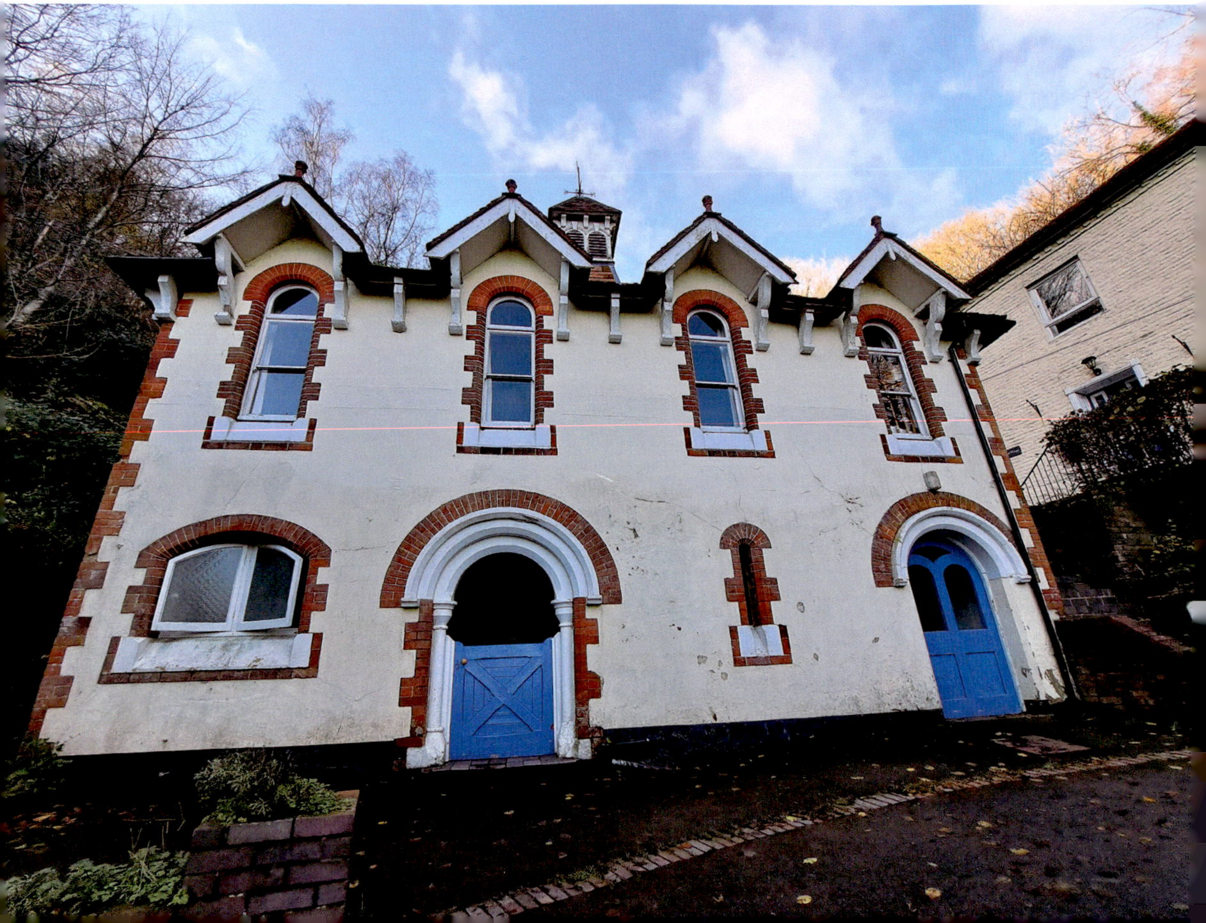

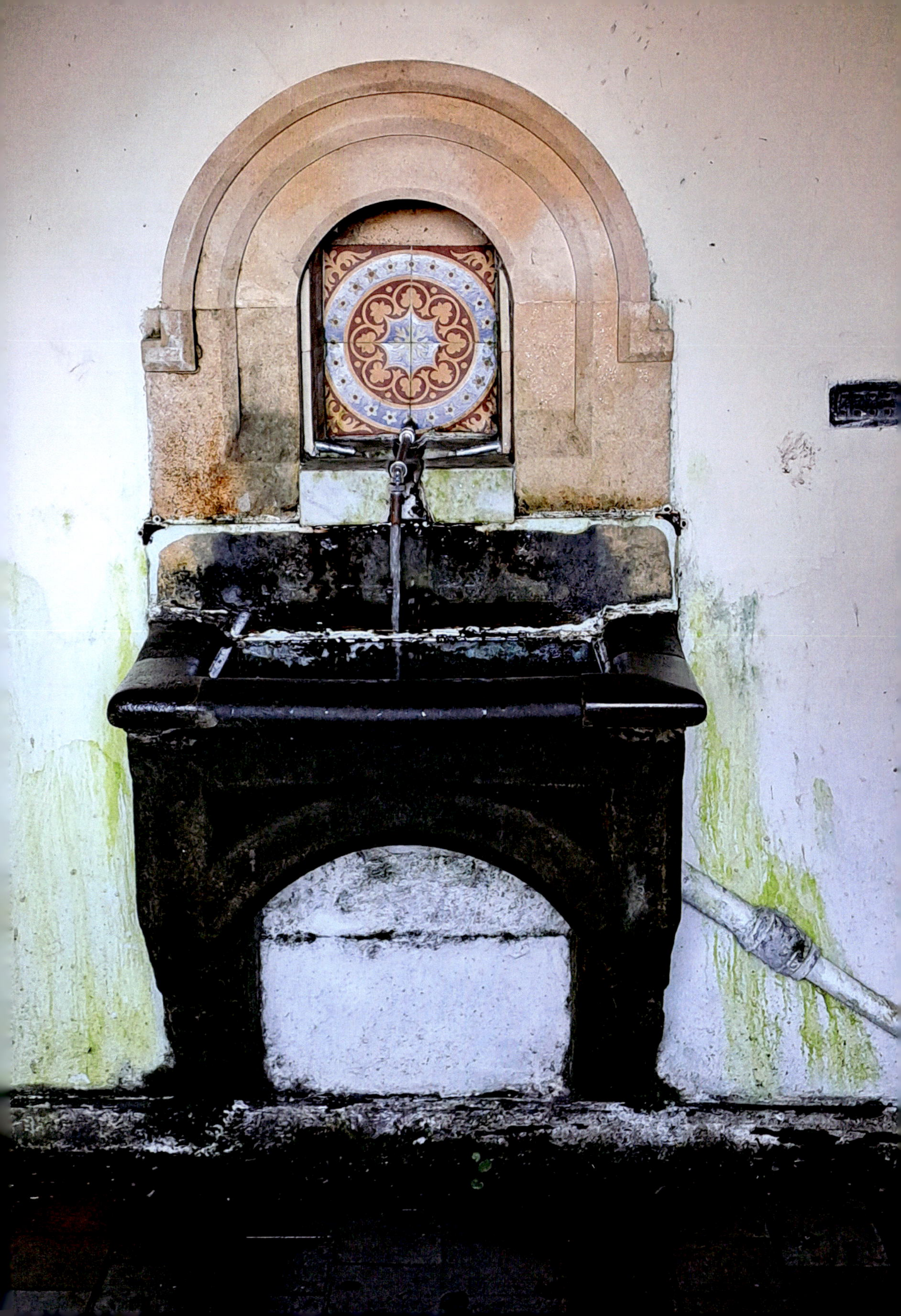

as Holy Well and subsequent pronouncement that the waters were pure. This statement was immortalised in 1757 in the statement by a contemporary chronicler that 'The Malvern Waters', says Dr John Wall, 'is fam'd for containing just nothing at all'.

Following this a modest bath house and pump room were built at the Holy Well site. The current building was built later, in 1843, and based apparently on a design from the German spa of Baden-Baden. By now, of course, the 'water cure' mentality had been introduced by Dr James Wilson operating from what was then the Crown Hotel on Belle Vue Terrace (since demolished and replaced by the Lloyds Bank building in 1892). At the new Well House both the consumption of and bathing in the waters were undertaken with a curative effect expected.

The pure spring water at Holy Well was first bottled here in 1622, though bottling on a commercial scale really began when Schweppes opened a bottling plant at Holy Well in 1850. The Holy Well is said to be the oldest bottling plant in the world. The plant passed into new ownership in 1890 but the operation had ceased by the 1960s when the site fell into dereliction. In 1972 John Parker bought the site and with the aid of the Civic Trust carried out extensive restoration in the mid-1970s. Water bottling recommenced at Holy Well and continued through the 1980s and 1990s. Later the site was purchased by Marion and Mike Humm, who have carried out extensive modernisation and provided tourist accommodation, as well as opening a visitor centre, all with the help of Heritage Lottery and matched funding. From December 2009 water bottling resumed and 1,200 bottles of water a day are currently produced. The Holy Well building was Grade II listed in the 1970s. The Holy Well is 'well dressed' annually in May during the Malvern Well Dressing Festival.

14. Park View (1845), No. 33 Abbey Road, Great Malvern, WR14 3HG

This Grade II listed building was built for Dr James Wilson as the first purpose-built hydropathic clinic in England. Three years earlier Dr Wilson had arrived in Malvern, which was already recognised for its many pure springs and bottled water bringing with him the practice of hydrotherapy.

Initially Wilson established his treatment centre at the Crown Hotel in Belle Vue Terrace (sited where now is Lloyds Bank) but transferred his business to the new premises, which was named Priessnitz House after the founder of modern hydrotherapy, though later being referred to as 'The Establishment'.

Vincent Pressnitz was the son of a peasant farmer in Austrian Silesia who revived the ancient medical practice of cold-water therapy now known as hydrotherapy and popularised it in the early nineteenth century. He founded the first 'water cure' establishment in the family farmhouse in Gräfenberg, an area similar to Malvern with its high steep hills and many pure water springs. Pressnitz ran a harsh regime

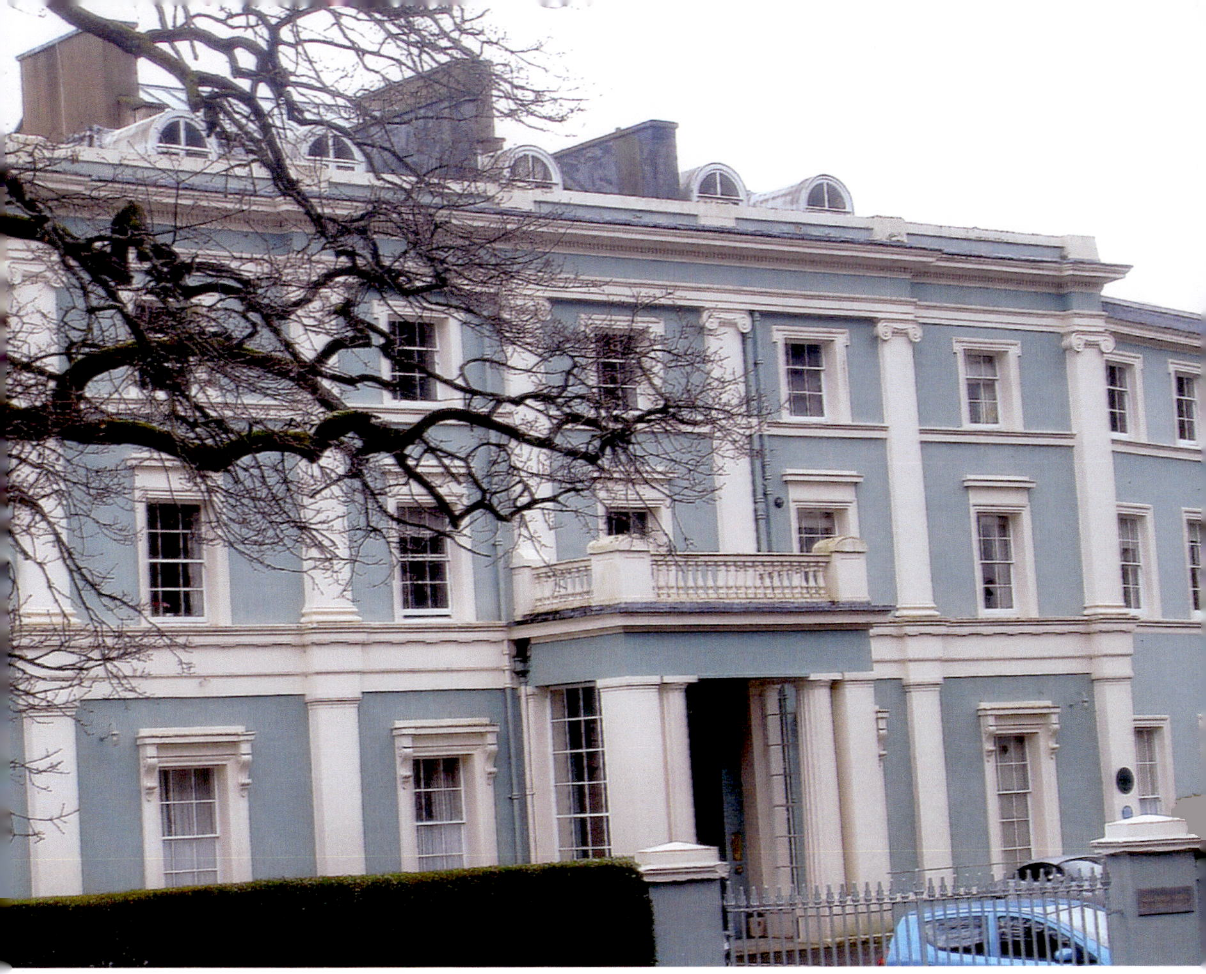

Above: Park View's front entrance.

Below: Park View's east-facing side.

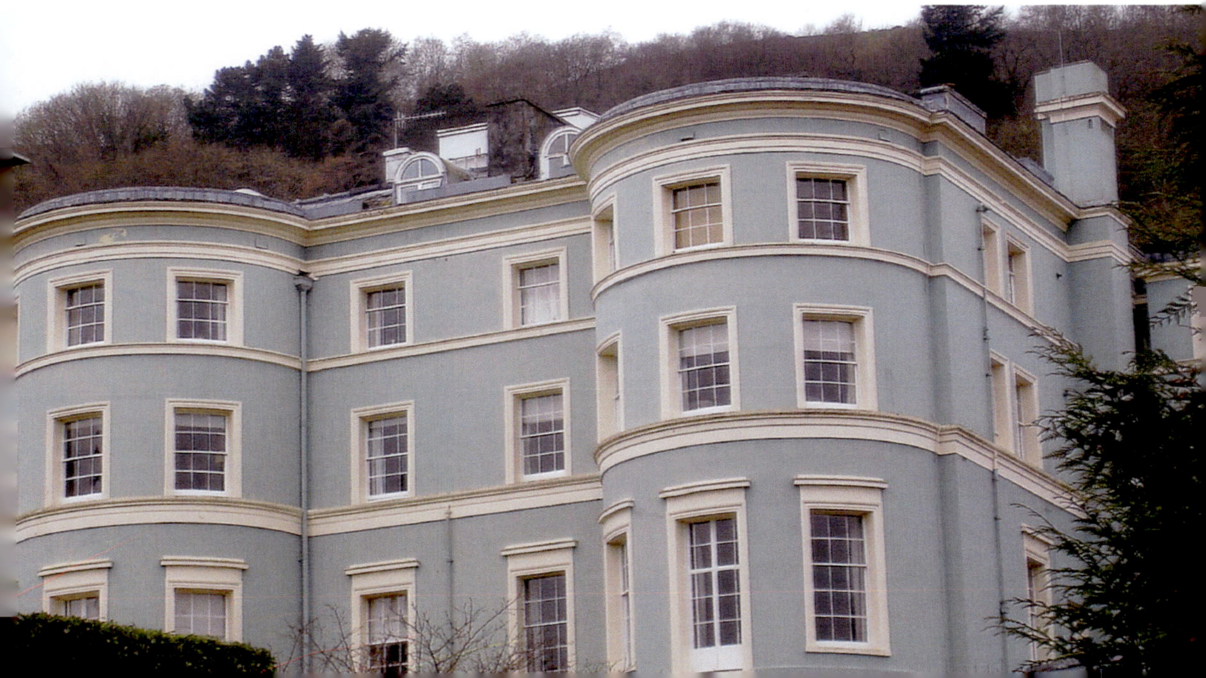

of early rising, cold baths, strenuous walks, waterfall douches, considerable spells wrapped in wet sheets and a spartan diet. He was inspired in this direction by his experience as a young man of being run over by a cart and suffering a number of broken bones. He was treated in the locally traditional way of being wrapped in wet strips of cloth continually soaked in cold spring water. Apparently, he was up and walking again within a fortnight and within a year back at work.

Dr Wilson operated a successful hydrotherapy business at The Establishment until his death in 1867. He continued the practices of Priessnitz, though without quite the spartan diet. Wilson and his successors did not relent on the water cure treatments; the cold baths and showers were strictly enforced and have been described in detail in an amusing book titled *Three Weeks in Wet Sheets: the diary and doings of a moist visitor to Malvern.*

However, in 1905 disaster struck. A sewage pipe from a property up the hill leaked into the water supply of The Establishment, which resulted in several guests becoming very ill with typhoid. Three people died in the outbreak and although the hydrotherapy business limped on, confidence was lost. The new trend of sea bathing was becoming popular and visitors in search of cold water and healthy air increasingly went to the seaside rather than the inland spas – the boom years of hydrotherapy were over.

In 1920 The Establishment was converted into the County Hotel, its upmarket aspirations encouraged by the building's classical appearance, its Greek Doric porch columns and east-facing double bows.

One famous name who stayed at the County Hotel was author Evelyn Waugh. He was based here when researching his first novel *Brideshead Revisited*, which it is believed was based on Waugh's observations and experience of the Lygon family of nearby Madresfield Court in the 1930s. Later in 1942 the County Hotel became a centre for the billeting of government scientists working on the development of radar, as well as American scientists from Harvard University and the Massachusetts Institute of Technology.

In 1992 the Malvern Civic Society placed a plaque commemorating Dr James Wilson's work at what is now Park View and a memorial to Wilson and his work has been placed at the corner of Abbey Road and Priory Road.

Park View is today a well-maintained building consisting of apartments, some with beautiful views across the Vale of Evesham.

15. The Abbey Hotel (1848/9), Abbey Road, Great Malvern, WR14 3ET

Following the demolition of the old Abbey House William Archer had the Abbey Hotel designed by S. W. Daukes and built in the Jacobean style of the earlier building.

There have been a number of additions to the original since, such as the Gothic half-timbered wing near the gates in the 1870s and twentieth-century annexes at

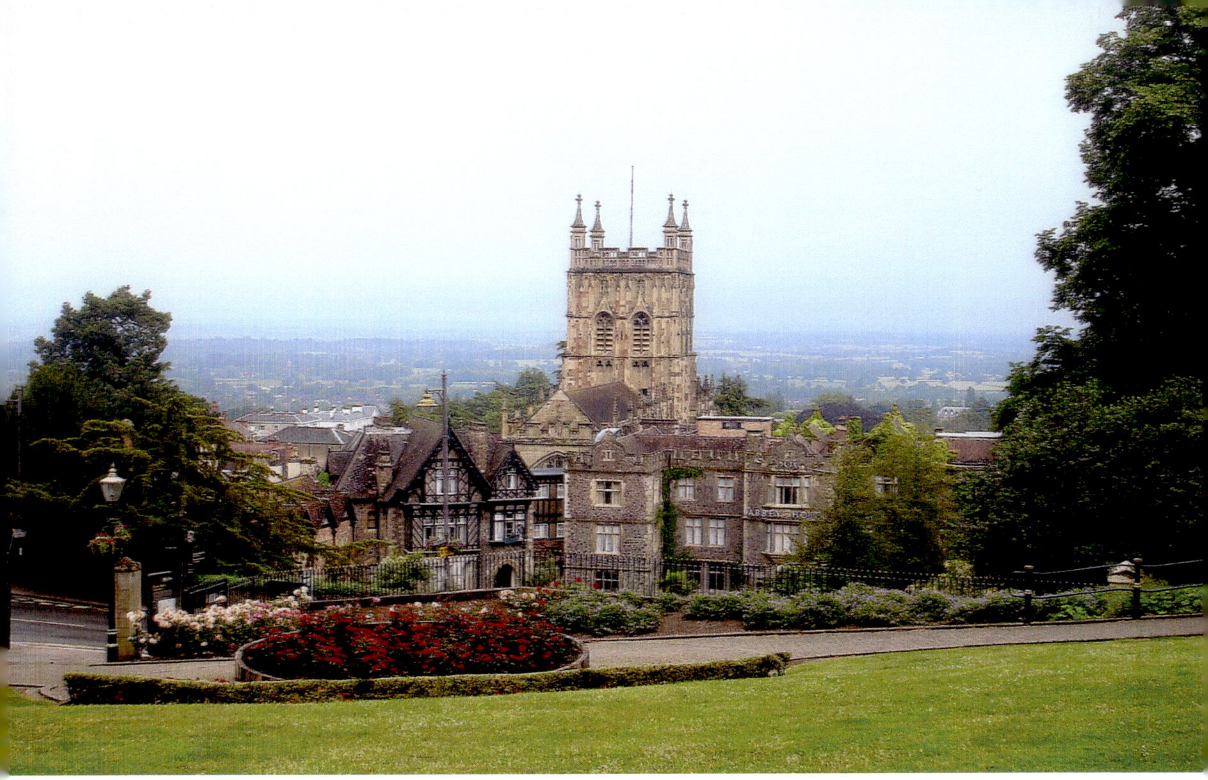

Above: The Abbey Hotel with the priory church tower and Vale of Evesham beyond.

Below: Entrance to The Abbey Hotel.

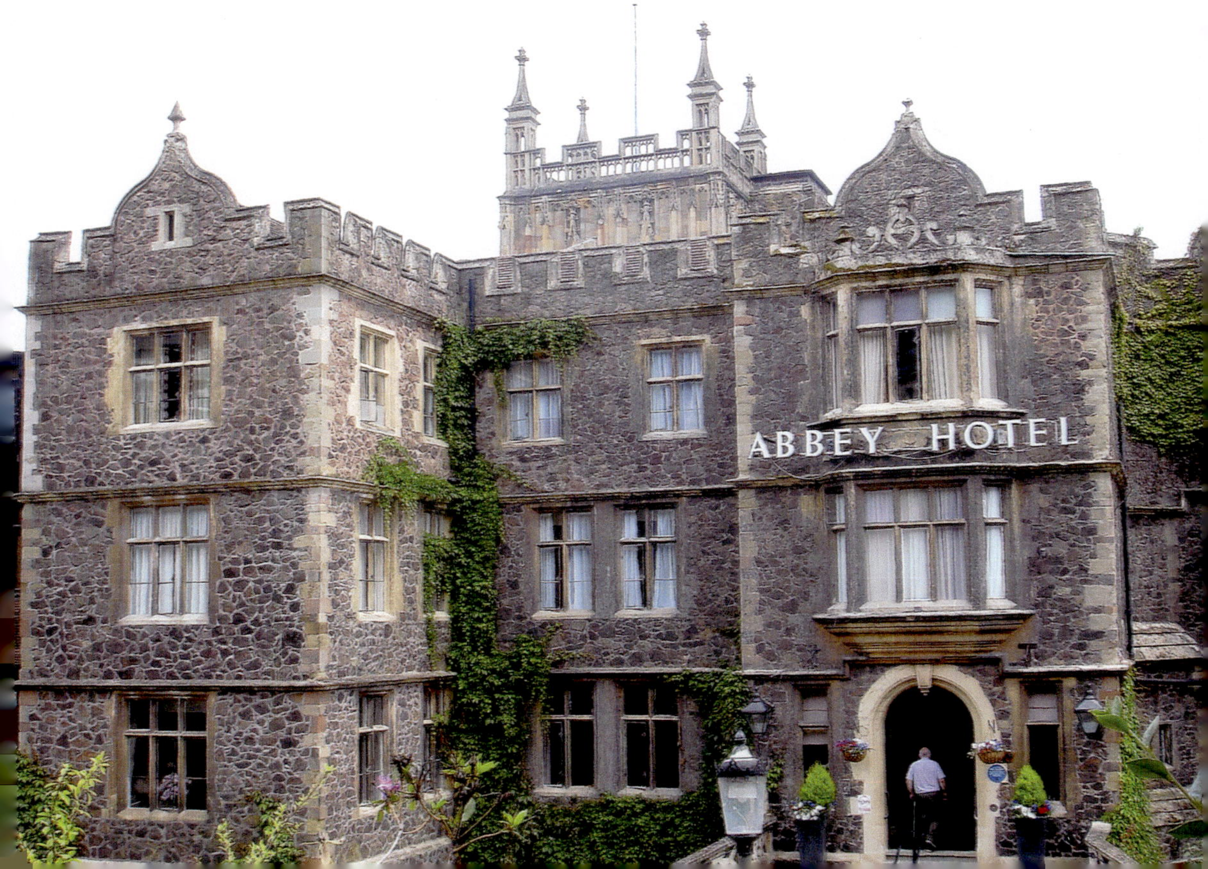

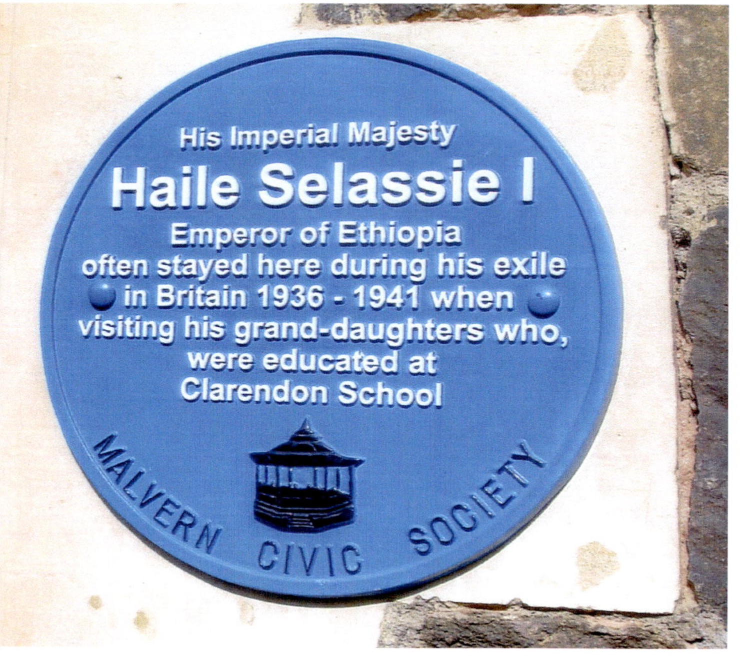

Plaque commemorating presence of Haile Selassie at The Abbey Hotel.

the southern end of the building. Much of the exterior of the Abbey Hotel is today covered in attractive Virginia creeper.

During the 1930s the Emperor of Ethiopia Haile Selassie I often stayed at the hotel whilst in exile in Britain and visiting his granddaughters, who were being educated in Malvern at the time. A blue plaque commemorating his visits was placed by the front entrance of the Abbey Hotel by the Malvern Civic Society in 2011.

The Second World War saw the hotel taken over initially by the Ministry of Information and later by the Royal Air Force. Today the Abbey Hotel is part of the Sarova Hotels group, and has had a £1 million upgrade and now boasts 103 en-suite modern bedrooms. Its location near the hills and the oldest parts of Great Malvern makes it an ideal centre from which to explore the locality.

16. Aldwyn Tower (1850), No. 21 St Ann's Road, Great Malvern, WR14 4RE

This striking Italianate-style tower of a building was built as a hotel during the onset of the building boom as Malvern's reputation as a spa town grew. It was named the Aldwyn Tower Hotel after Aldwyn, the hermit who first founded a monastic community locally that later became the Great Malvern Priory.

The hotel's most famous guest was probably the seven-year-old Franklin D. Roosevelt, the future president of the United States who was recovering from a bout of tuberculosis, presumably having received some form of 'water

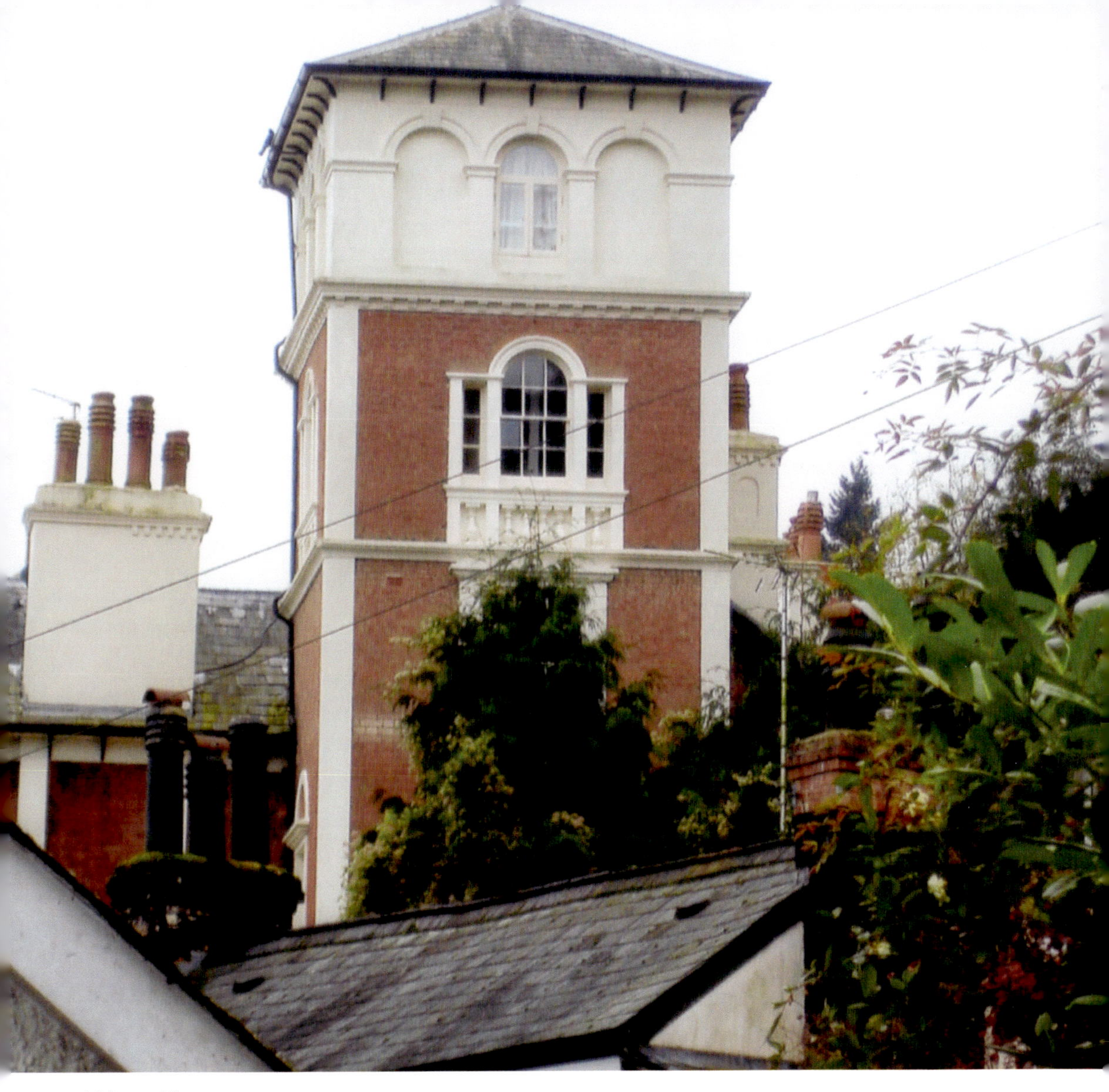

Aldwyn Tower.

cure' treatment. Obviously, Malvern's reputation as a health-giving spa was widespread!

Today the former hotel has been divided into quality apartments and has been Grade II listed.

17. Tudor House (1852), No. 15 Wells Road, Great Malvern, WR14 4RH

This magnificent building designed by Samuel Sanders Teulon was built in 1852 for Dr James Gully, another enthusiastic hydrotherapist who was persuaded by his colleague Dr James Wilson to come to Malvern to practise his similar business here.

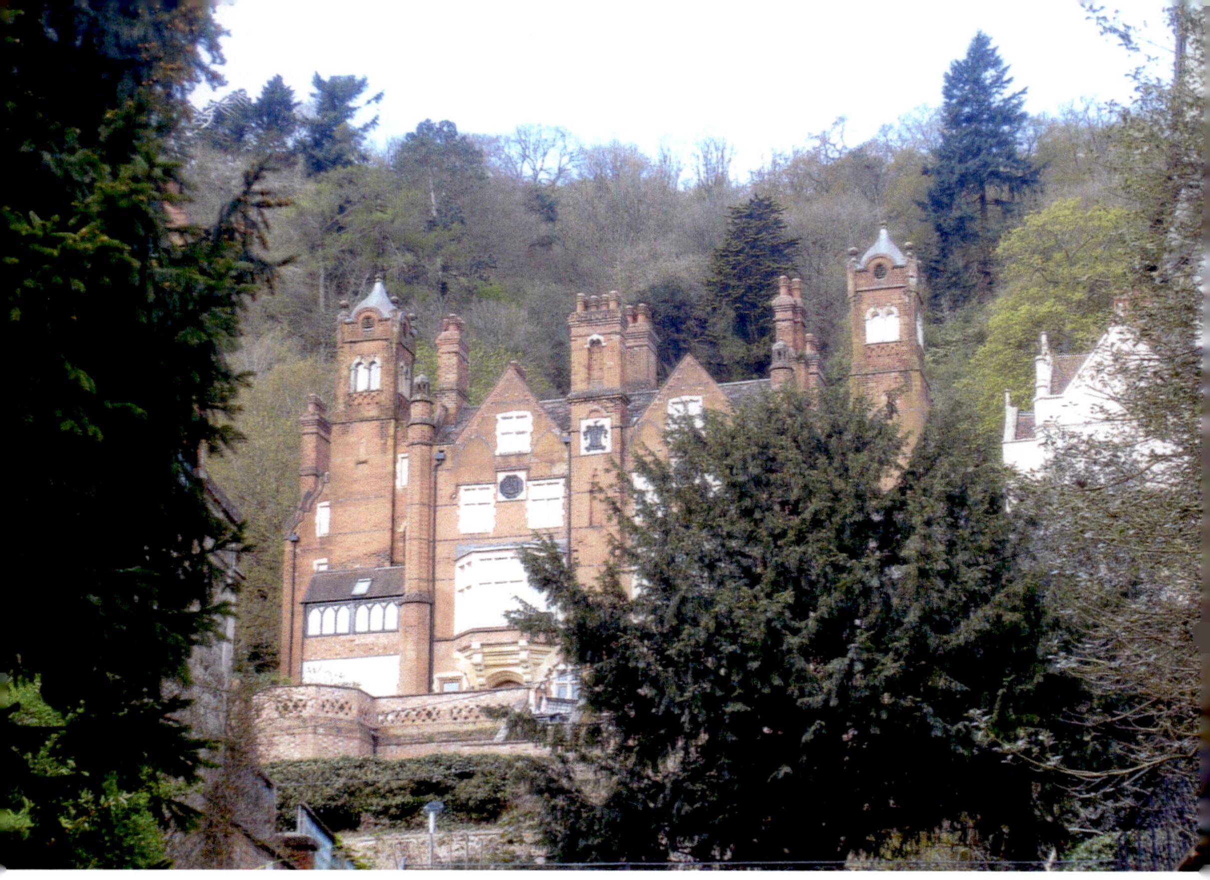

Above: Tudor House, seen from Abbey Road.

Below: Tudor House, seen from Wells Road.

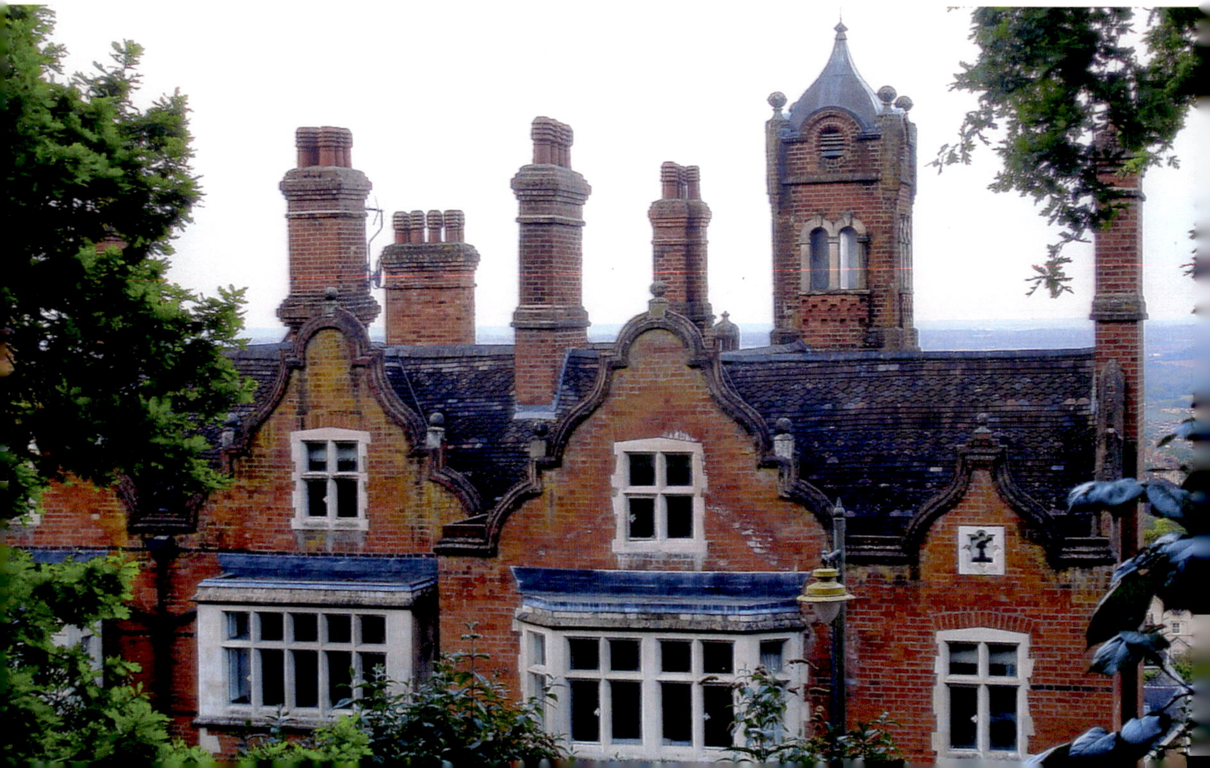

Dr Gully arrived in October 1842 and leased Holyrood House and Neubie House where he treated male patients initially. When Tudor House, described by architectural author Niklaus Pevsner as of 'lively Jacobean style', opened ten years later Gully's male patients were moved into the new premises. Female patients were accommodated in Holyrood and Neubie Houses and the old and new premises were connected by a bridge to allow medical staff to move between the two. Patients, however, were strictly segregated into the two houses. The connecting bridge became known as the 'Bridge of Sighs'.

Today the building is Grade II listed and currently houses residential apartments.

18. Malvern House (1859), No. 35 Abbey Road, Great Malvern, WR14 3HG

Right next door to the now duck egg blue Park View where Dr James Wilson established his main hydrotherapy centre you will find Malvern House. This red-brick Jacobean-style building accommodated more 'water cure' patients as Dr Wilson's business continued to grow in popularity.

After Dr Wilson's death in 1867 the building became a lodging house. Apparently, George Bernard Shaw stayed here several times in the 1930s whilst attending the Malvern Festival. In 1927 Malvern House became the Malvern Hotel. Today it consists of residential apartments.

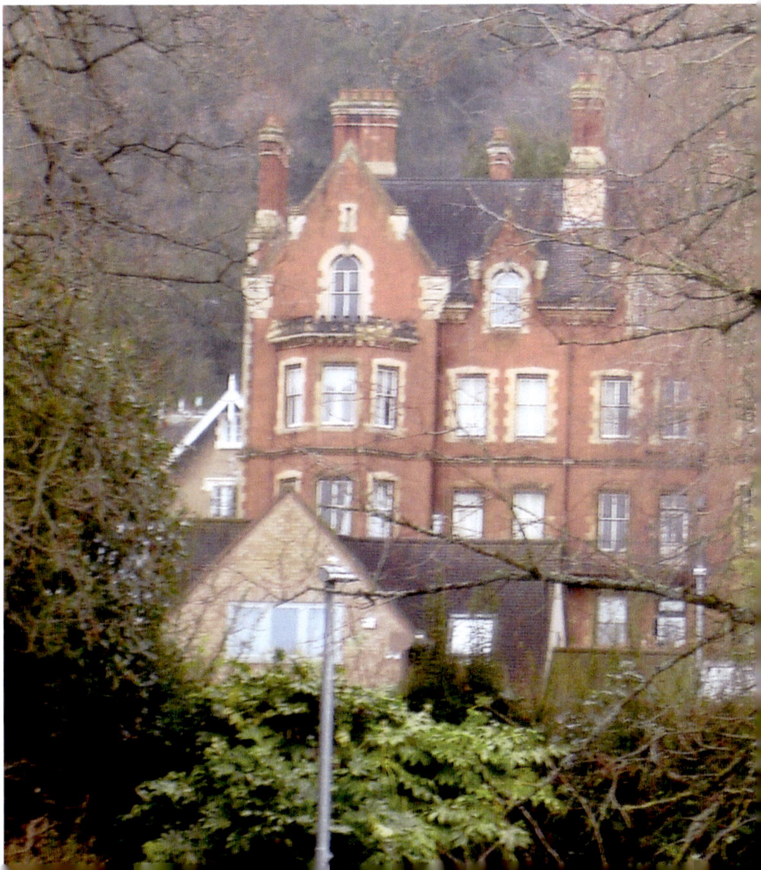

Malvern House.

Just down the road at No. 53 Elmsdale was another water cure establishment, this one operated by yet another James, Dr James Marsden. With the demise of the 'water cure' craze the place became a school for young ladies known as The Ladies College. This, in turn, closed in 1881 and today the building, in common with many others like it, has been divided into flats.

19. Great Malvern Station (1860–62), Station Approach, Malvern, WR14 3AL

With the increasing number of visitors comings to Malvern during the boom in the 'water cure' business the presence of a railway station became necessary. Sponsored by Lady Emily Foley, among others, the station was designed by local architect Edward Wallace Elmslie and opened in 1860, though construction continued until 1862.

The station was built with Malvern ragstone in the French Gothic style. The attractive canopies over the platforms are supported by iron columns topped by beautiful carved and painted floral creations by sculptor William Forsyth. Lady Foley had a first-class waiting room included for her own exclusive use. This has now become a tearoom and anyone can use it.

This fine Victorian building has recently had a considerable refurbishment and has been Grade II listed. Outside the station is a trough for horses to drink out of, fed by

Victorian canopies and ironwork, Great Malvern station.

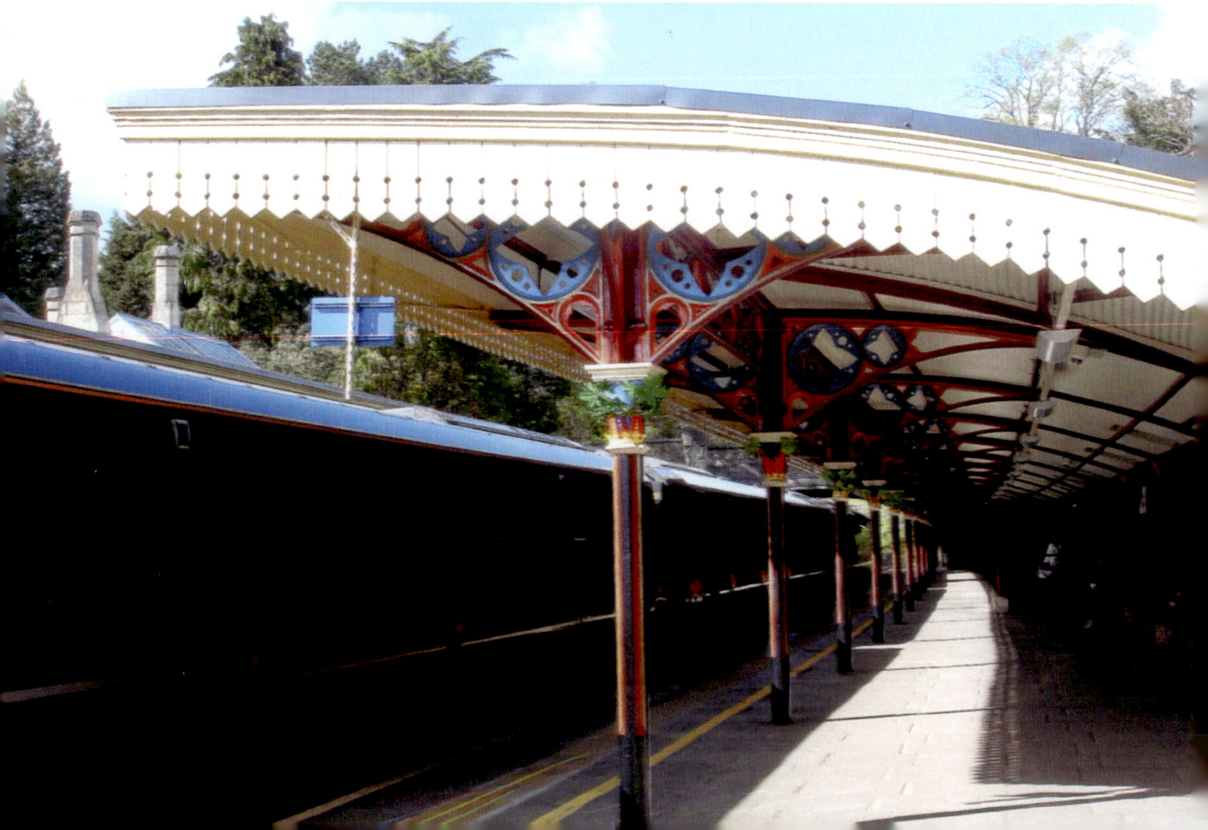

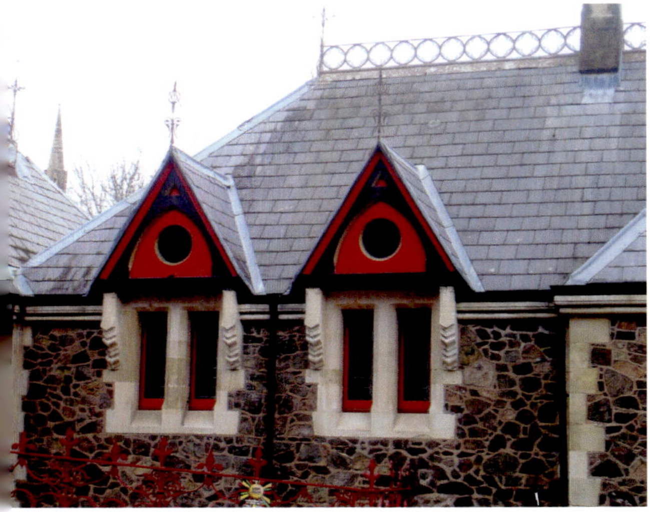

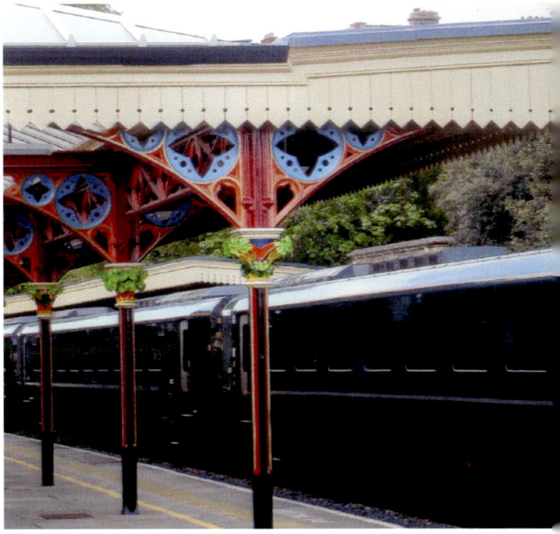

Above left: 'French Gothic' architecture, Great Malvern station.

Above right: Beautifully decorated ironwork at Great Malvern station.

Right: Detail of William Forsyth's sculptural work at Great Malvern station.

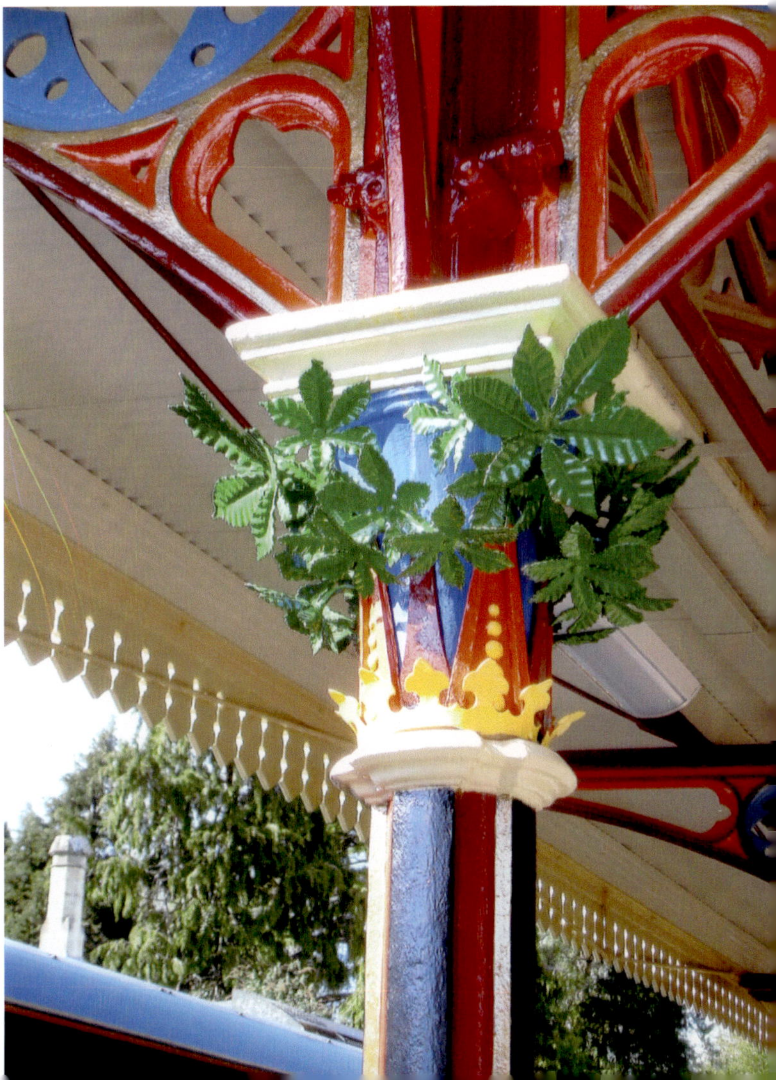

one of the many springs dotted around the town. The trough or 'well' is dressed every year during the Well Dressing Festival, a regular spring event in Malvern.

There is also an underground tunnel linking the railway station to the grand building across the road, which, at the time it was built, was the Imperial Hotel. The tunnel, now disused and blocked off, is known as 'The Worm' and is also a Grade II listed structure.

A recent addition to Great Malvern station is a new museum called The Technology Station, which tells and illustrates the story of Malvern's contribution to technological development. The museum shows how the Telecommunications Research Establishment and its successors contributed to the development not only of radar but eventually of such technology as LED displays and touchscreens. The museum is open limited hours but free to enter, with donations welcome to keep it going.

20. Malvern St James Girls' School (1860/61), No. 15 Avenue Road, Great Malvern, WR14 3BA

Originally built as the Imperial Hotel and designed by E. W. Elmslie, this impressive Victorian Gothic building was connected to Great Malvern station by an underground tunnel allowing guests to access both hotel and station undercover.

Malvern St James Girls' School's main building, formerly the Imperial Hotel.

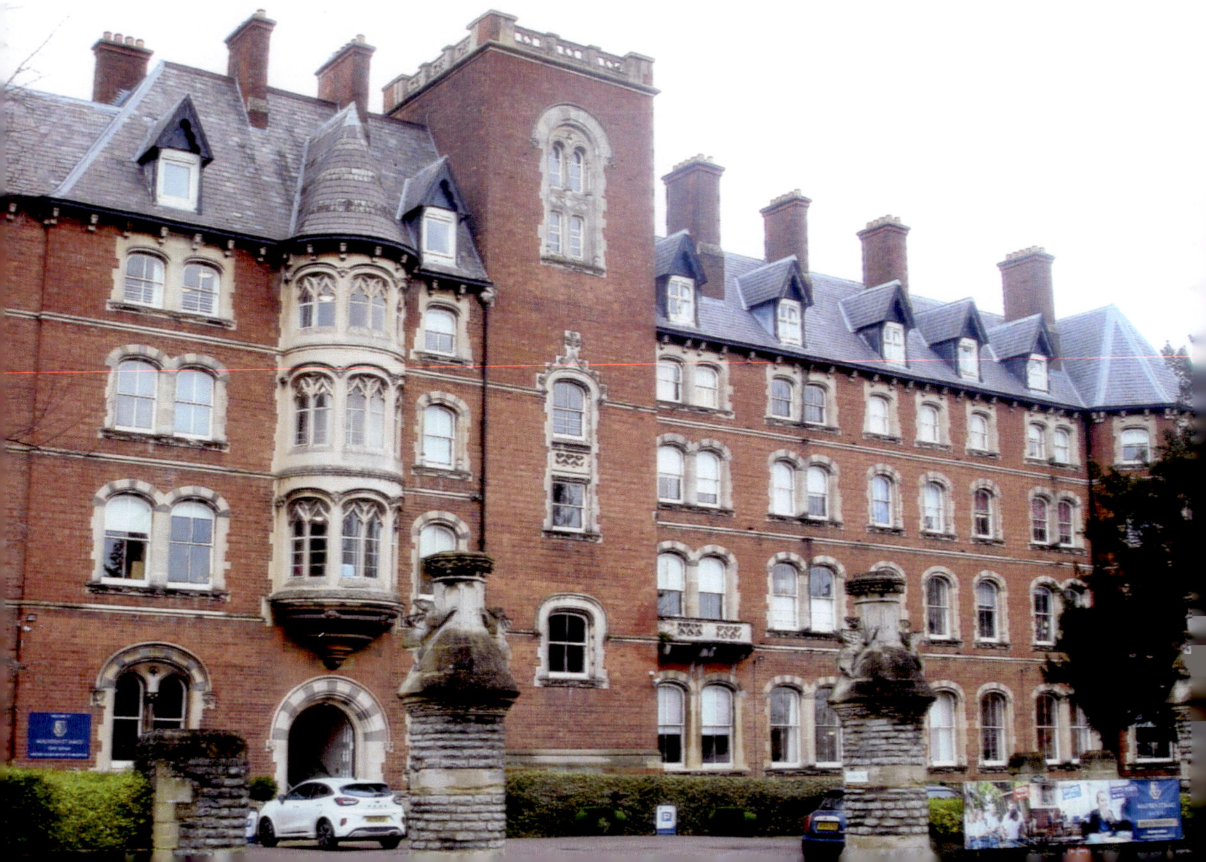

The nineteenth century saw not only a boom in the establishment of hydropathic accommodation but also schools and colleges, and in 1893 the Malvern Girls' College was founded. As hydropathy fell out of favour in the early twentieth century visitor numbers fell and hotels had a leaner time. The large Imperial Hotel was presumably no longer as viable and was sold to the girls' college in 1919. Since then, this building has functioned as the main part of the now named Malvern St James Girls' School.

21. St Wulstan's Church (1861–62), Wells Road, Little Malvern, WR14 4JL

This Grade II listed church, designed by Benjamin Bucknell and built in Victorian Gothic style, was extensively refurbished from 2004 onwards, with the roof being replaced and extensive restoration carried out within the church.

St Wulstan, to whom the church is dedicated, was the Bishop of Worcester from 1062 to 1095. Wulstan succeeded in abolishing the slave trade between Bristol and Viking Ireland and survived the Norman Conquest to become a trusted adviser to William I.

Inside St Wulstan's Church. (By kind permission of St Wulstan's Church)

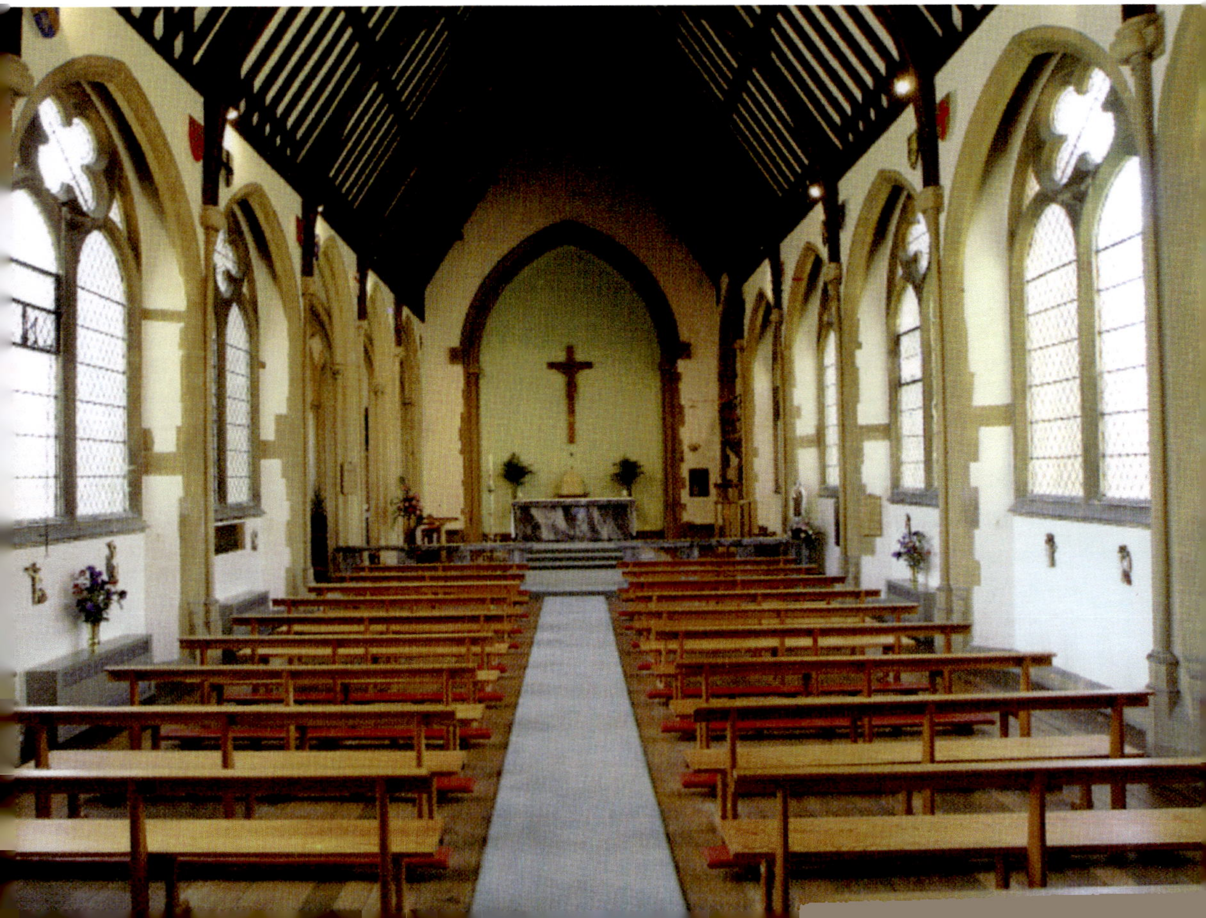

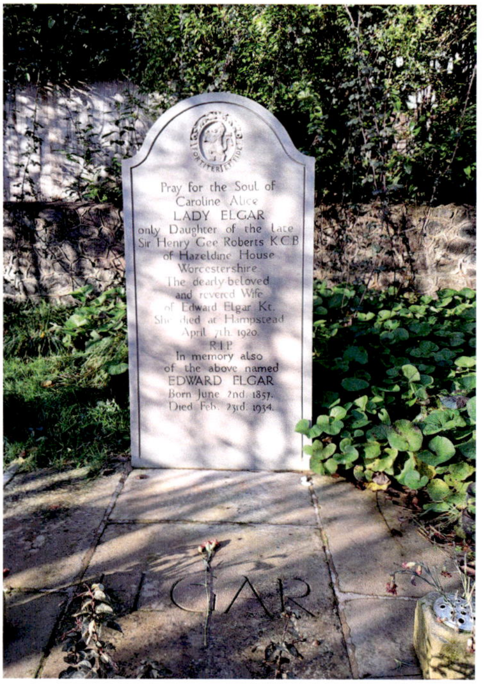

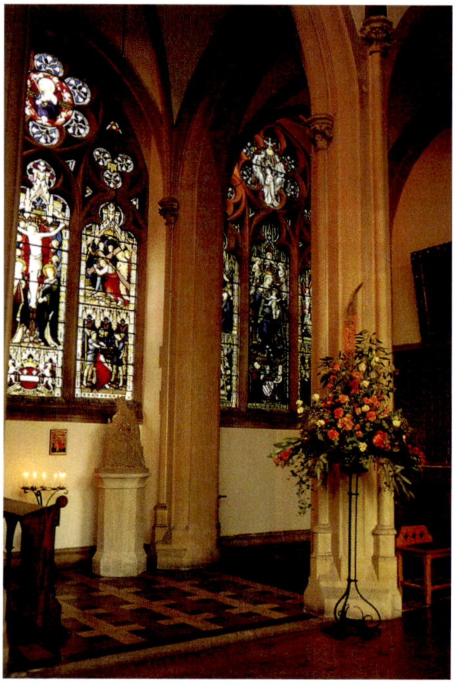

Above left: Grave of Sir Edward and Lady Alice Elgar at St Wulstan's Church. (Photo by Nathan Adams)

Above right: The Lady Chapel, St Wulstan's Church. (Photo by Dona Haycraft. By kind permission of St Wulstan's Church)

The graveyard of St Wulstan's contains the grave of both the composer Sir Edward Elgar and his wife Lady Alice Elgar. The grave has a separate Grade II listing from the church.

St Wulstan's Church is today owned and administered by the Benedictine Community of Downside Abbey. The church can be opened to visit by arrangement.

22. Elmslie House (1862–66), No. 8 Avenue Road, Malvern, WR14 3AG

This fine example of a Victorian Gothic-style villa was designed by local architect Edward Wallace Elmslie for his own use. Elmslie named his new home 'Falston'. Stone sculptural work is believed to have been by William Forsyth. This was but one of a number of such properties designed by Elmslie in this part of Malvern.

In 1922 the building was acquired by Lawnside school and was named 'Lawnside Grove'. The headmistress of the school allowed the buildings facilities to be used by producers, performers and guests attending the Malvern Festivals

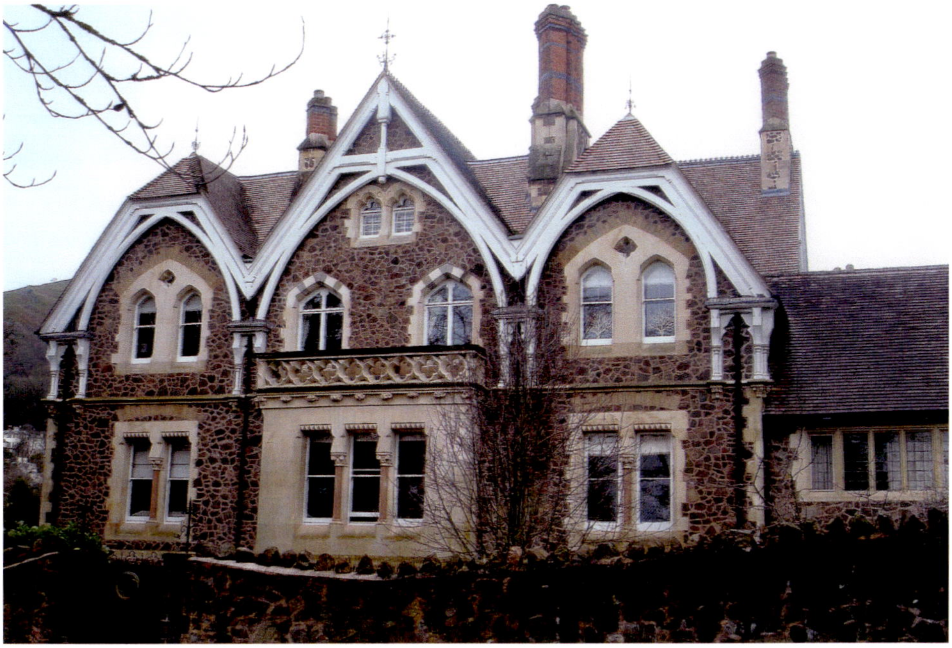

Elmslie House, Avenue Road, Great Malvern.

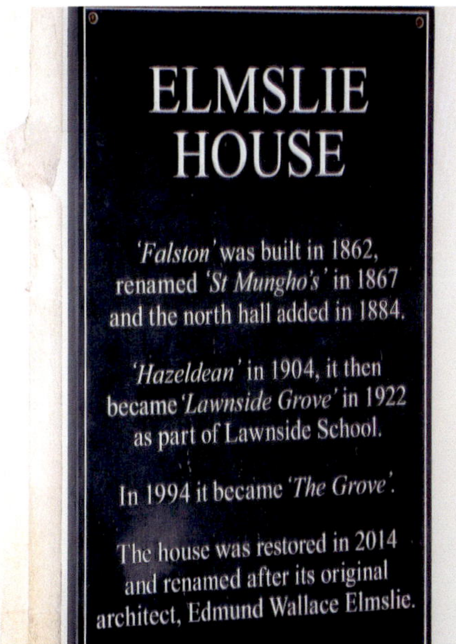

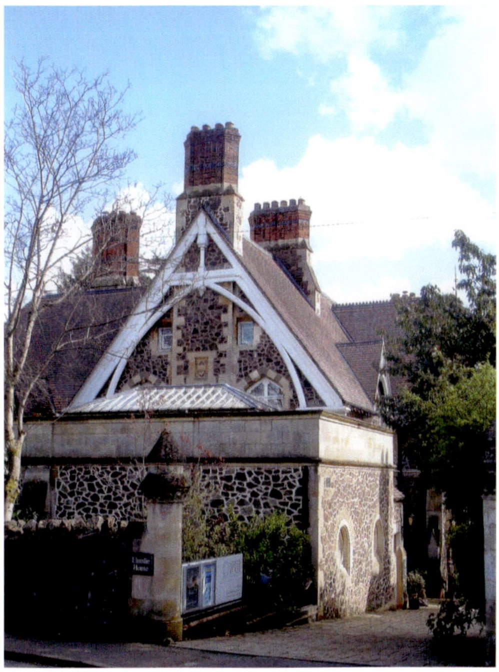

Above left: Potted history plaque of Elmslie House.

Above right: Entrance to Elmslie House in Avenue Road.

between 1929 and 1939. Notable guests included George Bernard Shaw, J. B. Priestley and Dame Laura Knight.

Lawnside sold the house in 1994 and it was then named 'The Grove'. Twenty years later the house was restored and renamed again after its original architect.

Today Elmslie House is both a family home and a locally important venue for art exhibitions, exercise and yoga classes, craft workshops, concerts and other events. Every two years Elmslie House hosts Blue Magpie Contemporary Craft Fairs.

23. Malvern College (1863–65), College Road, Malvern, WR14 3DF

This, perhaps one of the most spectacular of buildings in a town of spectacular buildings, was designed by Charles F Hanson and built of local Cradley stone in Early Tudor style between 1863 and 1865 as the main building for Malvern College, which had been founded just a year earlier in 1862.

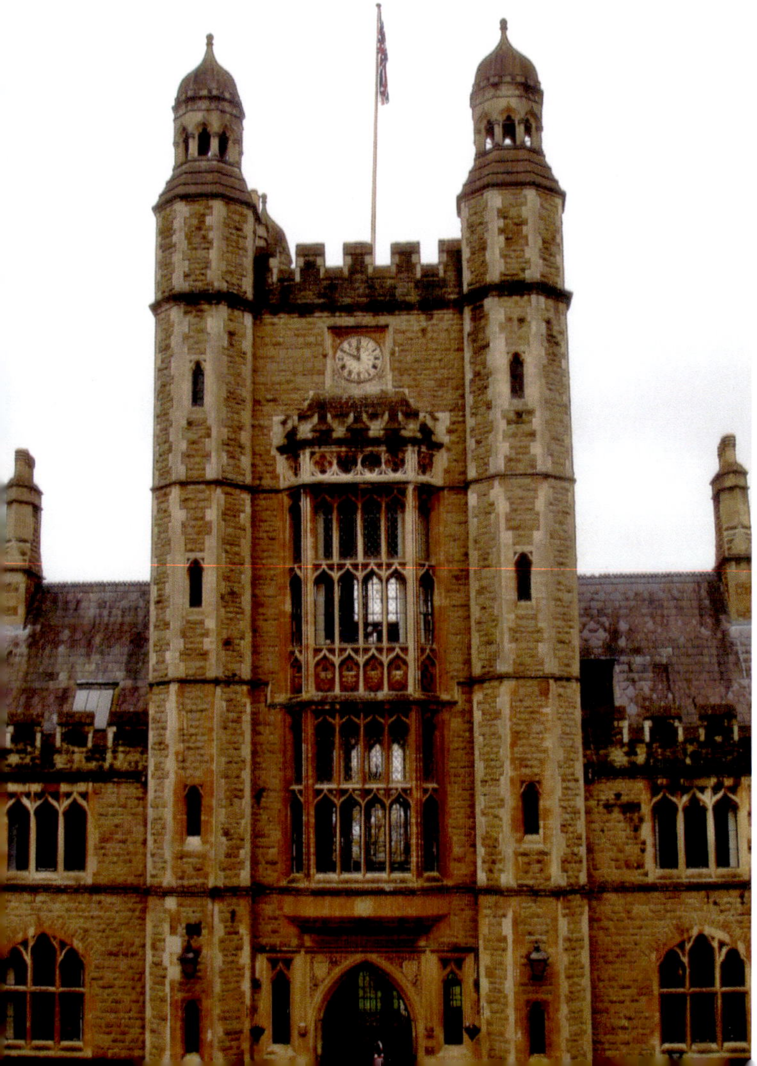

Malvern College gatehouse from College Road.

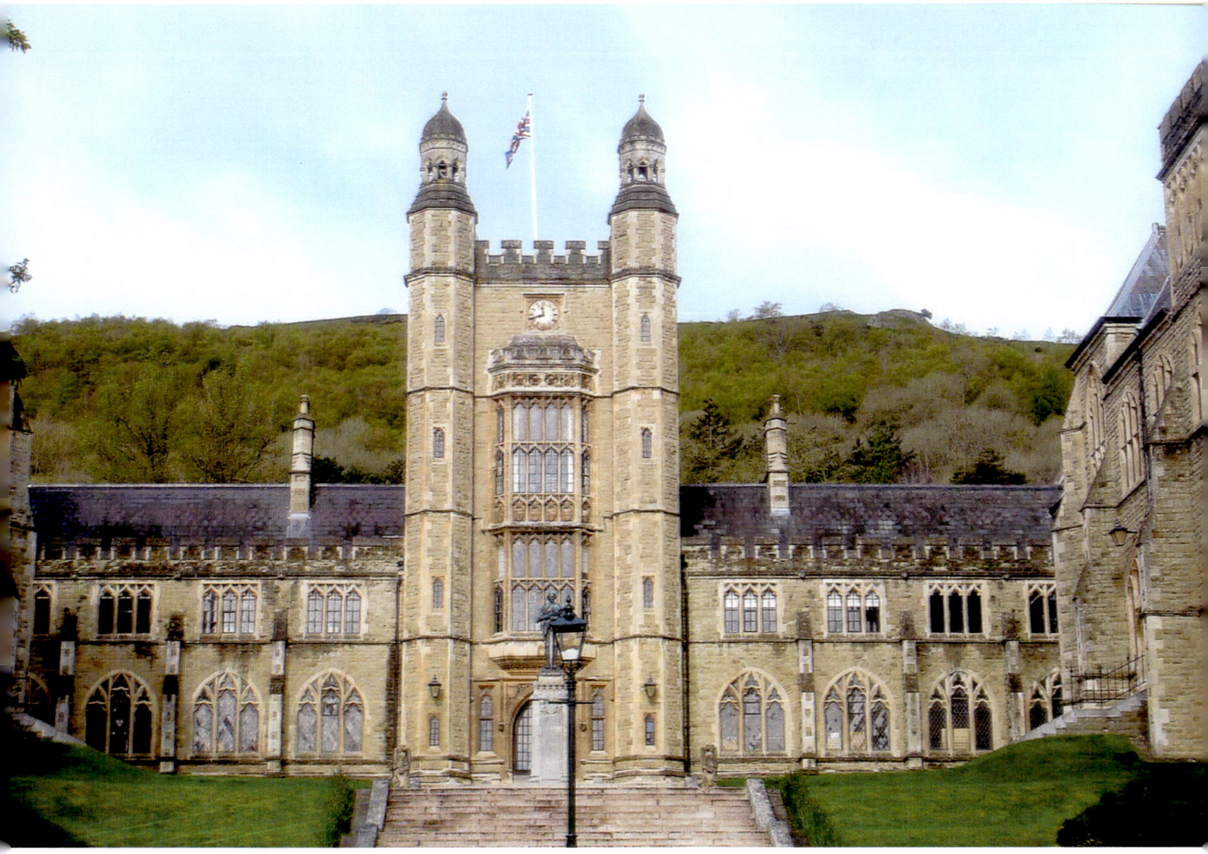

Malvern College main building from the east.

The gatehouse is striking from whichever angle you look at it, as you might expect as part of Malvern's most prestigious educational establishment. The chapel to the south of the college was added by Sir Arthur W. Bloomfield in 1897/99. The war memorial at the rear gatehouse entrance was by Sir Aston Webb and placed here in 1922. The prominent bronze figure of St George atop the monument was created by Alfred Drury.

During the Second World War Malvern College was home to the Telecommunications Research Establishment (TRE) from 1942 to 1946. A green plaque near the front entrance to the college describes the 'boffins' who worked for the TRE as having developed radar and pioneered radio astronomy and modern computing. The TRE after the Second World War moved to St Andrews Road, Malvern, where they eventually became the Defence Evaluation and Research Agency (DERA) and later QinetiQ.

The novelist C. S. Lewis attended Malvern College for a term during 1913/14. He became great friends whilst at Oxford University with George Sayer, who was later Head of English at Malvern College. Both Sayer and Lewis enjoyed the local

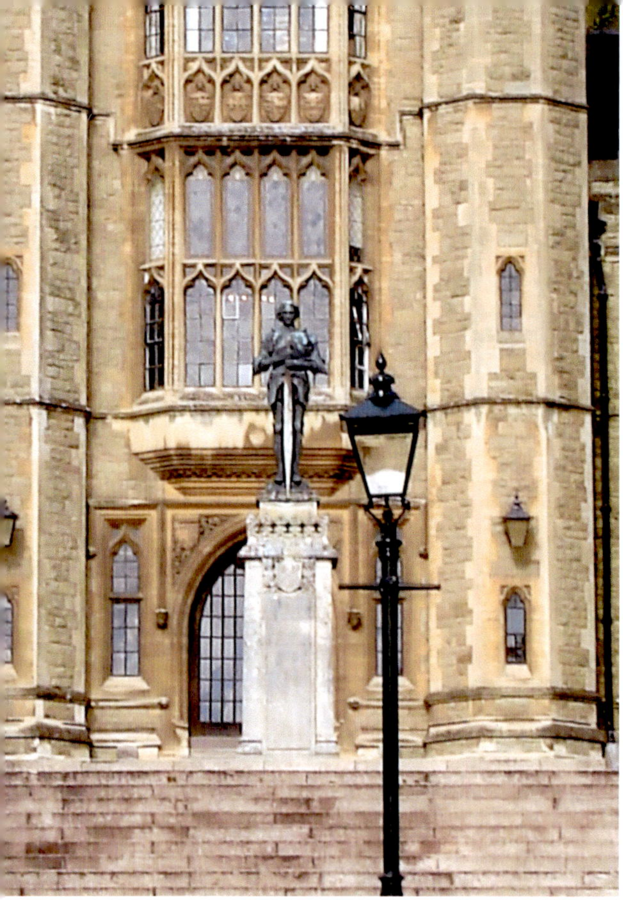

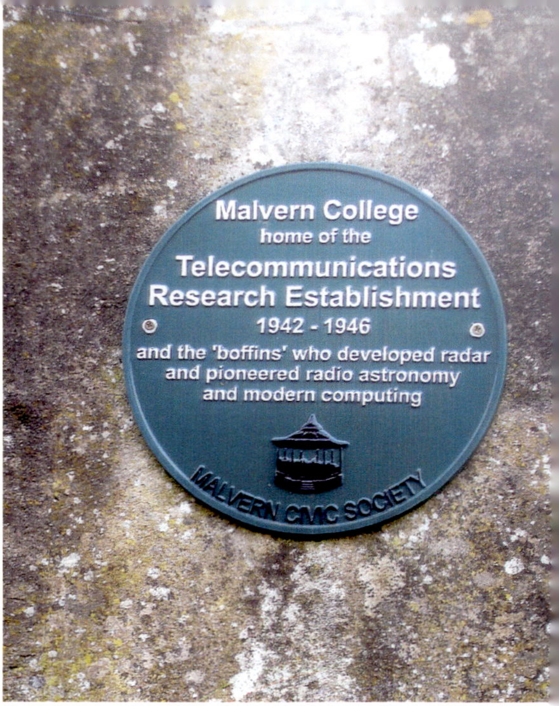

Above: Green plaque at the front entrance to Malvern College.

Left: War memorial and bronze St George statue at rear entrance to Malvern College.

hostelries and walks in the Malvern Hills along with J. R. R. Tolken, the author of *The Hobbit* and *Lord of the Rings*.

Today Malvern College is a most successful fee-charging, co-educational boarding school that also accepts day pupils. The college's campus covers some 250 acres and includes excellent playing fields. It also had overseas campuses in Egypt, China, Hong Kong and Japan. Malvern College's main building is Grade II listed.

24. Wesleyan Methodist Church (1865–66), Lansdowne Crescent, Great Malvern, WR14 2AW

This soaring church building was designed by John Tarring and built to replace an earlier Wesleyan chapel. The church tower certainly lifts the eye heavenwards and impresses with its battlements and pinnacles, typical of Victorian Gothic architecture. The church is built from Malvern stone.

Inside, the columns that support the church roof are capped with colourful floral decorative sculpture by William Forsyth, very reminiscent of his work in Great Malvern railway station. The floral theme is continued in the stained glass of the east window, installed in 1886.

Talking of windows, from the outside the church windows appear much higher in extent than they do inside. The answer to this puzzle is that the ceiling of the church was in effect lowered by the installation of a false one only half the height of the original to deal with poor acoustics within the building. The lowered ceiling much improved sound quality within the church, though the chancel ceiling has now been restored to its original height.

The basement of the church once played host to a primary school but, again, acoustics were a problem, with the sound from each classroom disturbing its neighbours. The school was eventually relocated to just off Pickersleigh Road where it is now known as Malvern Primary School.

The Wesleyan Methodist church is an active participant in the Malvern branch of 'Churches Together'.

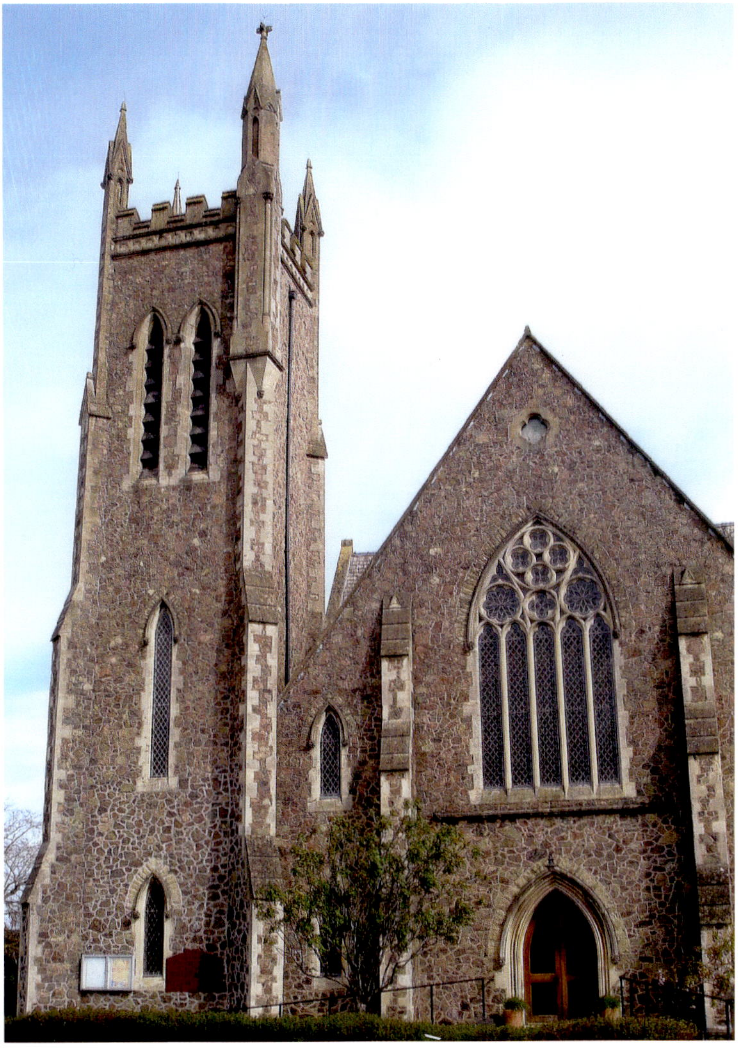

Wesleyan Methodist Church, Lansdowne Crescent, Great Malvern.

25. Madresfield Court (1863–88), Madresfield, Malvern, WR13 5AJ

There has been a house here since at least the twelfth century. The earliest mention, in 1086, has the site in the possession of Urse d'Abetot, the sheriff of Worcestershire. By 1196 the manor belonged to the de Bracy family until the de Bracy heiress married into the Lygon family in the fifteenth century. The property has since then continued in the family down to the present day, having never been bought or sold throughout its history. William Lygon had the house rebuilt in 1584–93, replacing the fifteenth-century medieval house.

The Madresfield Court we see today is a more recent affair still, in the main, hence the dating I have given it for this entry.

In 1815 another William Lygon became the first Earl Beauchamp. The fifth Earl Beauchamp commissioned architect P. C. Hardwick to commence a thorough remodelling of the house in 1863, which subsequently continued until 1888. The moated manor house became a 'Victorian fantasy', more or less a complete reconstruction with nearly every room altered in some way and each very different from the others. There were also new rooms added, a tower with a spire and timber bell turret and a wing of reception rooms. After twenty-five years of work Madresfield Court had been transformed.

A little later in 1902 the chapel was added, which contains what has been described as an exceptionally complete example of Arts and Crafts-style decoration. This was begun in 1902 by the Birmingham Group of craftsmen for Countess Beauchamp as a wedding present for the seventh Earl Beauchamp. The work continued until 1923.

Outside the building is no less interesting. A rock garden and grotto was produced by James Pulham and Son using Pulham's own innovation, 'pulhamite', an artificial stone made from rubble cased in cement. The garden extends over two levels. There is also an interesting pavement pattern in the form of a maze.

Madresfield Court. (Courtesy of Madresfield Estate/Ray Main)

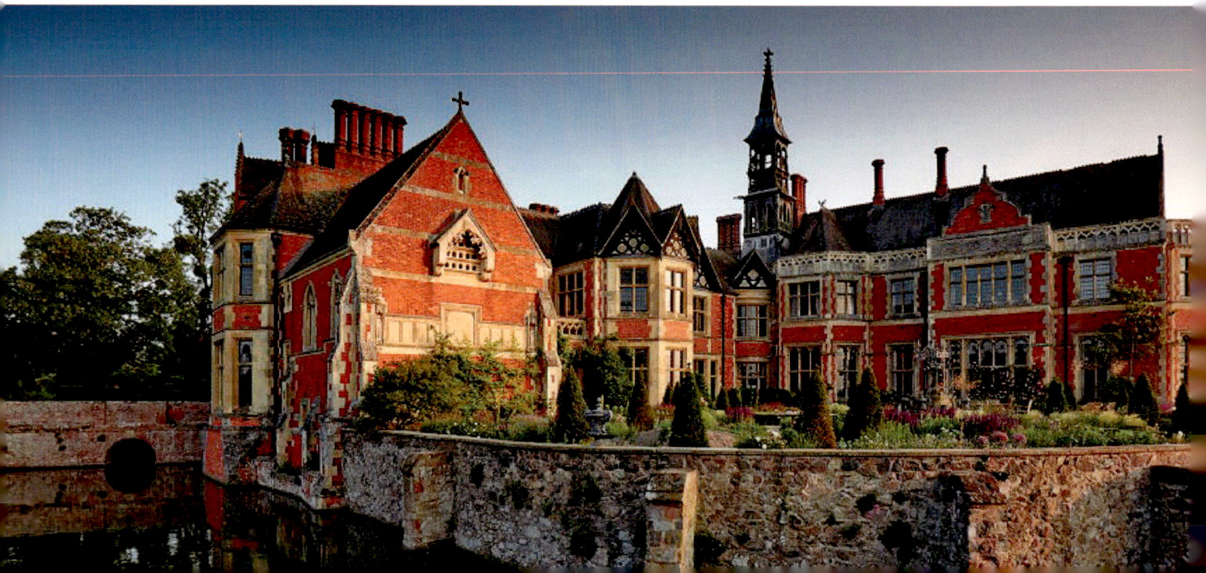

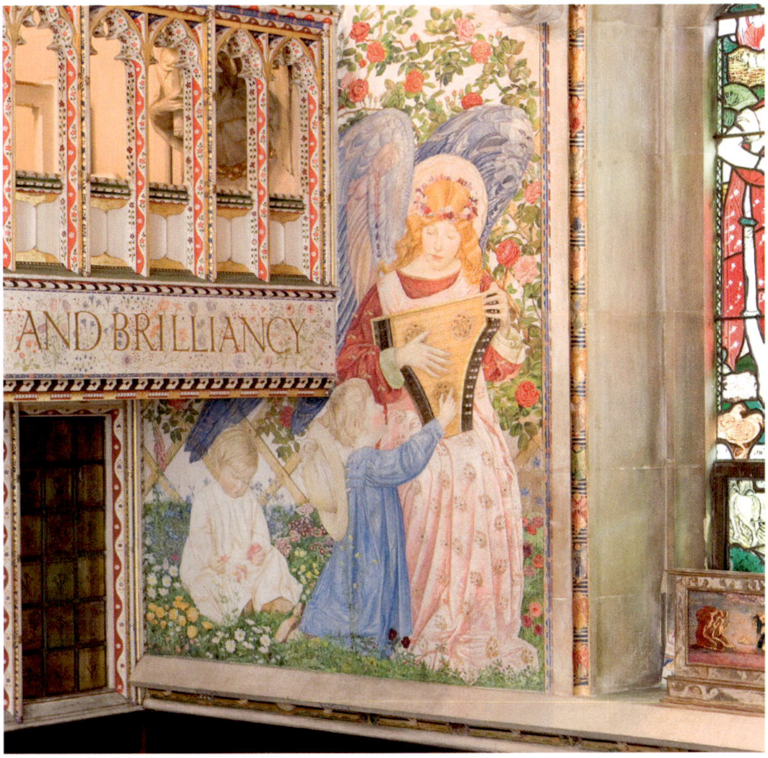

Madresfield Court Chapel. (Courtesy of Madresfield Estate)

Apart from the very interesting building itself Madresfield also has a literary connection. Novelist Evelyn Waugh became a close friend of the Lygon family, firstly through knowing Hugh Lygon, the second son of William, the seventh Earl Beauchamp, from his days at Oxford University and later his three sisters Mary, Sibell and Dorothy. Waugh stayed at The County Hotel (now Park View) in Malvern in 1931 whilst taking riding lessons locally but later became absorbed into the family and social life at Madresfield Court. It is certain that his famous novel *Brideshead Revisited* was based on his observations of life at Madresfield. Some of his characters are clearly based on members of the Lygon family, whilst he describes details of the interior of Madresfield Court such as the decoration of the chapel as being in the fictional Brideshead. *Brideshead Revisited* was published in 1945.

During the Second World War Madresfield Court was apparently being considered as the place to which the royal family would be evacuated in the event of Hitler's forces invading England in the south-east of the country. In fact, the government of the day was to be relocated to Worcestershire, far from London and the south-east.

Today Madresfield Court is a Grade I listed building and other buildings on the estate are Grade II listed. Madresfield Court is not generally open to the public but tours can be arranged by emailing tours@madresfieldestate.co.uk.

26. The Council House (formerly Priory Park Mansion) (1874–80), Avenue Road, Great Malvern, WR14 3AF

Described by Pevsner as Malvern's 'largest and best' Victorian Gothic house, what is now known as The Council House was originally built as a mansion for Alfred Miles Speer, a London-based businessman who made his fortune importing bird and bat guano from Peru for use as fertiliser.

Speer commissioned architect Henry Haddon to design the house, which took six years to complete. The Council House, although not open to the public, is highly interesting to view from the outside, which is public land, Priory Park, the one-time gardens of the mansion. Carvings are in the main by William Forsyth and the stained glass by Heaton, Butler and Bayne. There are many interesting features to the building itself including on the south-eastern corner a large polygonal oriel projecting from the top of a hexagonal shaft, on the eastern side a large domed conservatory, and ornate chimneys, grotesques and on the northern side an interesting pinnacle tower.

Following the departure of the Speers family this fine building was put to other uses. From 1909 to 1925 it served as a boy's preparatory school until sold to

The Council House, formerly Priory Park Mansion.

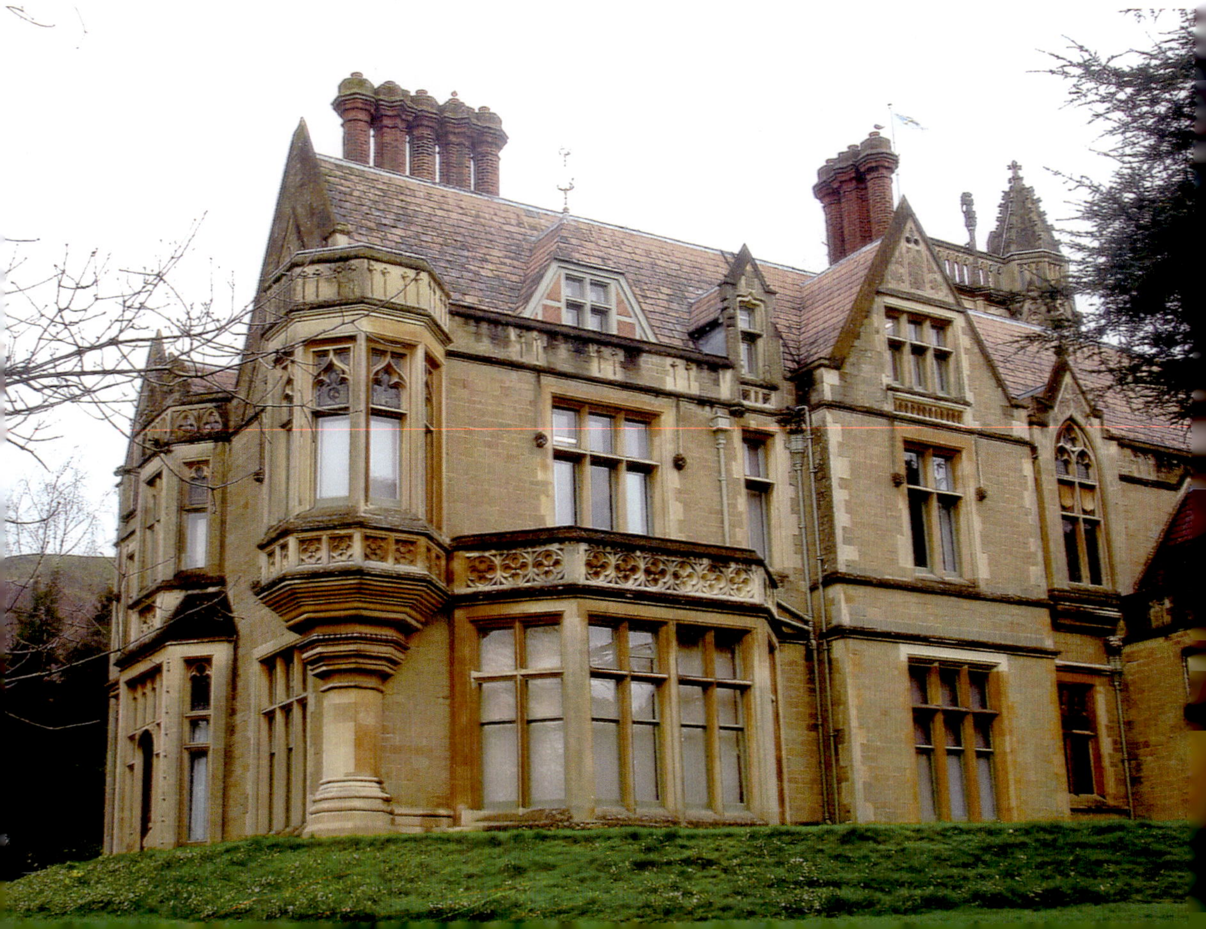

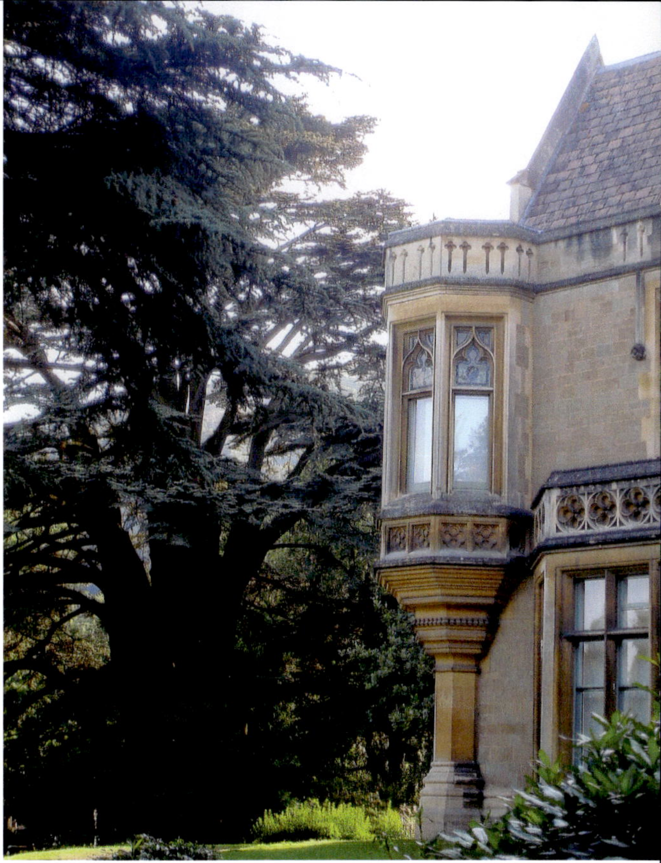

Right: Oriel on the south-eastern corner of The Council House.

Below: Domed conservatory on the east side of The Council House.

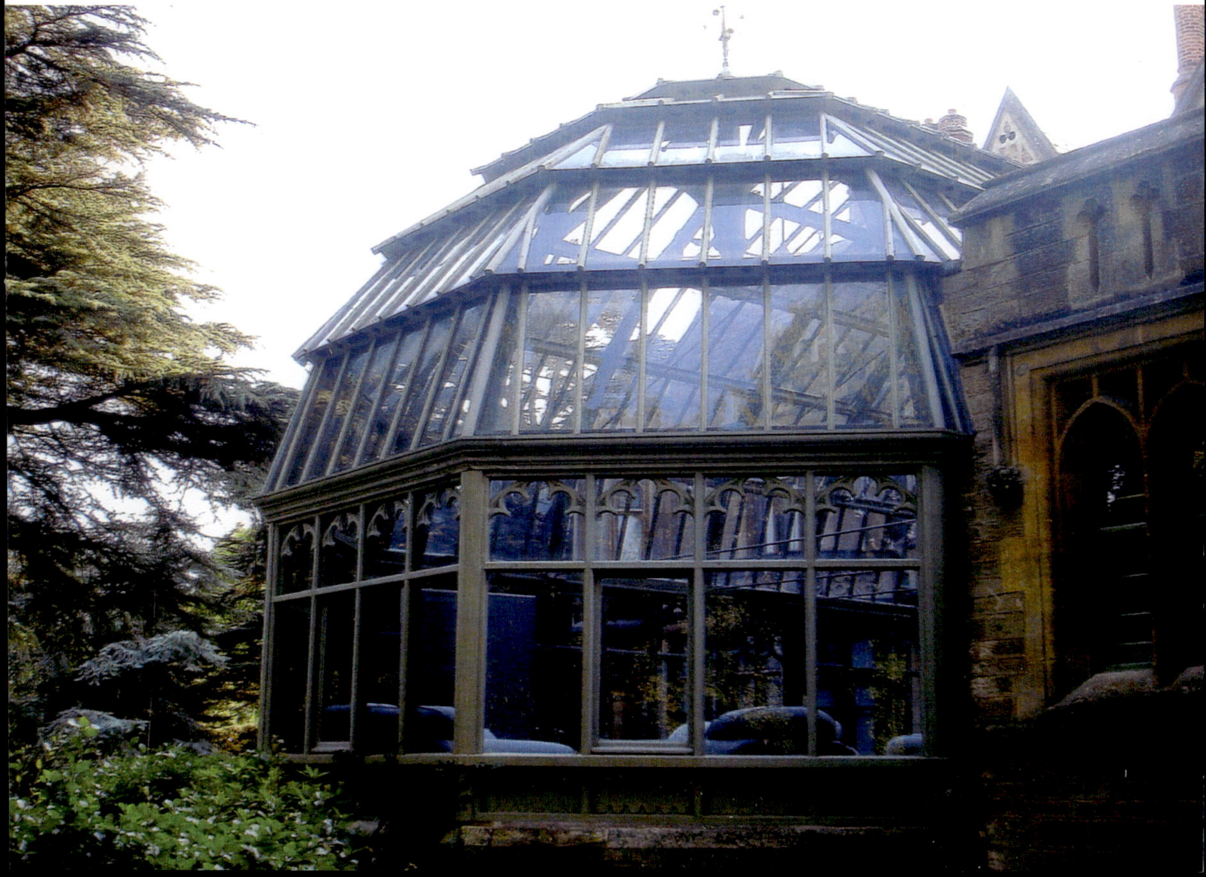

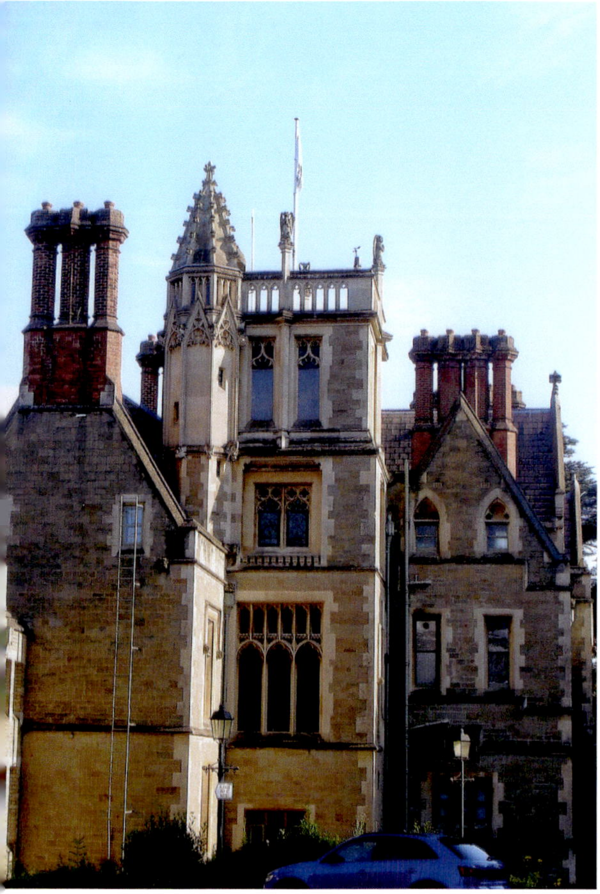

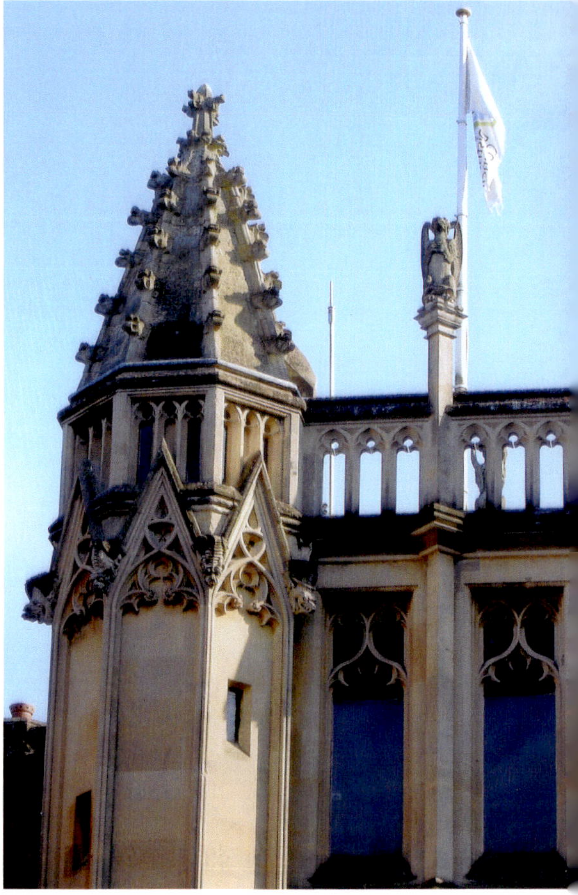

Above left: North side of The Council House.

Above right: Pinnacled tower, The Council House.

the local district council and is today the main administrative centre for Malvern Hills District Council. The exceptional quality of the architecture has earned The Council House a Grade II* listing.

27. The Bandstand (1875), Priory Park, Great Malvern, WR14 3AF

Priory Park is a most attractive enclave of Great Malvern with its superb collection of fine trees, ornamental ponds and a beautiful new wooden sculpture of the swimming *Malvhina,* carved by Tom Harvey, an artistic embodiment of the spirit of springs and flowing water. The park's most traditional centrepiece, however, is the Victorian bandstand, erected here in 1875, a must have for any genteel Victorian park.

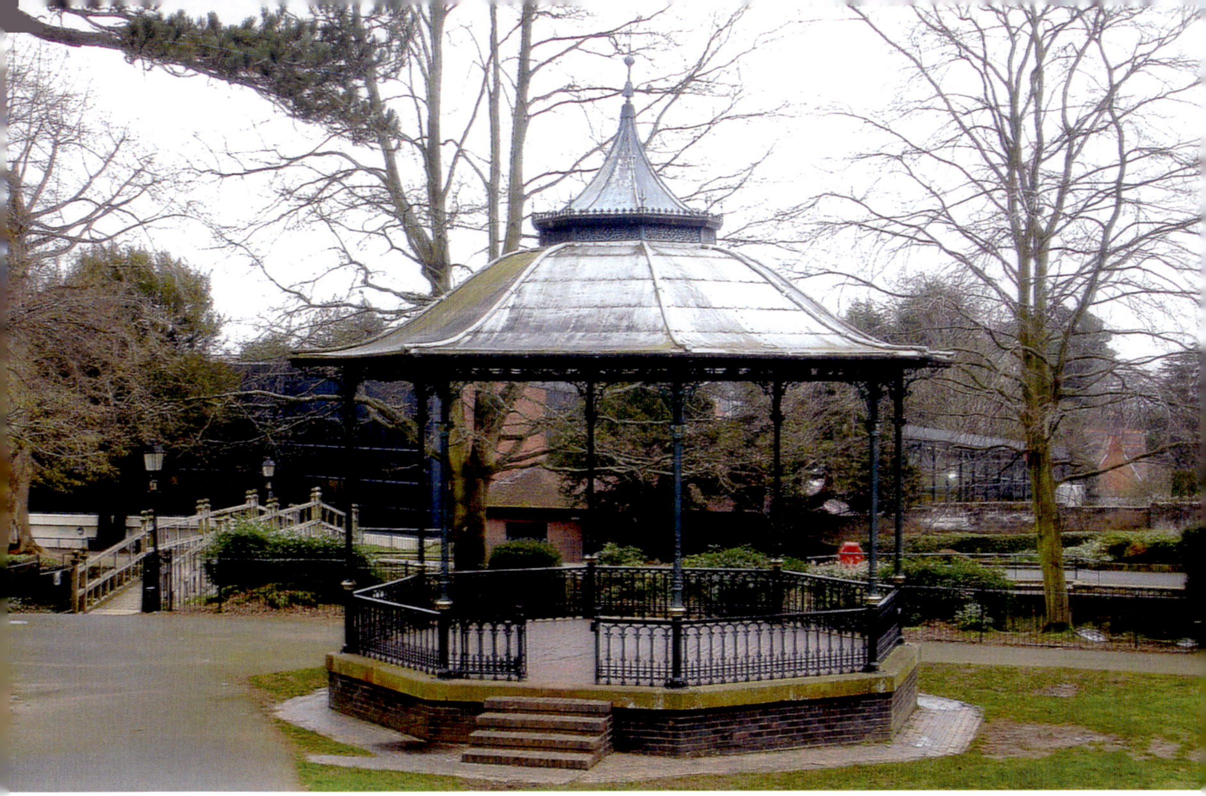

Above: The Bandstand in Priory Park.

Right: Carved *Malvhina* sculpture by Tom Harvey.

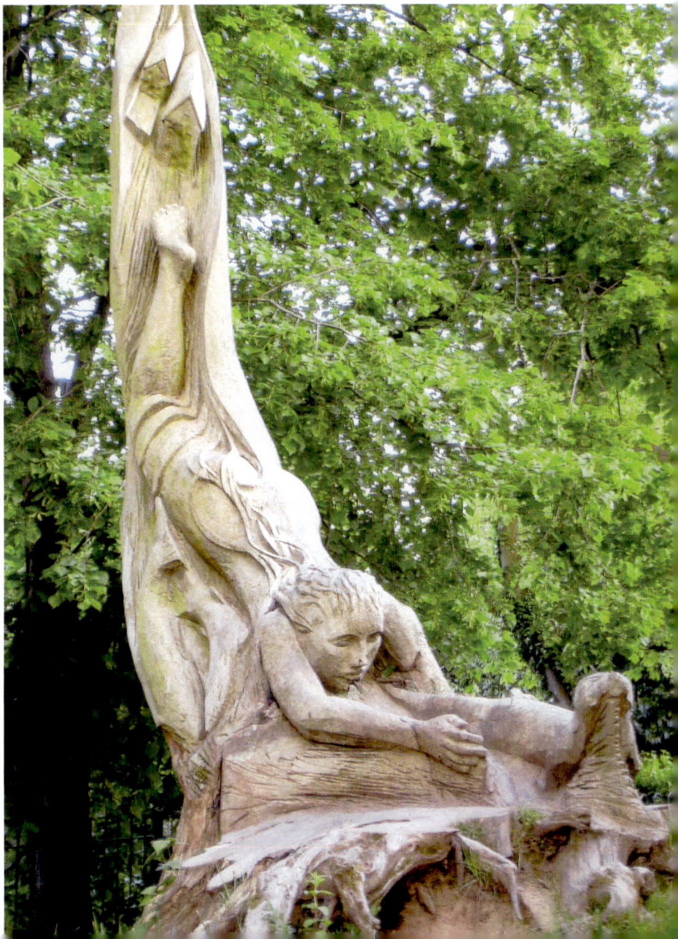

The ironwork of this bandstand was carried out by W. Macfarlane and Company, a Glasgow-based business. The bandstand was used as a podium for entertainment for decades, but in the 1950s was move to Victoria Park in Malvern Link. Here, it did not get the same use or attention and over the years deteriorated and suffered from vandalism. In 1984 the Malvern Civic Society succeeded in arranging for its return to Priory Park where it today once again hosts Sunday summer concerts and other entertainments. The bandstand is a Grade II listed structure.

28. Lloyds Bank (1892), No. 48 Belle Vue Terrace, Great Malvern, WR14 3LZ

This address was once the Crown Hotel until in 1842 Dr James Wilson arrived to set up his 'water cure' business, which, along with that of Dr James Gully, propelled Malvern into its boom years of the mid- to late nineteenth century. Dr Wilson bought the Crown Hotel and renamed it Gräfenberg House, after the Austrian village of Gräfenberg where the modern age of hydrotherapy began, courtesy of the work of Vincent Priessnitz from whom Dr Wilson had learnt the practice. It was here that Dr Wilson set up his first hydrotherapy centre, later moving onto a larger building in Abbey Road, now known as Park View.

Lloyds Bank, formerly the site of the Crown Hotel.

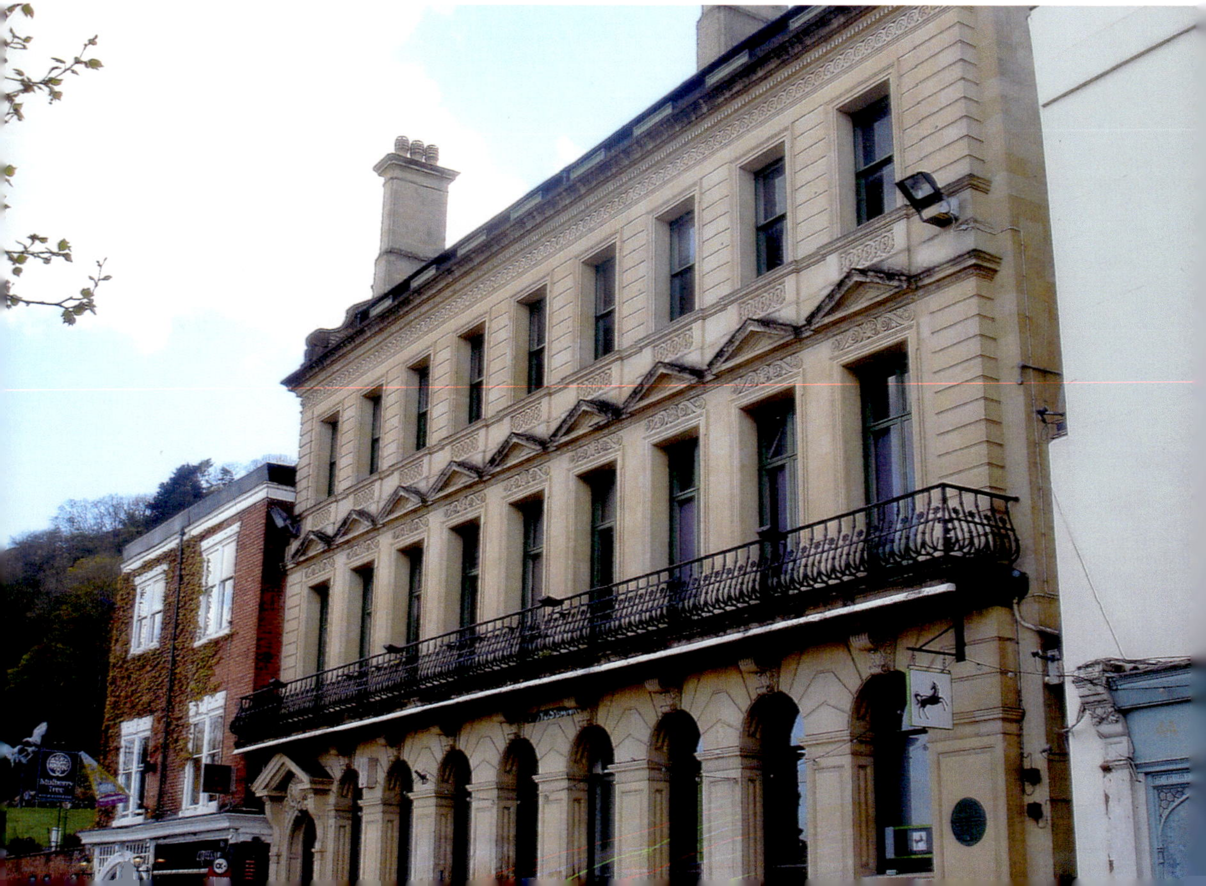

By 1892, with the popularity of the 'water cure' waning, Gräfenberg House had been demolished and a new, Italianate-style building had arisen in its place designed by Birmingham architect J. A. Chatwin for the Worcester and County Bank. In 1930 the building was enlarged for Lloyds Bank, who have operated a branch here ever since.

29. Malvern Public Library (1905–06), Graham Road, Malvern, WR14 4HU

Malvern came late to the concept of public libraries, whereas many English towns introduced them through the second half of the nineteenth century. Some local residents were opposed to the idea fearing the cost to the public purse but money was raised by American businessman Andrew Carnegie and local philanthropist Charles Dyson Perrins and the foundation stone was laid on 5 February 1905 at a public event that attracted some 5,000 people. The building was completed the following year, with the library formally opening on 18 May 1906. The library building was designed by Birmingham architect Henry Crouch and built by James Herbert.

Malvern Public Library is an attractive red-brick building constructed in Edwardian baroque style with large ionic pilasters flanking the entrance and two

Malvern Public Library.

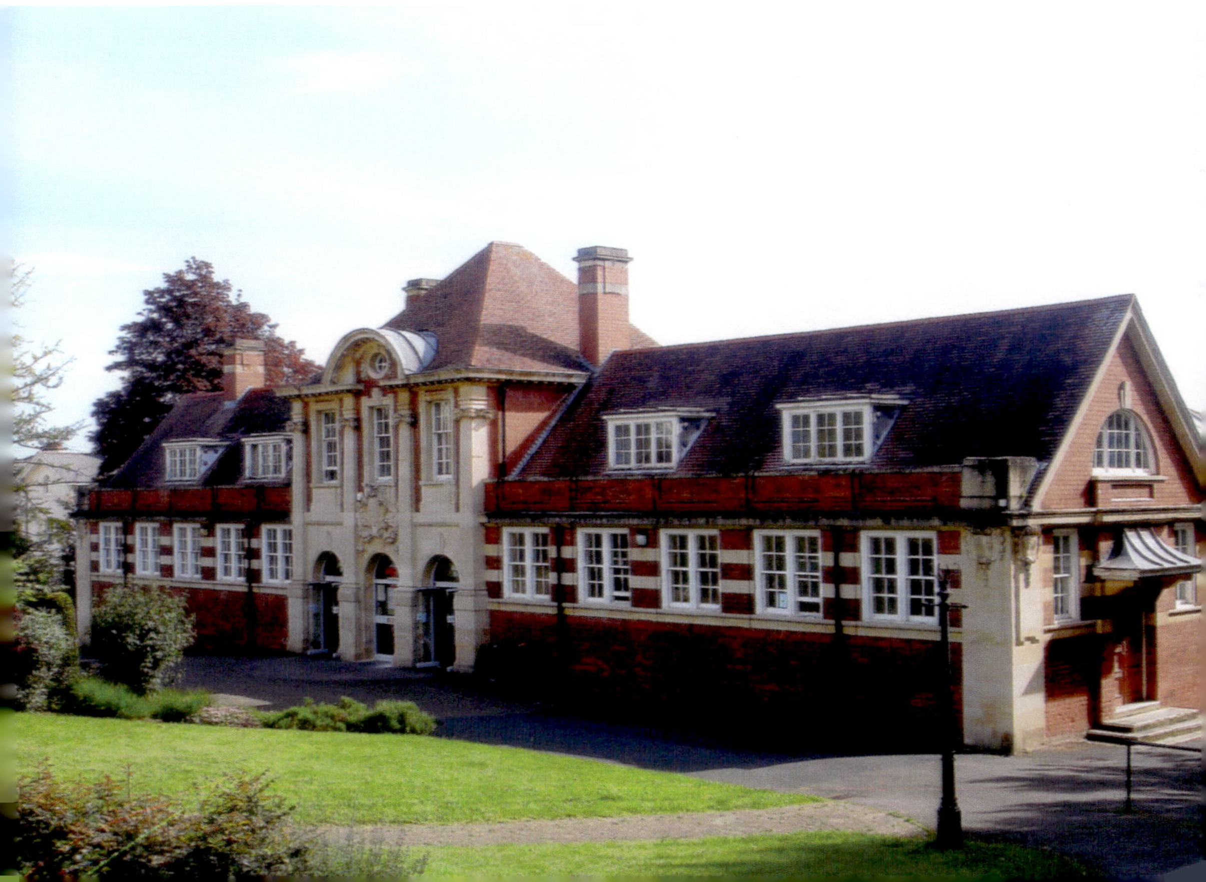

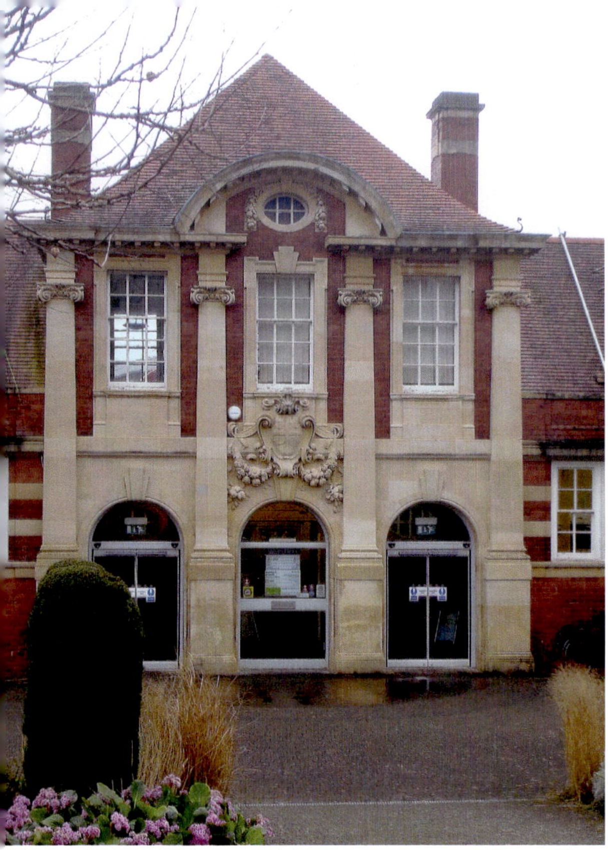

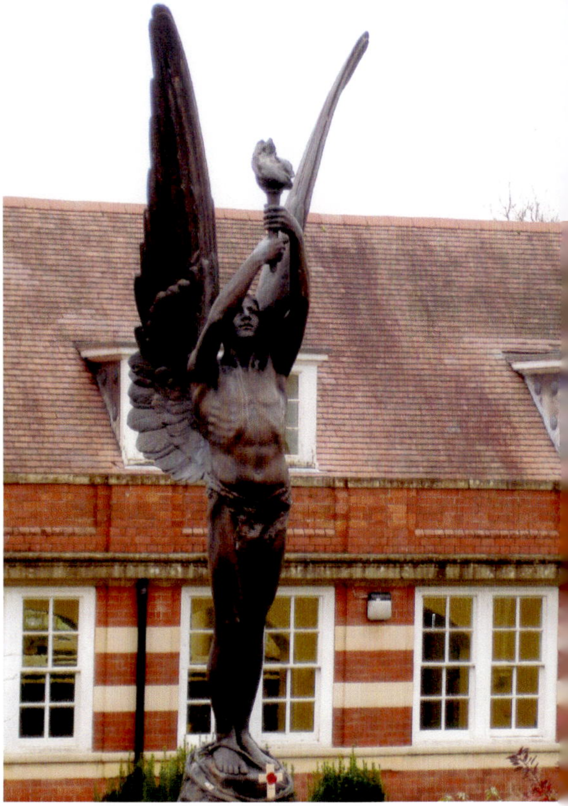

Above left: Malvern Public Library front entrance.

Above right: War memorial, Malvern Public Library.

single-storey wings adjoining the central two-storey main building. Extensions to the building were made by M. W. Jones in 1937 and Worcestershire County Council Property Services in 2005 on the eastern (rear) side.

In front of the main entrance to Malvern Library stands a large bronze angel statue with uplifted wings. This is a war memorial and was designed by Sir Aston Webb and Sons. The torch held in the figure's hands, the *Torch of Truth*, is by Richard R. Goulden. The memorial statue was completed and installed here in 1923.

Malvern Public Library has proven a popular and well-used local facility and has evolved over time, now incorporating computer and Wi-Fi access, a café and a job centre, as well as providing the traditional book lending and local research facilities common to many public libraries throughout the country. However, as of 2024, a new innovation has been introduced called Libraries Unlocked. This allows library members to access the building outside normal hours within a twelve-hour period, in this case 8 a.m. to 8 p.m. Library users can therefore enter and leave the building using their library cards when the facility is not staffed. I'm sure there may be varied opinions on this but hopefully it is working well.

Another recent development has been the establishment of a sensory garden with weekly sessions teaching people how to grow herbs and vegetables using organic methods. Malvern Public Library continues to develop and provide important community services to the town's residents.

The library building itself is Grade II listed.

30. Morgan Motor Company (c. 1914), Pickersleigh Road, Malvern Link, WR14 2LL

Entering Malvern Link from Great Malvern on the Pickersleigh Road the traveller sees an interesting road sign featuring an image of a Morgan car, which of course is recognising the important role the Morgan Motor Company has in the life of Malvern Link.

Malvern Link has the honour of being where Britain's first motor car was manufactured, the Santler Dogcat, which took to the road in 1894. The Santler's first workshop was at a site now occupied by a retirement home called Santler Court in memory of the former car manufacturers. A purple plaque on the building commemorates the taking over of the motor works by H. F. S. Morgan in 1905, who patented and produced the first Morgan car, the 'runabout'.

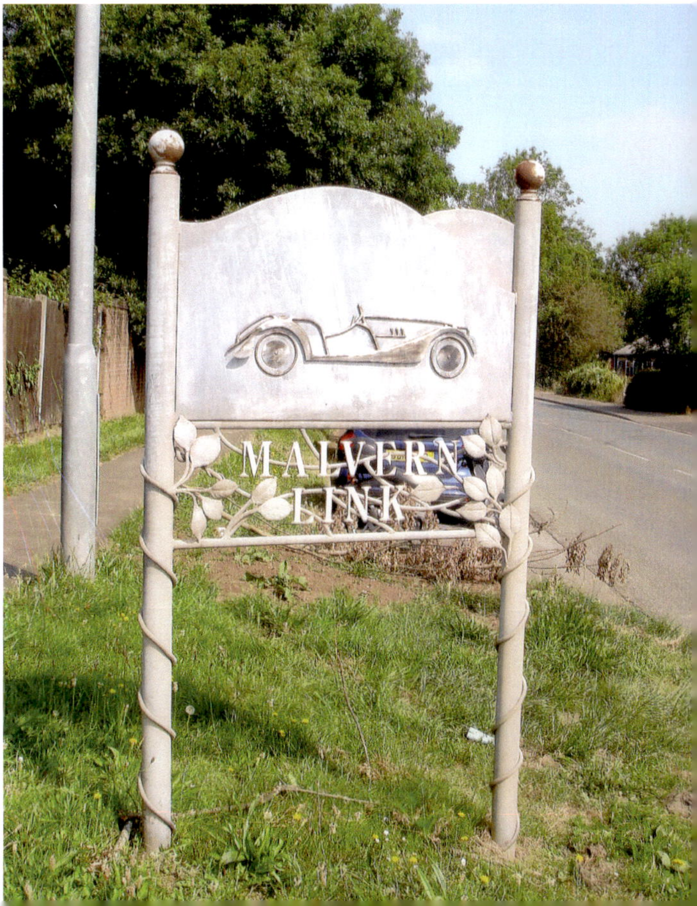

Entering Malvern Link.

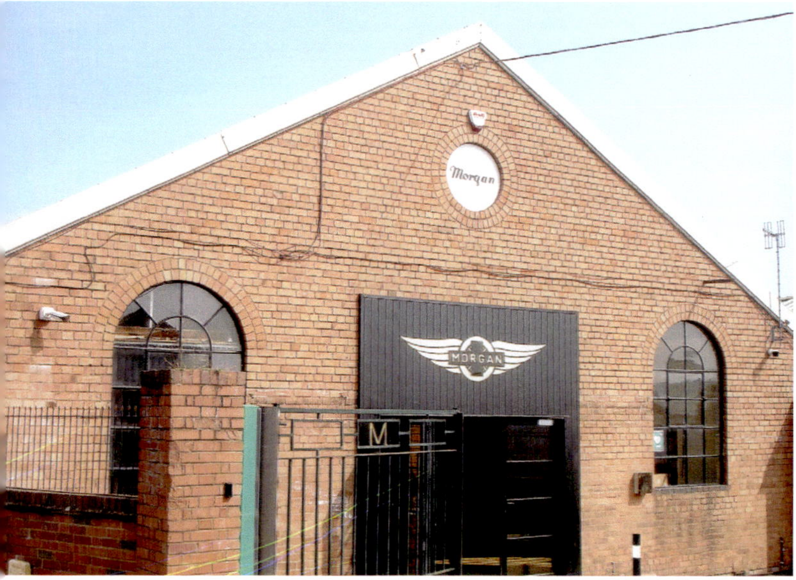

Left: Morgan Motor Company's Pickersleigh Road works.

Below: Morgan cars outside Pickersleigh Road works.

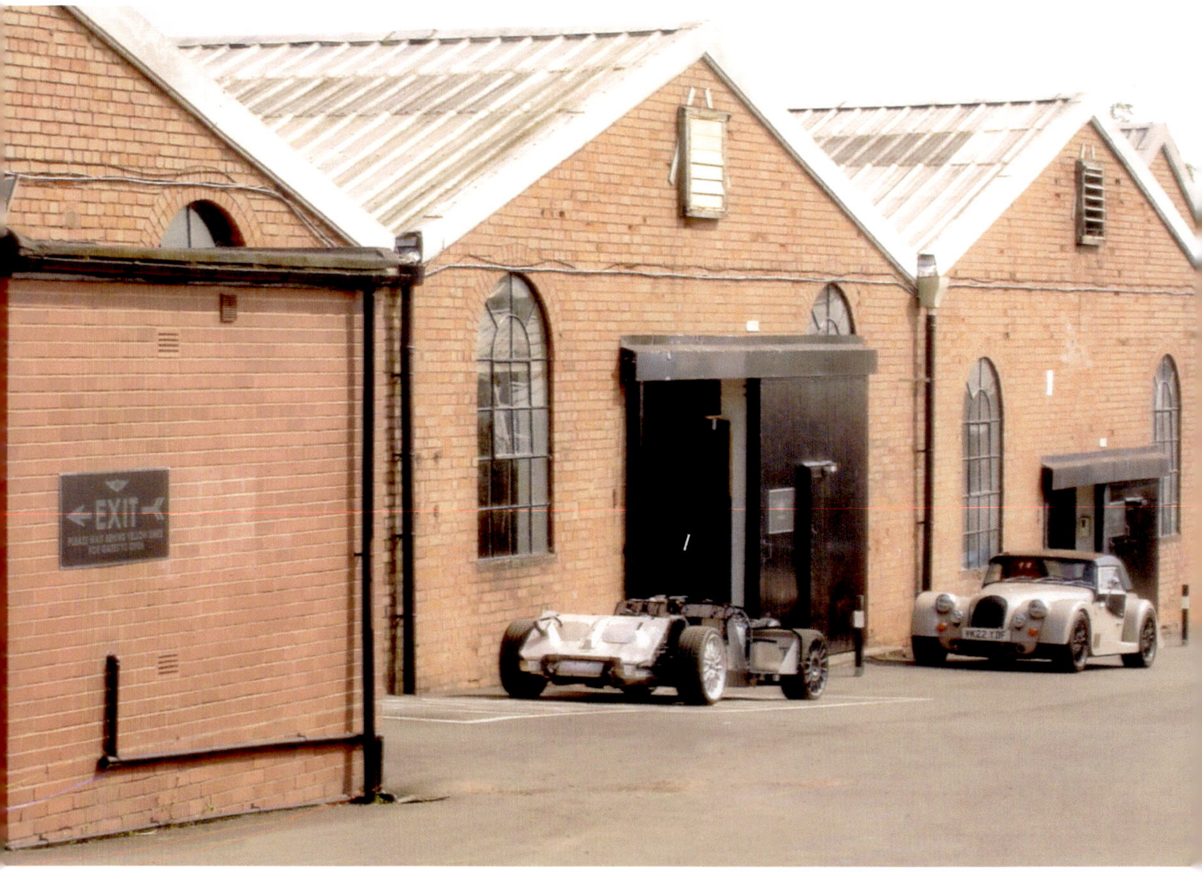

From 1914 the Morgan Motor Company produced a range of cars at the current address in Pickersleigh Road, just opposite the aforementioned road sign.

Here some 850 cars per year are assembled by hand – no mechanised mass production here. The average wait for a car is some six months, which has in the past given rise to criticism from some in the industry but the business model works; people are prepared to wait for a quality handmade vehicle, the like of which they will not find elsewhere.

The Morgan cars themselves were initially all three-wheelers, with the first four-wheeler produced in 1935. Now most cars produced here are four-wheelers. Wood is still used in their construction, the car bodies frame still being hand crafted entirely in ash wood. Some 220 people from in and around Malvern Link are employed by the Morgan Car Company, so it is a significant local employer. The company is recognised as the world's leading coachbuilder and has been producing new models every two years or so on average, the most recent being the Morgan Super 3 (in 2022) and the Morgan Midsummer (2024).

Just around the corner from the Morgan works is a new 'experience centre', of which I will say more later.

31. Malvern Theatres (1927–28/1977–98), Grange Road, Great Malvern, WR14 3HB

In 1885 privately owned Assembly Rooms had been constructed on this site in the beautiful Priory Park for the benefit of Victorian visitors and local people. After a long campaign, Dr Henry Jacob succeeded in bringing about the public ownership of the facilities and park in 1927. The local council embarked on a development programme that created the modern Malvern Theatres complex. Some of the buildings from this time, designed by A. V. Rowe, are still visible to the south end of the Theatres. These building works created a new concert hall, ballroom, and theatre, and shortly after a regular Malvern Festival became part of the annual cultural calendar. The festival was set up and directed by Sir Barry Jackson and George Bernard Shaw and included a drama festival where plays by C. Shaw, as well as J. B. Priestley, had their first performances.

The Malvern Festivals flourished between 1929 and 1939. The first British Film Festival was held here and from 1931 the composer forever associated with Malvern, Edward Elgar, brought his music here and provided, with George Bernard Shaw, the core of the festival programme. Touring plays also often performed here before going on to London's West End. The festivals stopped during the Second World War and didn't return until 1977 when once again Malvern attracted top touring companies and classical performers, but the buildings needed major refurbishment and this was forthcoming by way of a Lottery Grant, which allowed substantial modern development in 1997–98 by the Renton Howard Wood Leven Partnership on behalf of Malvern Hills District Council.

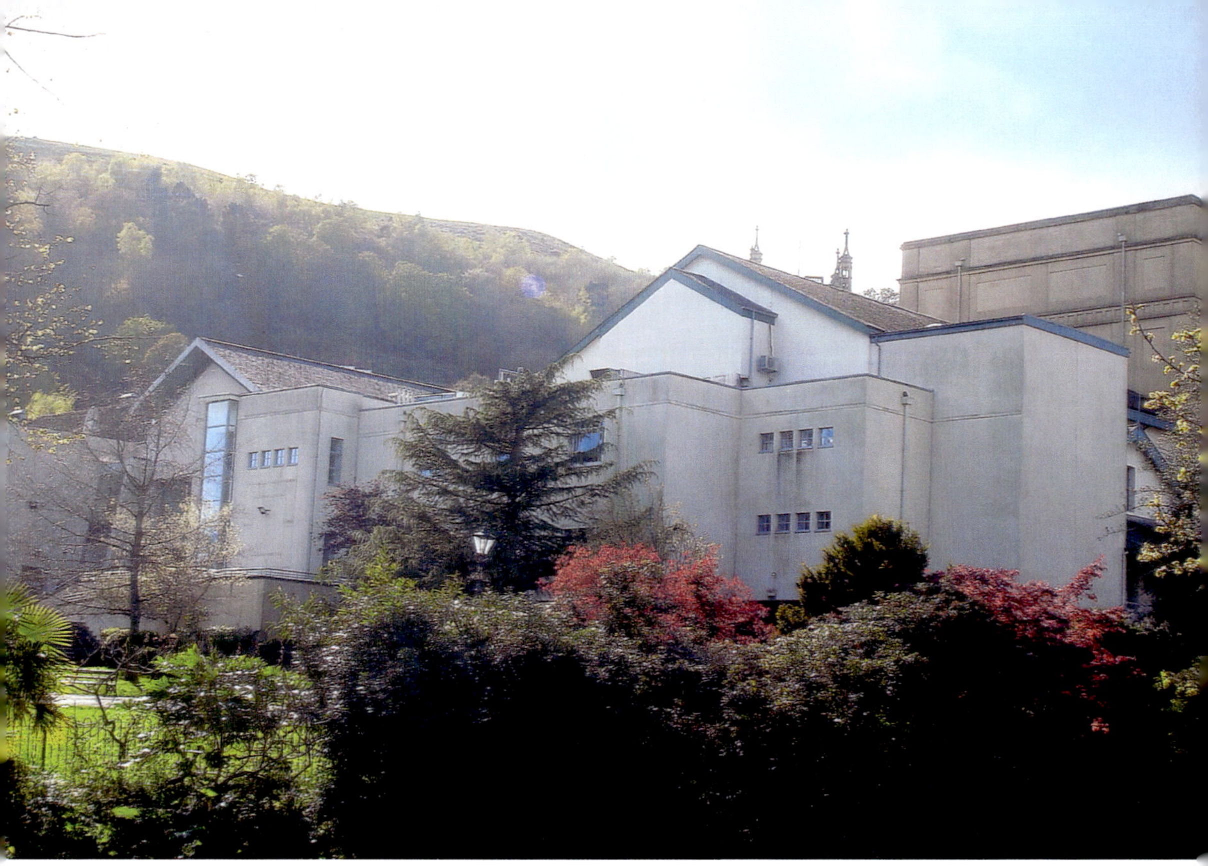

Above: Malvern Theatres in their landscape setting.

Below: Malvern Theatres today after reconstruction in 1997/98.

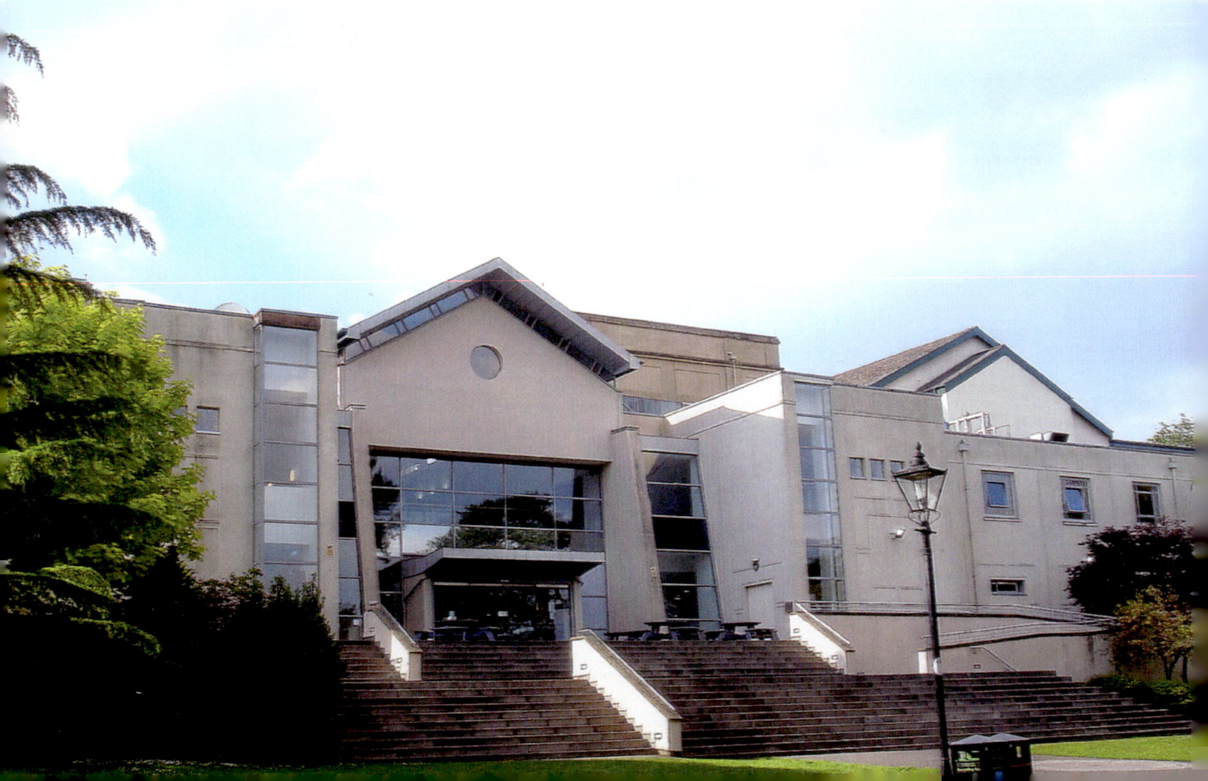

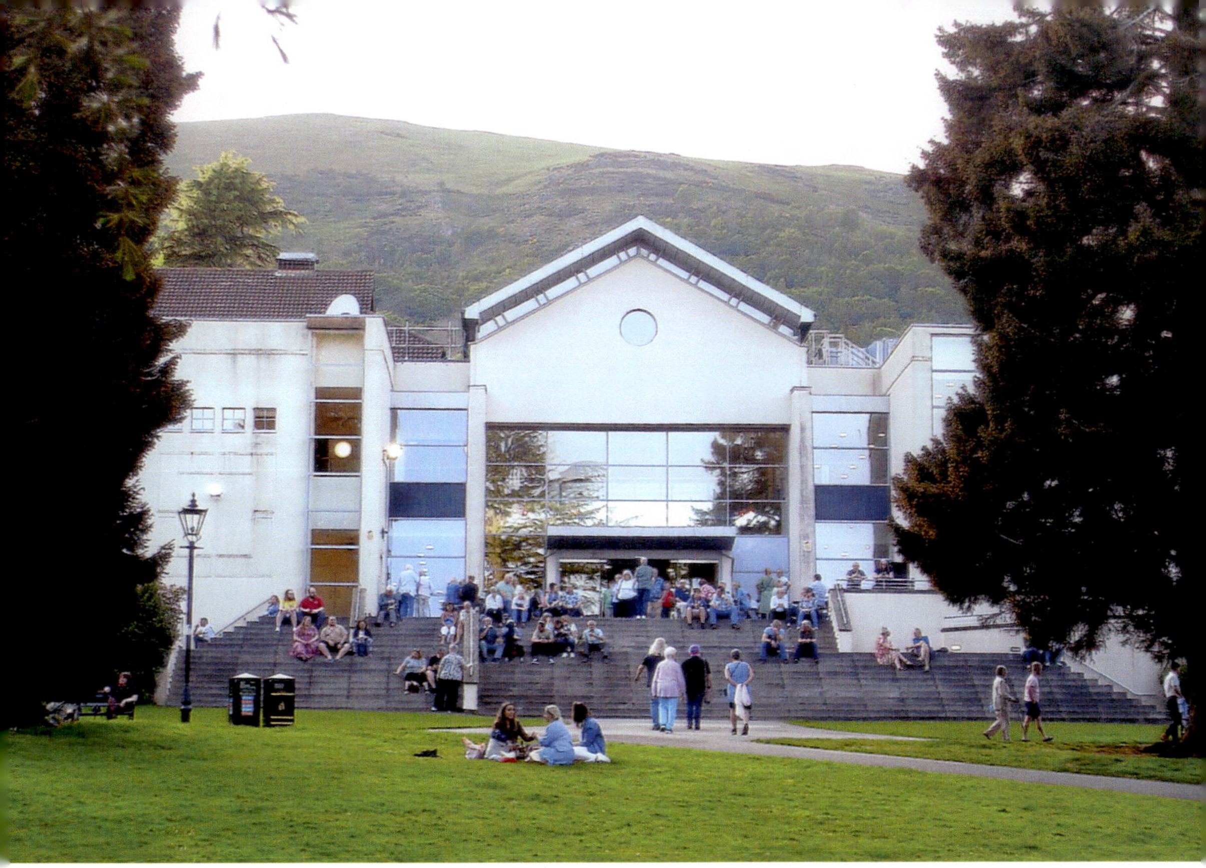

Above: Malvern Theatres with the Malvern Hills in the background.

Below: Close-up of the 1997/98 reconstruction work on Malvern Theatres.

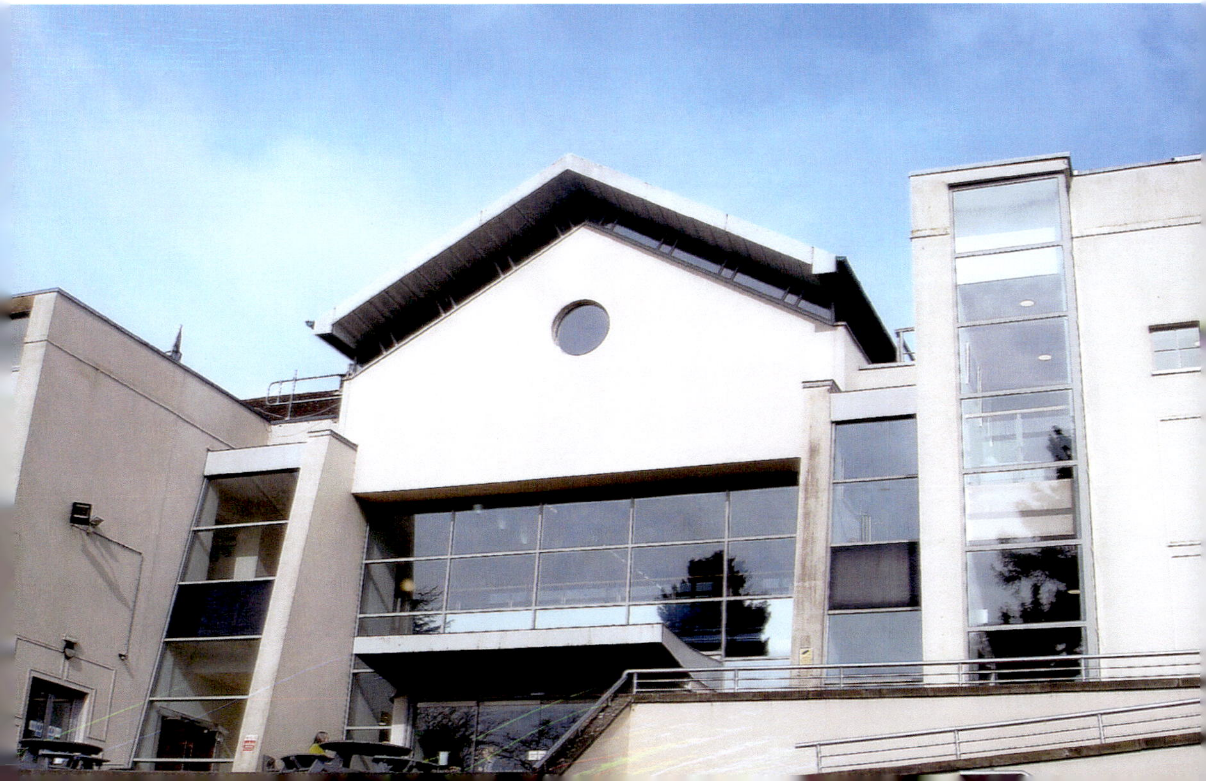

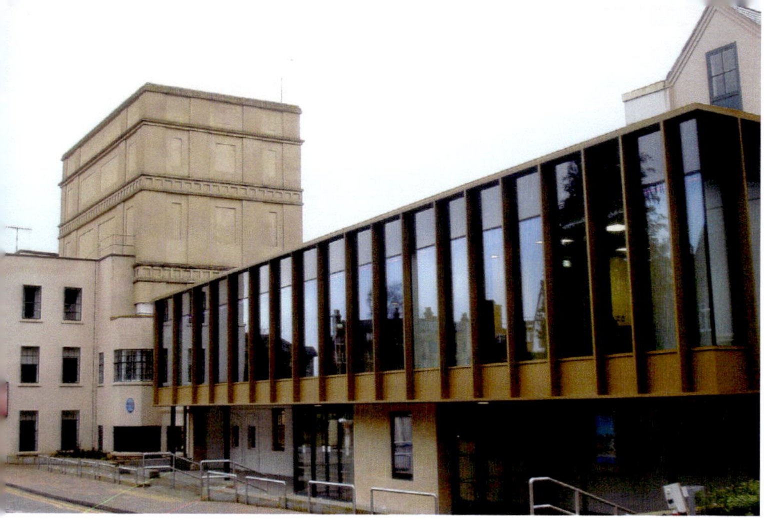

Grange Road entrance, Malvern Theatres, which was reconstructed in 2022.

Malvern Theatres now has, as well as extensive exterior refurbishment, a brand new 800-seat Festival Theatre, a 400-seat cinema, a new bar and restaurant and in 2022 a new wing at the Grange Road entrance was completed.

Today, Malvern Theatres has once again become a major cultural centre for the region.

32. The Water Cure (1931), No. 30 Church Street, Great Malvern, WR14 2AZ

This semi-rotund and rather pleasing looking building is of more recent origin than you might be forgiven for thinking. The style is Renaissance revival designed by F. C. Palmer for the National Provincial Bank, which subsequently operated

The Water Cure, No. 30 Church Street, Great Malvern.

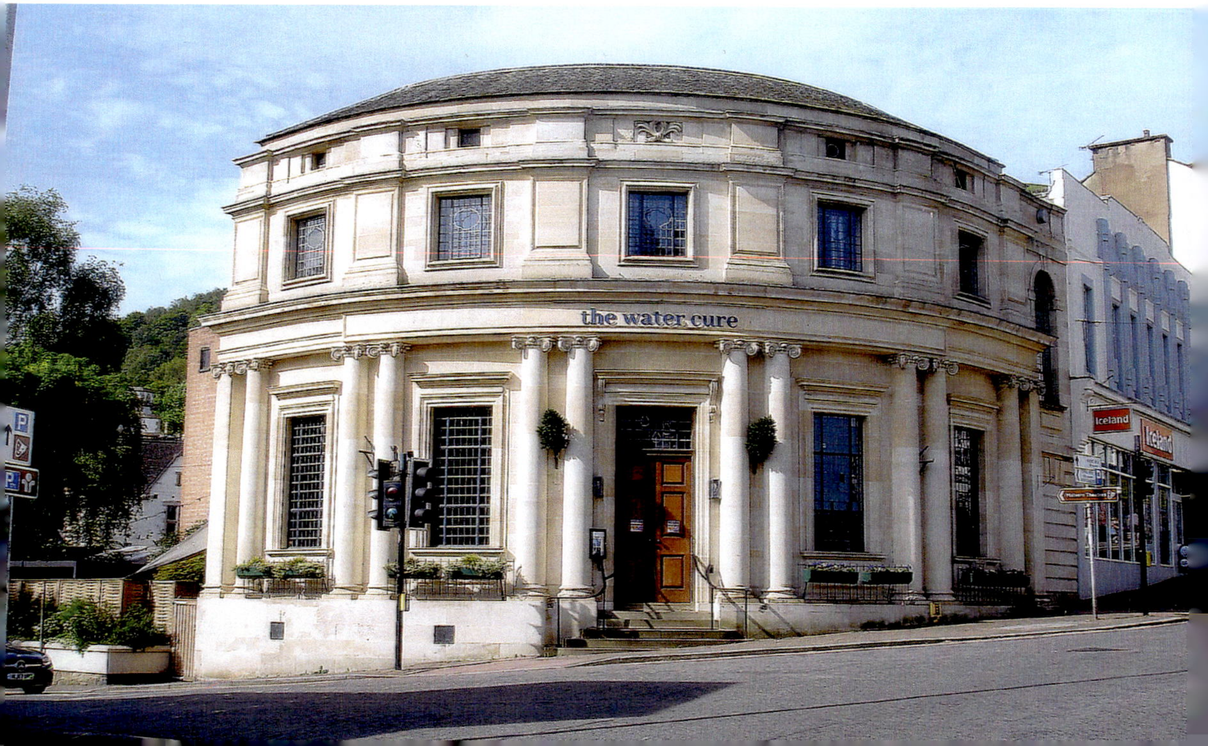

here until 1970 when it merged with the National Westminster Bank. National Westminster became, in time, 'NatWest' and they continued to run a branch here until 2017. Upon the closure of the branch of NatWest, four years of renovation work was commenced by the current owners, who converted the building into a stylish cocktail bar, which was opened its doors in 2021. As the current venue's name suggests the 'water cure' of Malvern's boom years in the nineteenth century has inspired the range of 'water cure'-themed cocktails served here by friendly staff, along with tasty snacks and sometimes accompanied by live music.

33. War Memorial Bus Shelter (1945–46), Court Road, Barnards Green, Malvern, WR14 3BY

This art deco-style bus shelter standing on the corner of Court Road and Barnards Green Road, topped by a clock tower, as well as serving its practical purpose, is also a rather unusual war memorial. Built, according to Historic England, in 1945, the brightly painted and regularly refurbished bus shelter contains a plaque dedicated to the men and women who lost their lives during the Second World War. As a war memorial this is unusual as it was erected after the Second World War and not

Barnards Green bus shelter war memorial.

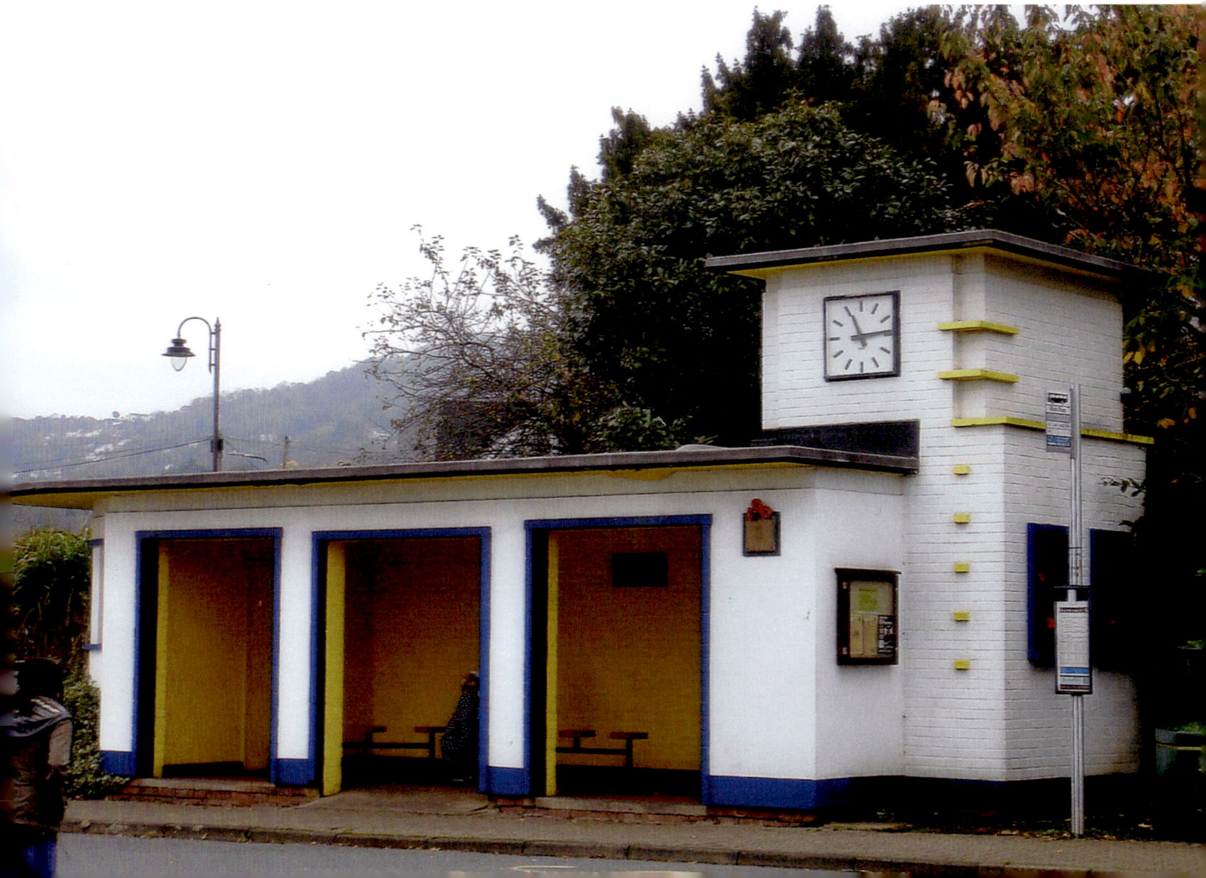

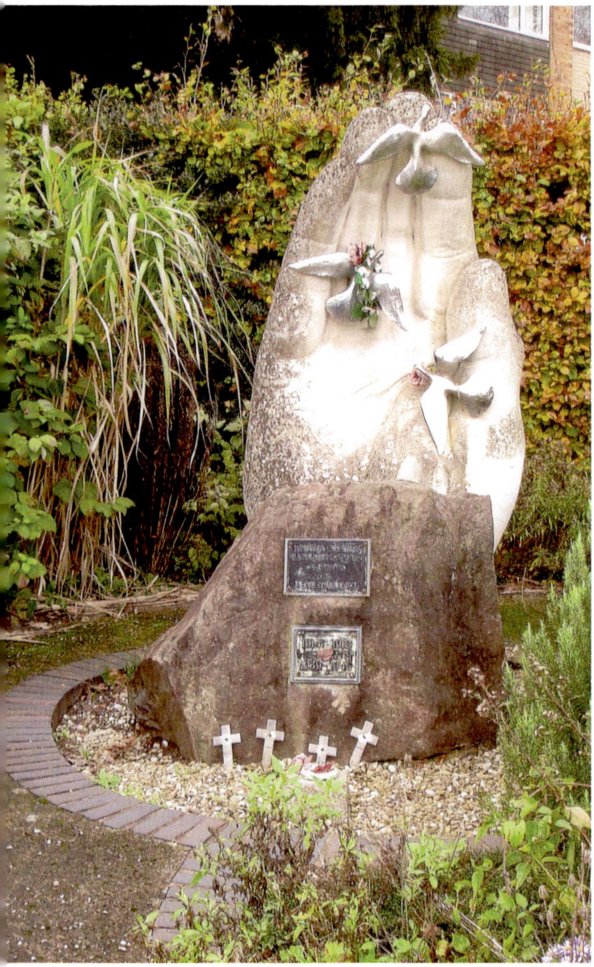

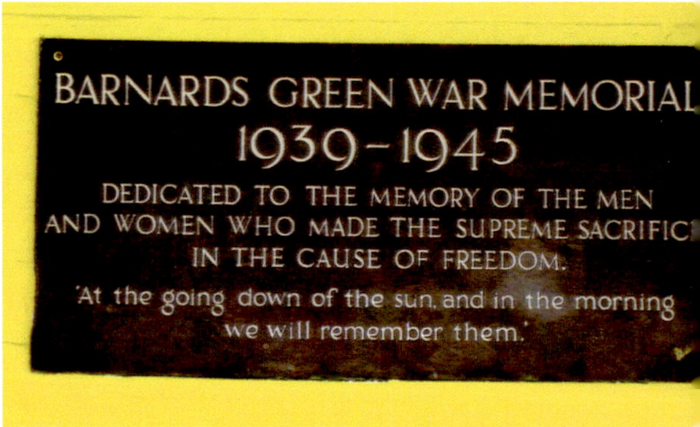

Above: Plaque inside Barnards Green bus shelter war memorial.

Left: *Hand of Peace* sculpture by Rose Garrard.

Opposite above: Hatfield House, Imperial Road, Great Malvern.

Opposite below: Close-up of Hatfield House.

the First, as most war memorials were. Also, its dedication is specifically for those lost in the Second World War. Despite the bus shelter's sombre connection it is a remarkably upbeat and cheerful little building and has also been Grade II listed.

Next to the bus shelter war memorial is a little circular memorial garden, in the centre of which stands a beautiful sculpture by sculptor Rose Garrard titled *The Hand of Peace*, which was installed here in 1999.

34. Hatfield House (1963–64), Imperial Road, Great Malvern, WR14 3AP

This interesting-looking building is a nice example of 1960s architecture. Designed by T. H. B. Borough and Maurice W Jones as a school house for St James Girls' School, the building has many polygonal projections like a cross section of a beehive when seen from the air. It was formerly used as middle school boarding

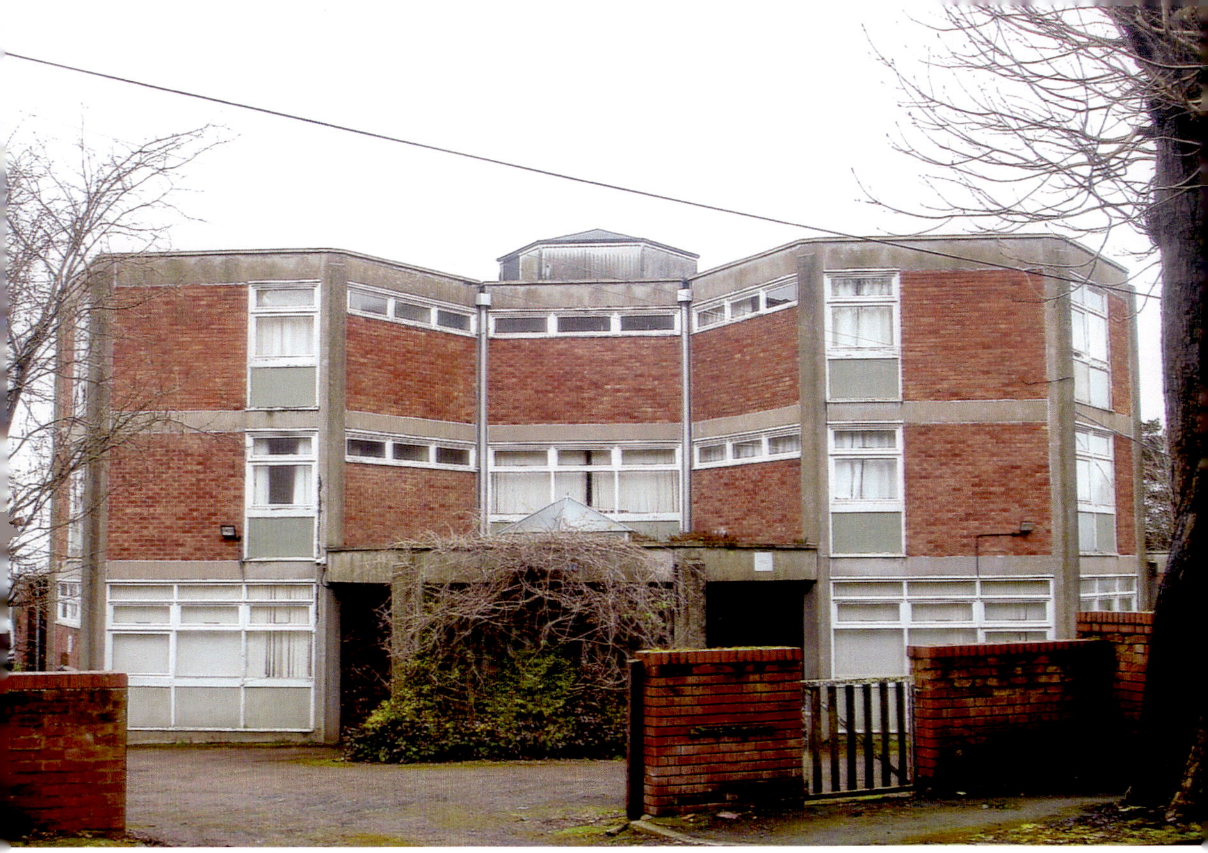

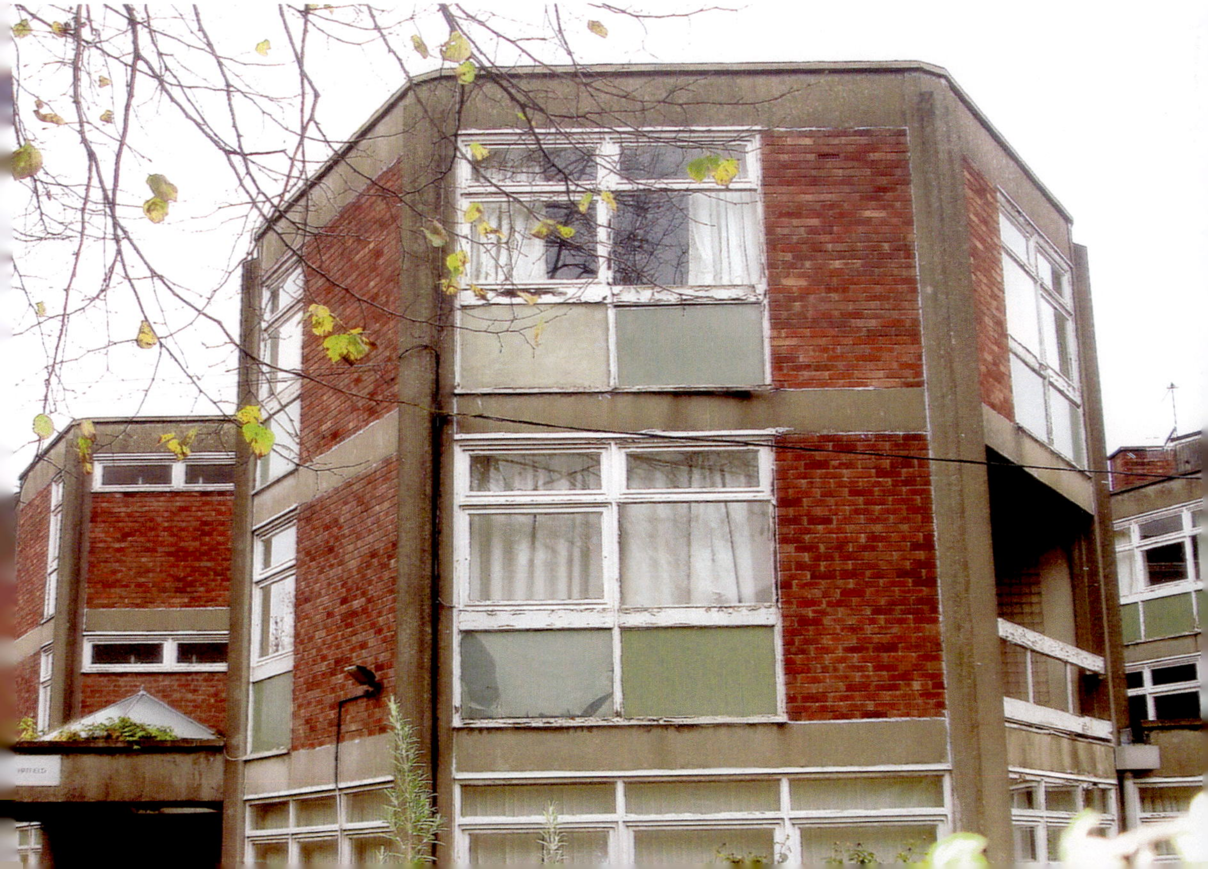

accommodation for fifty-two boarders and has two staff flats. Currently the building is up for sale for its development potential. I hope it is put to good use. To me it evokes my school days, the 'swinging sixties', the Beatles, Doctor Who, etc.

35. Hardwicke House (1965), No. 55 Abbey Road, Great Malvern, WR14 3HH

This modern block of flats is a something of a rarity in Malvern, unlike in most English towns and cities. It is named after an earlier Hardwicke House, built on this site in 1851 as a 'water cure' establishment for Dr James Marsden. With the demise of the 'water cure' business in Malvern, Hardwicke House became a boarding house, but by the mid-twentieth century had fallen into disrepair and was demolished in 1965. The modern Hardwicke House was built soon afterwards. I have not been inside but imagine some of the flats have good views over Malvern and across the Vale of Evesham.

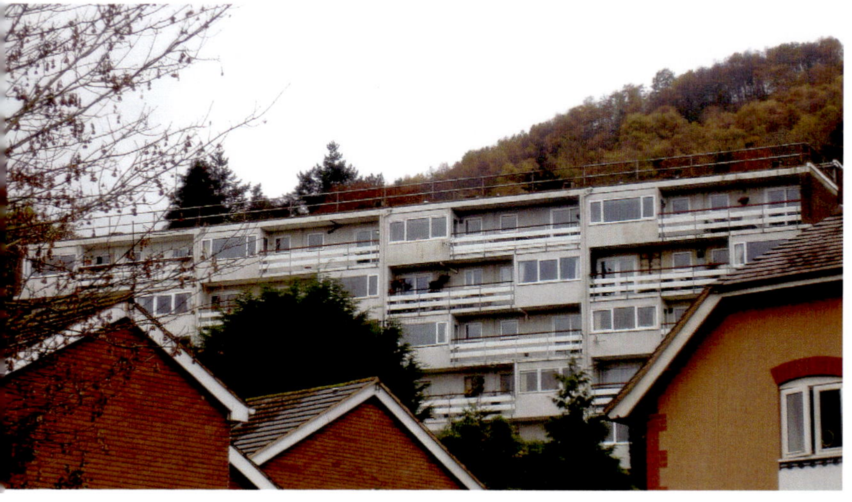

East side of Hardwicke House, Abbey Road, Great Malvern.

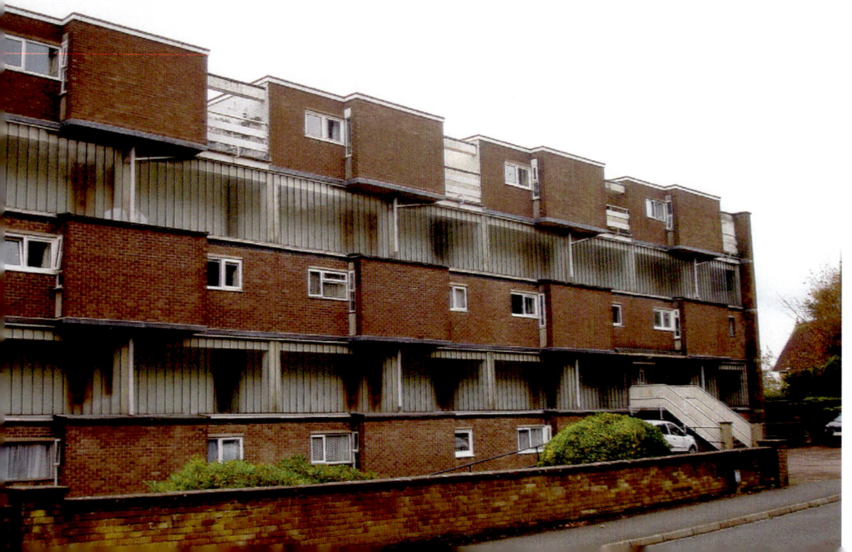

West side of Hardwicke House.

36. The Edinburgh Dome (1977–78), Imperial Road, Great Malvern, WR14 3AP

This building might seem more at home on the moon or in a science fiction film but it is here in Malvern, the only one of these 'Binidomes' ever built in Britain. The concept was developed by an Italian, Dr Dante Bini, in 1967. This particular dome was built for Malvern St James Girls' School by Godwin and Cowper, Oscar Fabor and partners and Norwest Holst.

An information plaque in Avenue Road explains how the dome was constructed. Apparently, the dome consisted of a 36-metre-diameter ring beam and two layers of neoprene sandwiching, a filling of expanding steel coil and wet concrete.

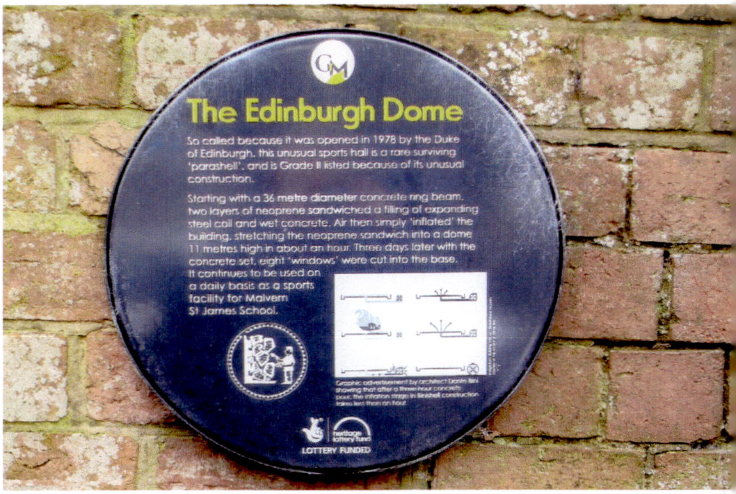

Right: The Edinburgh Dome information plaque in Avenue Road.

Below: The Edinburgh Dome.

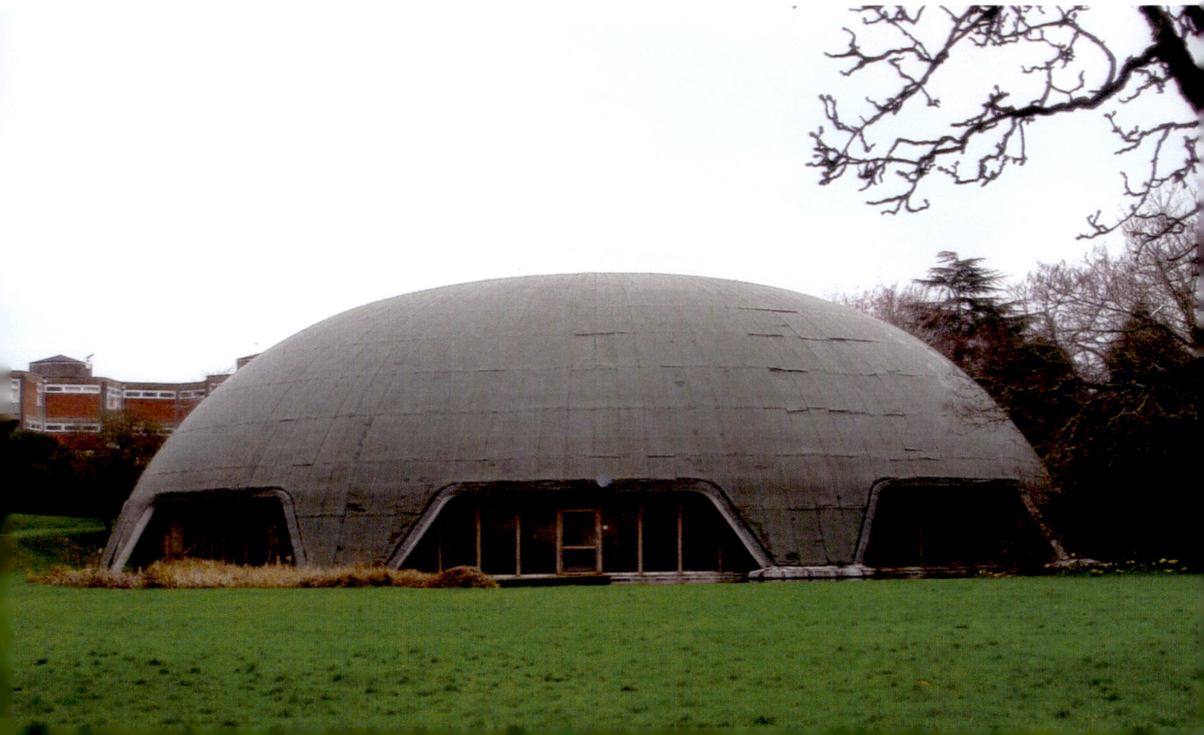

Air then simply 'inflated' the building stretching the neoprene sandwich into an 11-metre-high dome in about an hour. Three days later with the concrete set, eight 'windows' were cut into the base. The information plaque shows the process in diagrammatic form. The whole dome structure is set within a surrounding moat. In 1985 the exterior was clad in copper.

The Edinburgh Dome is so called because it was opened by the Duke of Edinburgh on 4 May 1978. Historic England, however, list the building merely as the 'Sports Hall'. This is indeed the dome's function but why change the name to a merely functional one? The Dome is today Grade II listed and is the only one of these to have been constructed in the country. It continues to operate as a sports hall for use by the school and other groups outside of school hours.

37. Malvern Splash (1989), Priory Road, Great Malvern, WR14 3DS

At one time there were a number of outdoor swimming pools or lidos around Malvern. One was at the British Camp Hotel, another at the Colwall Park Hotel (famously depicted in artist Laura Knight's painting *The Pool*) and the public lido at Priory Park). This latter was opened in the 1920s and was used by many for decades until its eventual demolition in the 1980s.

Malvern Splash swimming pool and leisure centre.

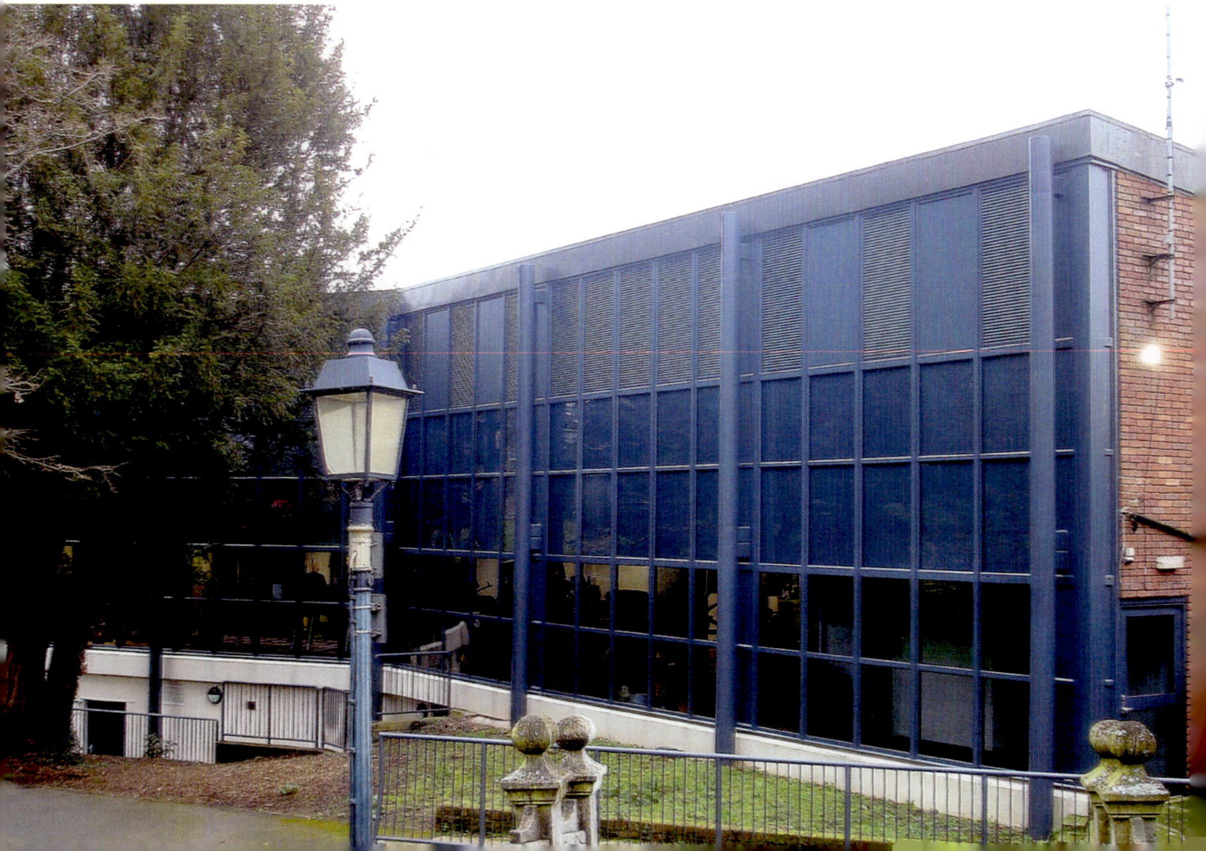

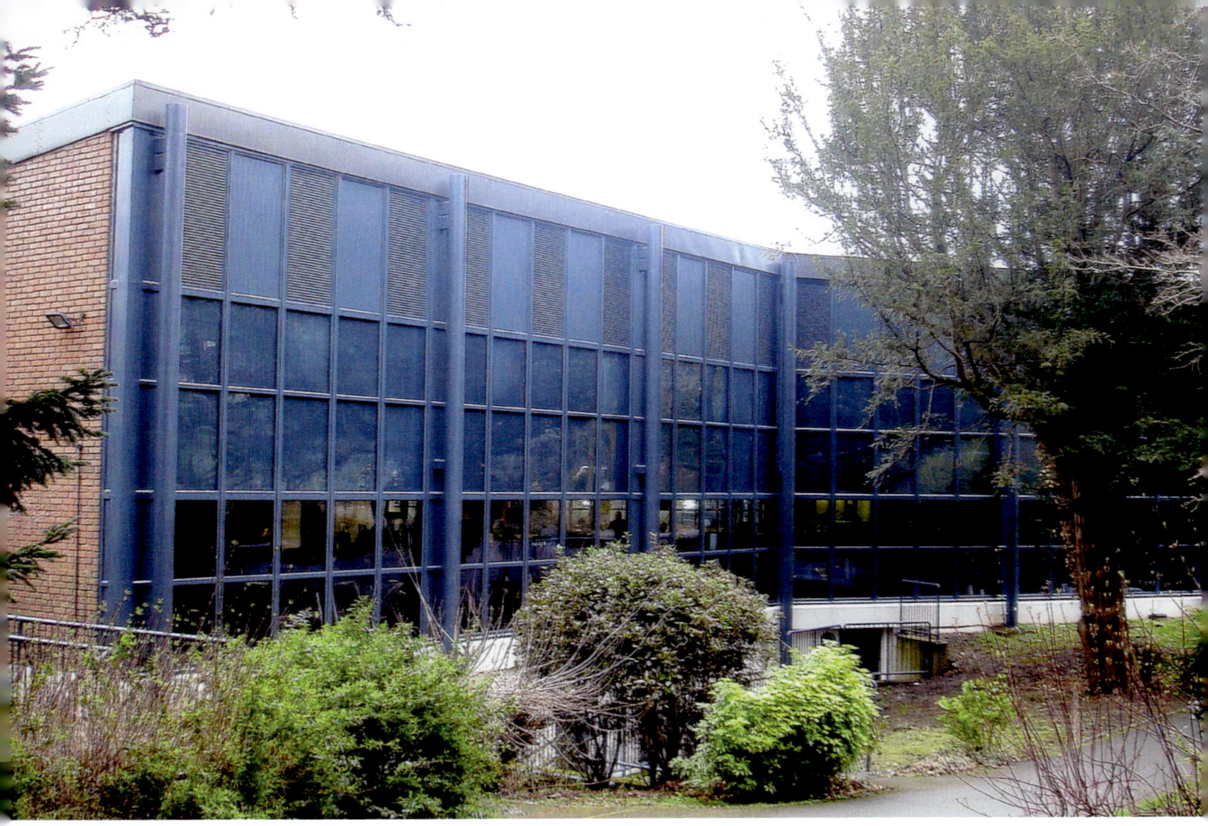

Malvern Splash swimming pool and leisure centre.

In 1989 a brand-new indoor swimming pool and leisure centre called Malvern Splash was constructed at the Priory Park site of the former lido. The new building was designed by Charles Smith with the Abbey Hanson Rowe partnership. It is today run by Freedom Leisure and considerable improvements have been made over recent years, particularly from 2021 to 2024. The leisure centre now boasts a cycling studio, a newly refurbished gym, a slide and wave machine in the pool area and various interactive play features. There are also some forty group exercise classes each week. At the time of writing improvements have been made to the changing rooms and other facilities and solar panels are being fitted to the roof to provide energy efficiency in an environmental-friendly way. Malvern Splash remains a popular facility and important amenity component of the lovely Priory Park.

38. The Lyttelton Well (1993), No. 6 Church Street, Great Malvern, WR14 2AY

Near the Church Street entrance to the priory church grounds is an interesting modern development on land where, in 1824, the local philanthropist Apphia Lady Lyttelton provided a Sunday school for children. The children received religious instruction and learned good manners. Later, in the 1880s, the Lyttelton Grammar School was established here, in a new building by Henry Haddon. The newly

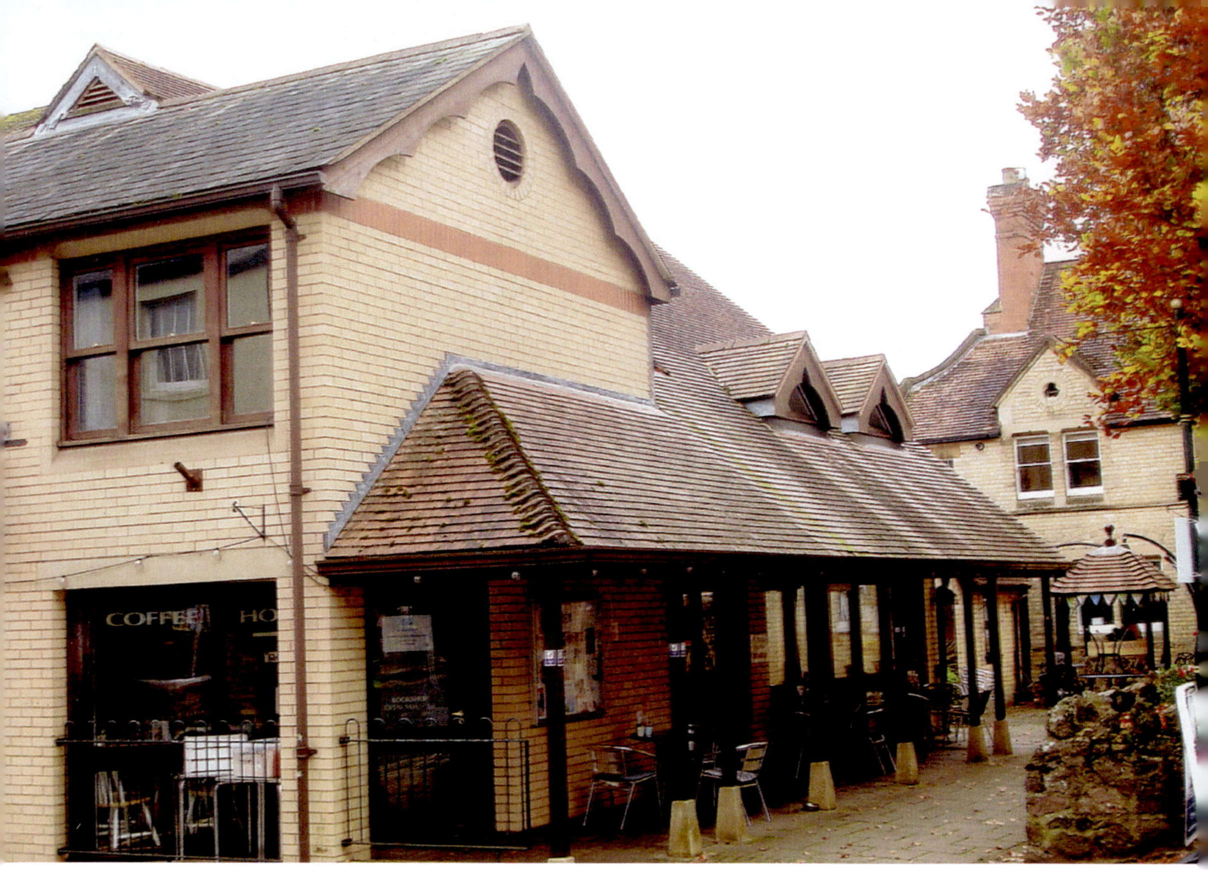

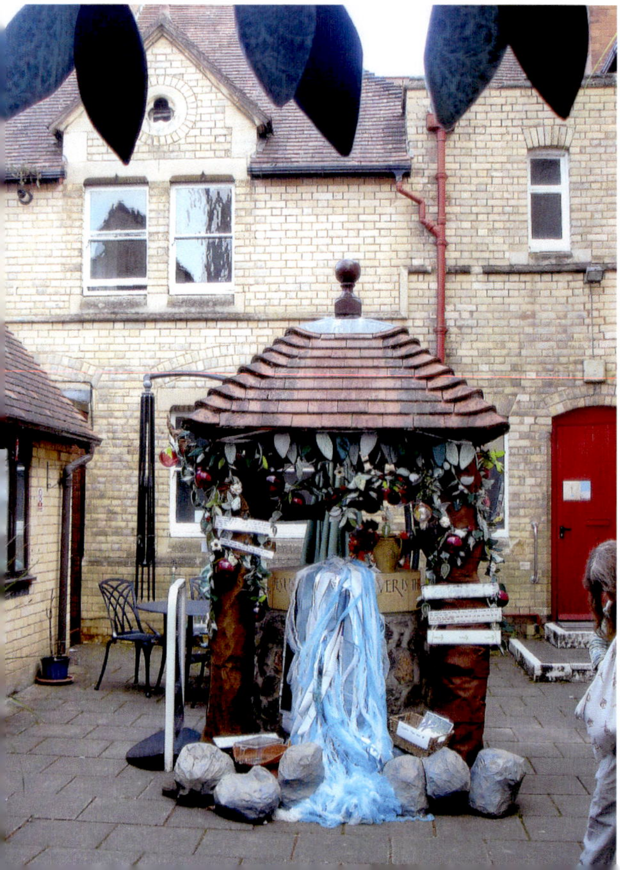

Above: The Lyttelton Well centre.

Left: A 'well-dressed' Lyttelton Well.

built ecumenical centre you see today incorporates part of the Victorian grammar school and has as its centrepiece an ornamental well known as the Lyttelton Well. The new building was designed by Bartosch and Stokes and opened in 1993.

The Lyttelton Well is a church-based community project backed and run by a group of twenty-two Malvern churches including the parish church, the former priory. The centre consists of meeting rooms, offices, a bookshop and a coffee shop. It provides a meeting place and counselling services for the local community and also houses the town's Tourist Information Centre, which is just opposite the well itself. This ornamental well is 'well dressed' along with wells and springs all around Malvern annually during the Well Dressing Festival that is held every May.

39. Belle Vue Island (Refurbished 1998–2000), Belle Vue Terrace, Great Malvern, WR14 4PZ

Originally this was the village green and still contains a small wayside cross, possibly medieval, from this early time. Subsequently this 'island' between what have become Belle Vue Terrace, Worcester Road, Church Road and Abbey Road has become built up with steps and platforms and gas lampstands to become a little park where one can rest and relax after a steep climb up Church Road. During the 1990s Malvern Hills District Council embarked on a major refurbishment of this enclave with the installation of interesting and informative features related to the history of Malvern. An information plaque tells us about the many gas lamps of Malvern. Once there were some 1,299 such lamps and there are still over 100 in working order, some of them here on Belle Vue Island. It is popularly believed that C. S. Lewis was inspired by the Malvern gas lamps to include one at the entrance to the otherworldly realm of Narnia in his children's story *The Lion, the Witch and the Wardrobe*. Lewis, however, was not able to confirm this to his friend George Sayer when asked directly about this. There was very likely some subconscious influence at work you might surmise, so perhaps the idea is not totally fallacious.

For many the centrepiece of Belle Vue Island is the beautiful sculpture in stone and bronze of *Malvhina* by Rose Garrard. The sculpture is named after a Celtic princess claimed by Victorian historian Charles Grindrod to have given rise to the name of Malvern itself. This romantic linkage may be fanciful but as an embodiment of the spirit of springs and flowing water elsewhere expressed as the Celtic water deity Ana or the Christian St Ann, patron saint of springs and wells, it makes perfect sense.

The water that pours from *Malvhina*'s bronze spout comes from three springs and collect in a main containing untreated spring water and then piped to the fountain via particulate, ultra violet and carbon filters before pouring out into the spiral decorated stone basin below. The water is safe to drink – I have filled

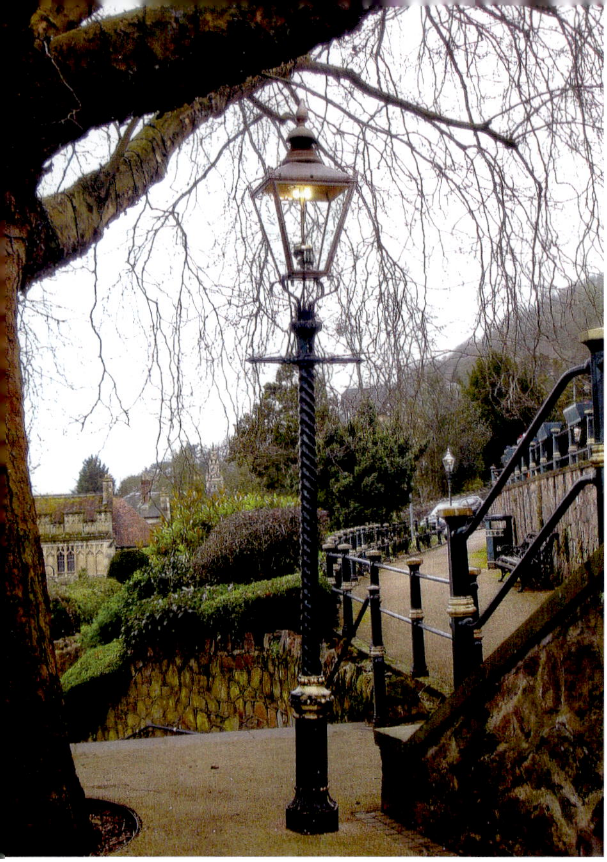

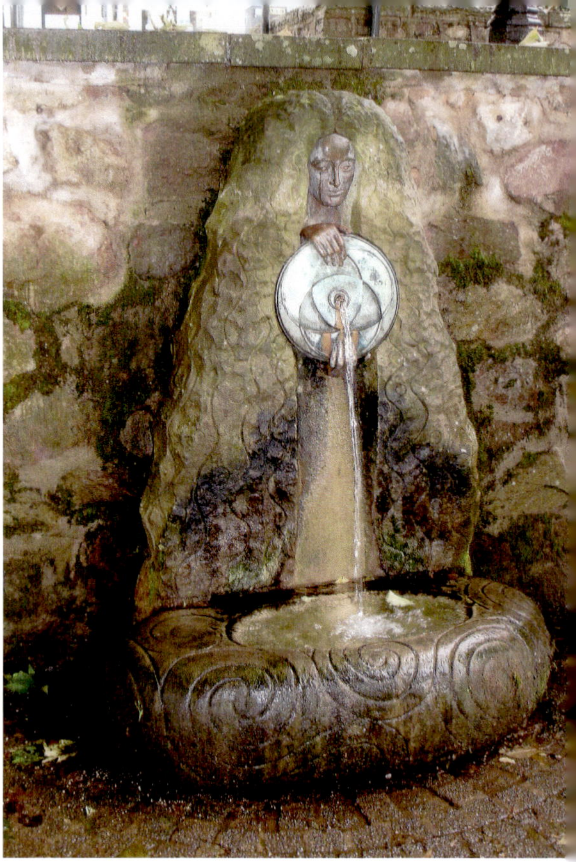

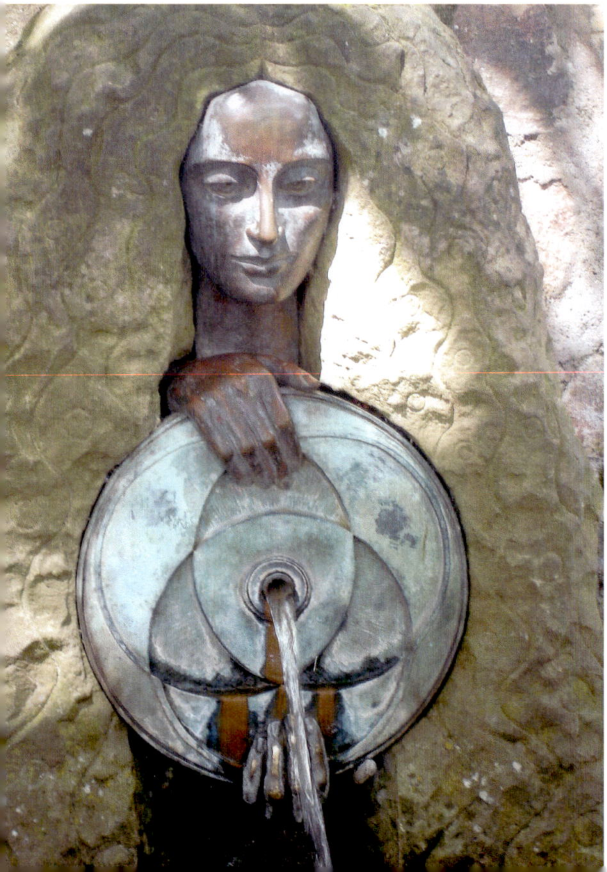

Above left: Gas lamp on Belle Vue Island.

Above right: Malvhina spout on Belle Vue Island.

Left: Close-up of *Malvhina* sculpture by Rose Garrard.

my water bottle from it several times and have often found here a similarly minded gathering of all and sundry with an assortment of bottles and containers for filling.

An annual Malvern Well Dressing Festival is held usually commencing on the early May bank holiday and run by the Malvern Spa Association, when you will find *Malvhina* and other spouts suitably decorated and celebrated.

The *Malvhina* spout was officially 'opened' on 4 September 1998. Another more recent sculptural depiction of *Malvhina*, this time in wood, carved from the remaining spur of a fallen tree by sculptor Tom Harvey, can be seen in Priory Park.

Not long after the unveiling of *Malvhina,* Rose Garrard produced another masterpiece on Belle Vue Island, the *Enigma Fountain.* This consists of four standing stones surrounding a spring or fountain with fourteen sides, each one bearing the initials of one of Sir Edward Elgar's friends 'featured' in his *Enigma Variations,* the piece of music that made his name, composed in Malvern in 1898. In front of the fountain stands a life-sized bronze statue of Sir Edward Elgar himself, looking across the road to where he used to frequent, the Bluebird Tea Rooms.

The *Enigma Fountain* was unveiled in May 2000 as part of The Malvern Spring Water Arts Project, which was established to bring pure spring water back to Great Malvern.

Below left and below right: *Enigma Fountain* with statue of Sir Edward Elgar.

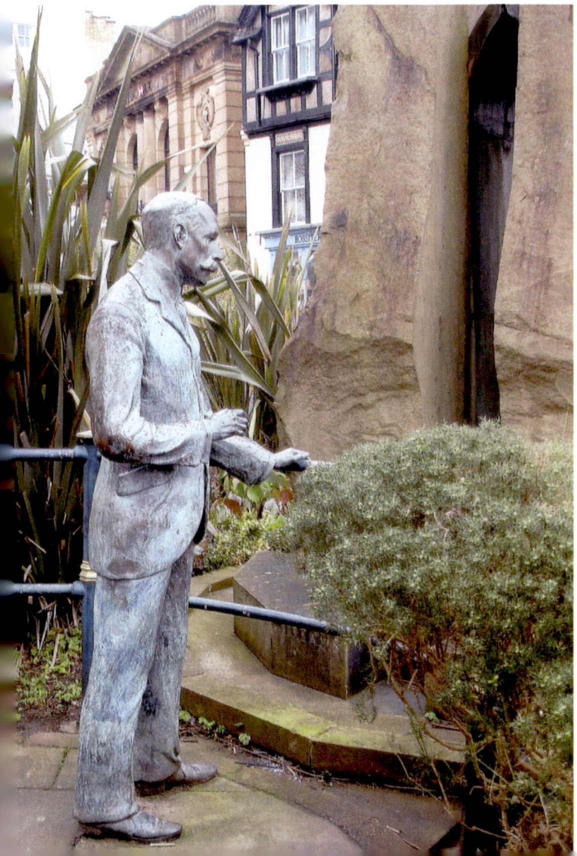

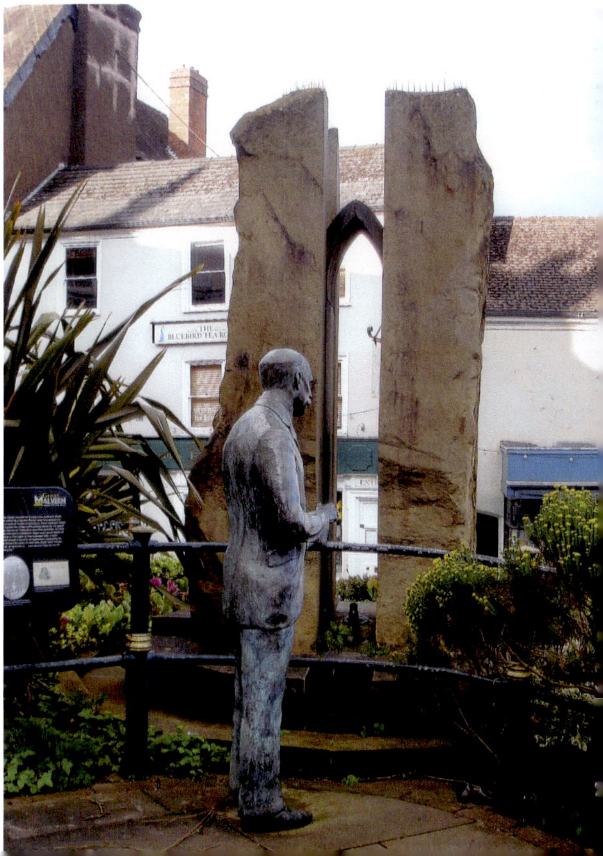

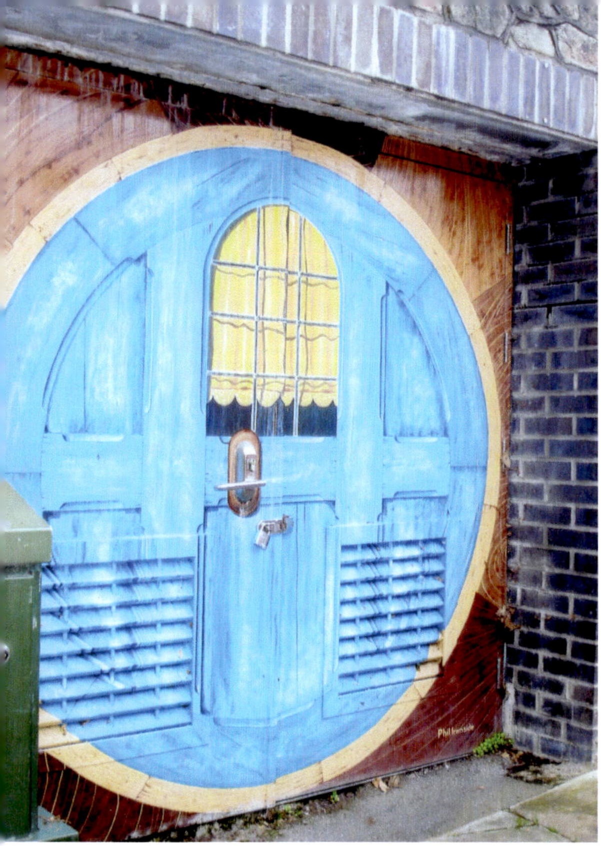

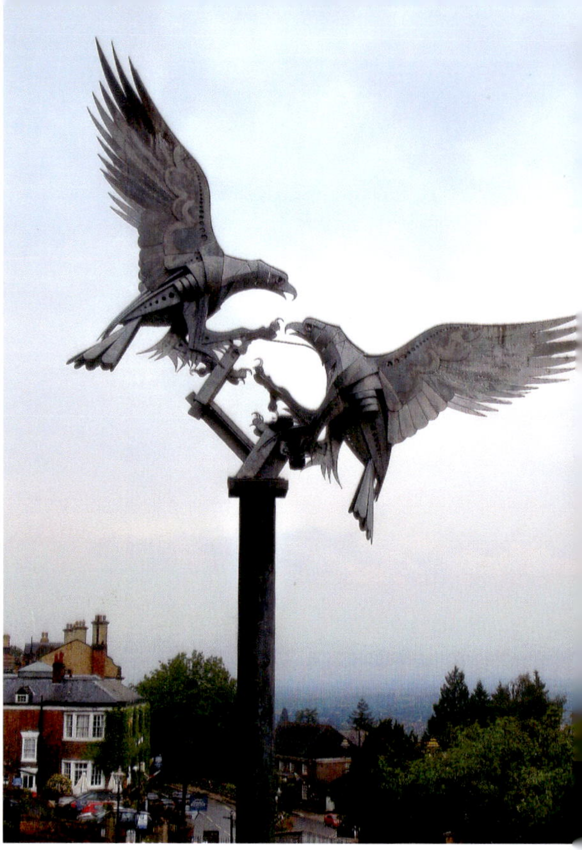

Above left: 'Hobbit door' on Belle Vue Island.

Above right: *Buzzards* sculpture by Walenty Pytel.

Another interesting feature of Belle Vue Island is the round double door created by local artist Phil Ironside in 2021. You will recognise it as the sort of door to a hobbit's home if you have seen the cinematic adaptations of J. R. R. Tolkien's *The Hobbit* and *Lord of the Rings*. The 'Hobbit Door', as it is known, is an artistic nod to the one-time presence in Malvern of Tolkien, who frequently visited the town and walked the hills with his close friends, author C. S. Lewis and Head of English at Malvern College, George Sayer. All three went walking together in the Malvern Hills and Sayer in particular helped and encouraged Tolkien in his work producing his now world-famous series of stories about Middle Earth. The distinct round 'Hobbit Door' is in fact the entrance to an electricity substation.

The whole Belle Vue Island enclave, apart from all its intrinsic interest, also hosts art exhibitions and music events on a regular basis.

Across the road, in Belle Vue Terrace, was once a large nineteenth-century private home called Rose Bank House. This was purchased by Charles Dyson Perrins, the grandson of one of the inventors of Lea and Perrins Worcestershire Sauce. The house was demolished in the 1950s but the gardens in which it was situated had been given by Charles Dyson Perrins to the townspeople of Malvern to enjoy. In 2012 Malvern Town Council restored the gardens and commissioned some striking bronze sculptures by Walenty Pytel. *Buzzards* can be seen across the road and further back in the parkland is *The Lark Ascending*. The park area provides spectacular views across the Vale of Evesham and Great Malvern, which also takes in a number of the fine buildings featured in this book. The ninety-nine steps ascending the hill behind the park lead up to the picturesque St Ann's Well described in an earlier entry.

40. The Theatre of Small Convenience (1999 Conversion), Edith Walk, Great Malvern, WR14 4QH

Malvern has a strong theatrical tradition so perhaps it is no surprise to find any unused or unusual space being pressed into service for this purpose. This one, named back in the late 1990s in tongue-in-cheek fashion as the Theatre of Small Convenience, was once a gentleman's lavatory block, that is until 1999 when local artist and puppeteer Dennis Neale opened the building as a theatre of the smallest of spaces.

The theatre building is a mere 16 feet long by 10 feet wide and could seat twelve people in its beautifully decorated interior. A wide range of performances at this tiny venue included both professional and amateur productions, puppet shows, poetry readings and storytelling. In 2002 the theatre was described in the Guiness Book of

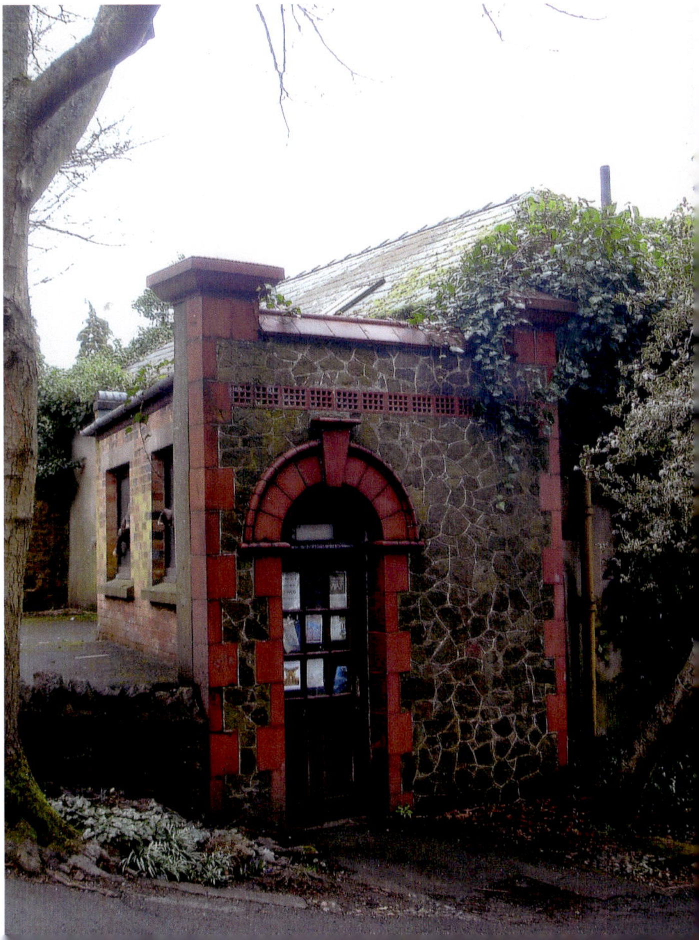

Former gentleman's lavatory block, now the Theatre of Small Convenience.

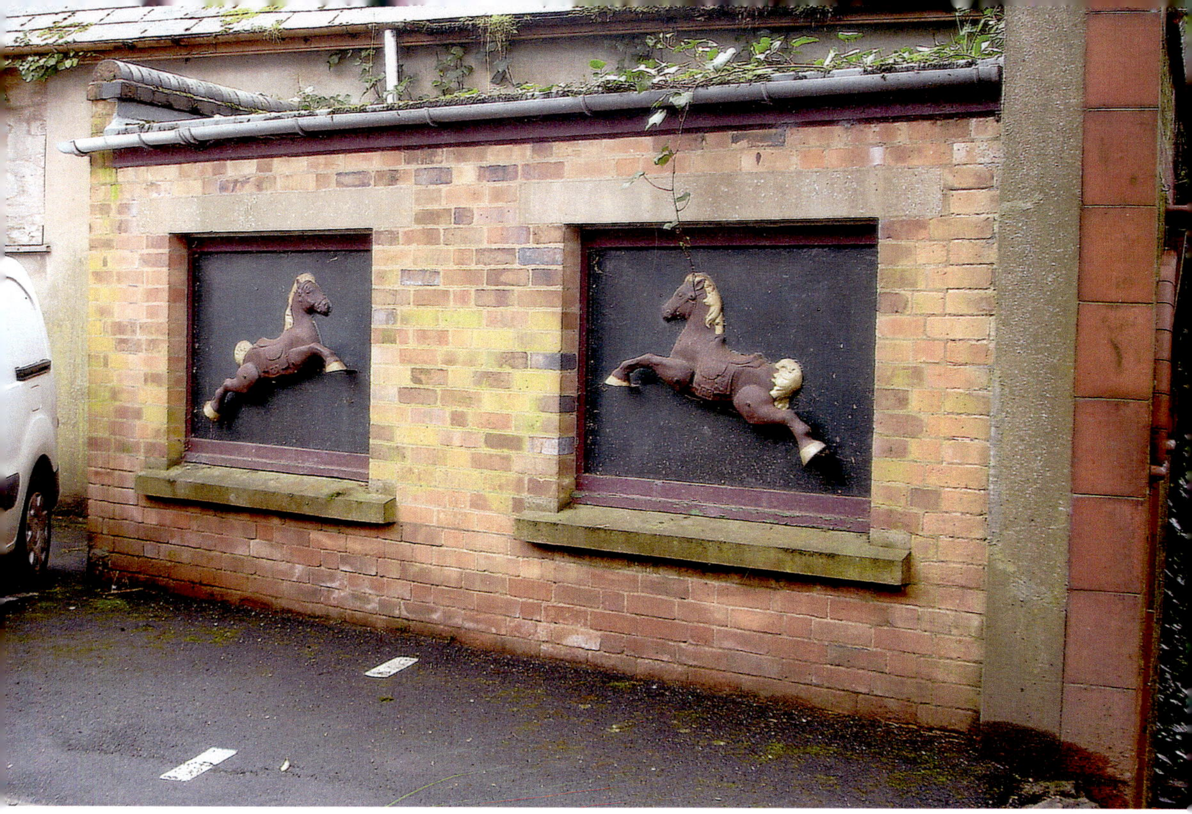

Interesting relief on the side of the Theatre of Small Convenience.

Records as the smallest theatre in the world. Dennis Neale continued to successfully run the theatre until his retirement in 2017. The theatre was then leased to the Warwickshire College Group by the building's owners, Malvern Hills District Council, from 2018. However, what with the Covid pandemic in 2020/21 and a fire caused by a faulty dehumidifier in 2021, the building deteriorated and remained closed for a few years.

All is not lost though as at the time of writing (October 2024) the Theatre of Small Convenience CIC has been set up to refurbish the premises and reopen it once again as a place of public entertainment, hopefully sometime in 2025. Malvern Hills District Council are passing the building to the new theatre community interest company by Council Asset Transfer. It could be that by the time you read this book the Theatre of Small Convenience will be up and running again as a quirky little venue for local and visiting theatregoers.

41. Malvern Cube Community and Arts Centre (Late Twentieth/Early Twenty-first Century), Albert Road North, Great Malvern, WR14 2YF

Malvern youth centre was operated from here until its closure by Worcestershire County Council in 2010. In response Malvern Youth Community Trust was formed, a charity whose aim was to run the centre with volunteers 'for the community by the community'.

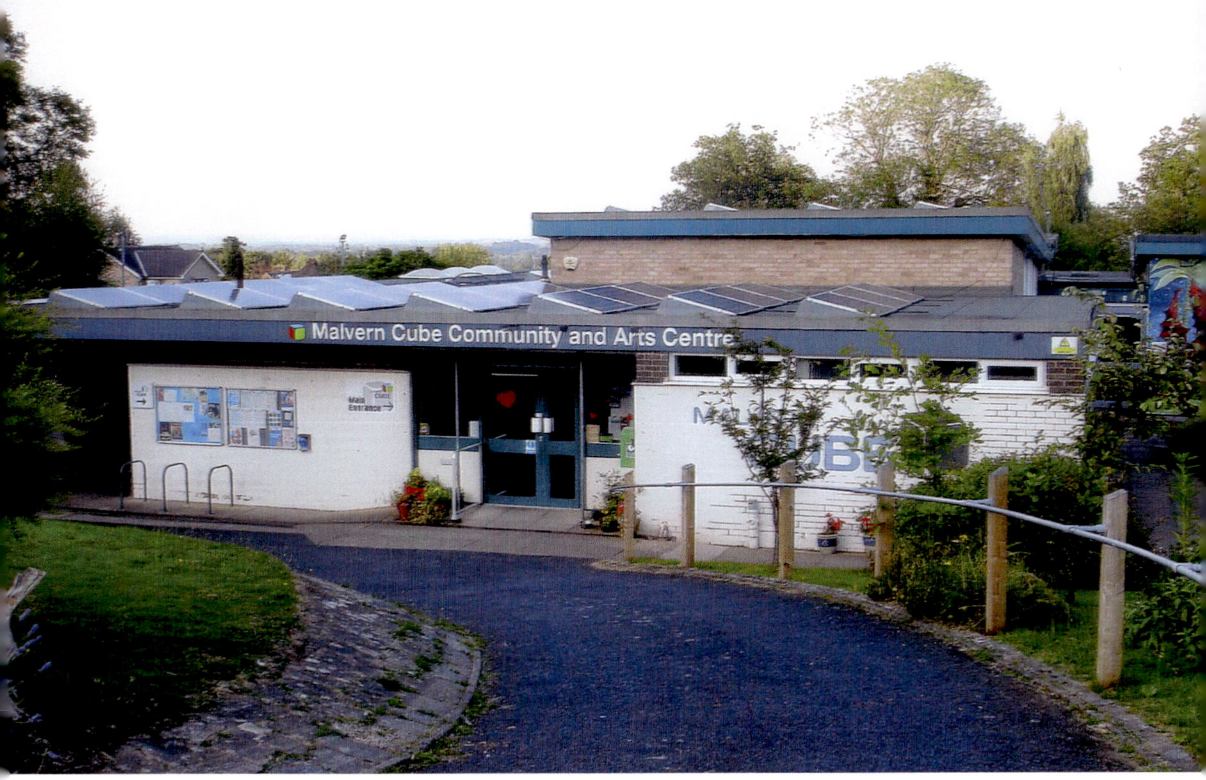

Above: Malvern Cube Community and Arts Centre.

Below: Community Garden at the Malvern Cube.

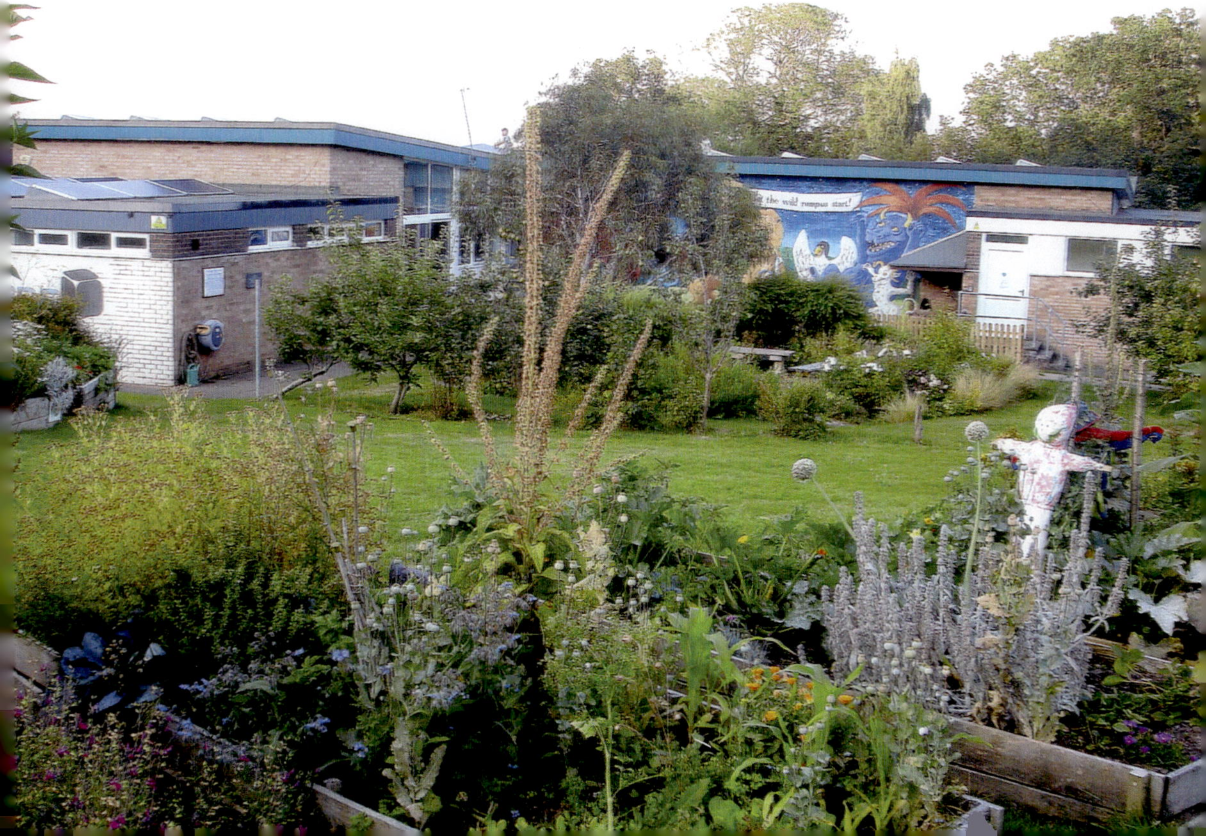

The centre has been described as a 'vibrant and inclusive space'. There are year-round performances and gigs, arts activities, a café and a community garden, produce from which is used to create the satisfying menu on offer. The Malvern Cube Community and Arts Centre was opened its doors in 2012 and continues to be a popular meeting and activity space for Malvern residents.

42. Malvern Technology Centre/QinetiQ (c. 2000), St Andrews Road, Malvern, WR14 3PS

The site of these modern buildings, obscured from easy viewing by fine meshed wire fencing and tightly secured access gates, has an interesting history. Originally a training area for both army and naval recruits, it once housed a sprawling expanse of tented accommodation and a brick battleship for training young sailors – one of them I think was my father. The naval training facility was there to provide basic training and was called HMS Duke.

From 1942 to 1946 Malvern saw an influx of government scientists and American scientists from Harvard and the Massachusetts Institute of Technology. Initially these scientists worked from Malvern College, as we have seen earlier, whilst being billeted around Malvern in schools, private homes and hotels (including the former hydropathic establishment now known as Park View).

Malvern Technology Centre/QinetiQ. (Photo by Nathan Adams)

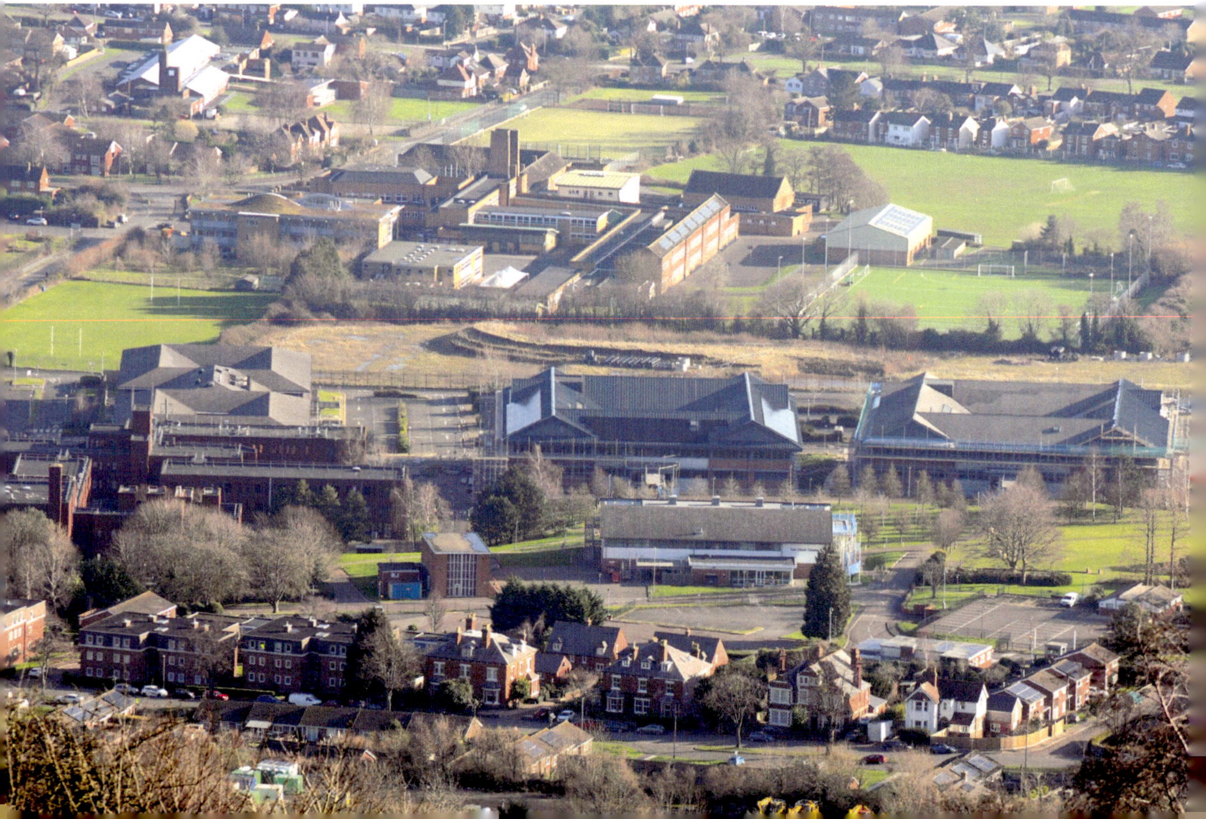

With the end of the Second World War the scientists and technicians of what had become known as the Telecommunications Research Establishment (TRE) moved out of Malvern College to the site of the now closed down HMS Duke, just off St Andrews Road. The organisation worked on many, at the time, secret projects throughout the war and afterwards, which resulted in the development of much of the technology we take for granted today, including radar, radio astronomy, meteorological radar, thermal imaging, touchscreens, LED displays, air traffic control and flight simulators. In 1953 TRE became the Radar Research Establishment and not long after the Royal Radar Establishment (RRE), which in turn was renamed the Defence, Evaluation and Research Agency (DERA) until early twenty-first-century privatisation created QinetiQ. The 1950s buildings were upgraded by Design Works Services *c.* 2000 and are those we see today. Important work continues with satellite communications and cyber security developments ongoing. In fact, it was as long ago as 1969 that the world's first geosynchronous orbit communications satellite Skynet 2B was developed here.

In 2018 developers Square Bay purchased 25 acres of this site for the construction of new private housing and a residential care home.

You can learn much more about the scientific and technological achievement of Malvern's recent history from The Technology Station, a small museum established at Great Malvern railway station in 2024 and run by volunteers. Check for opening times before visiting.

Elgar Court Care Home.

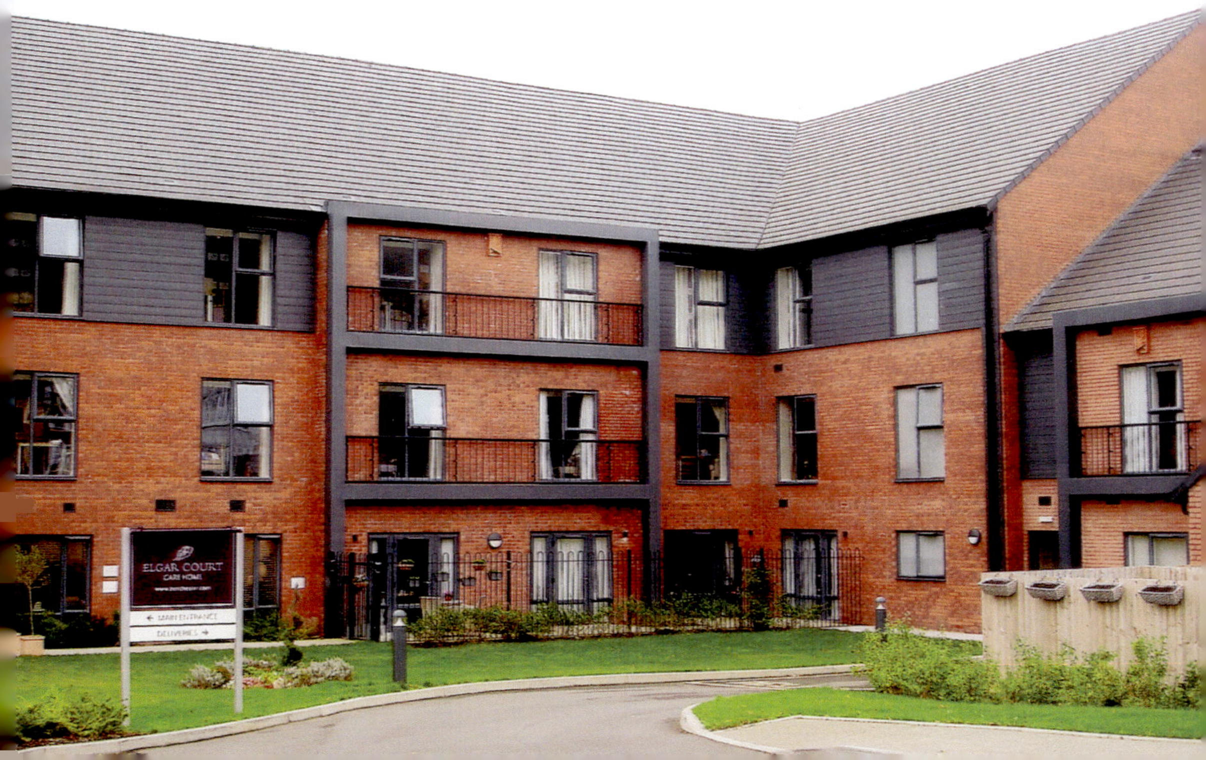

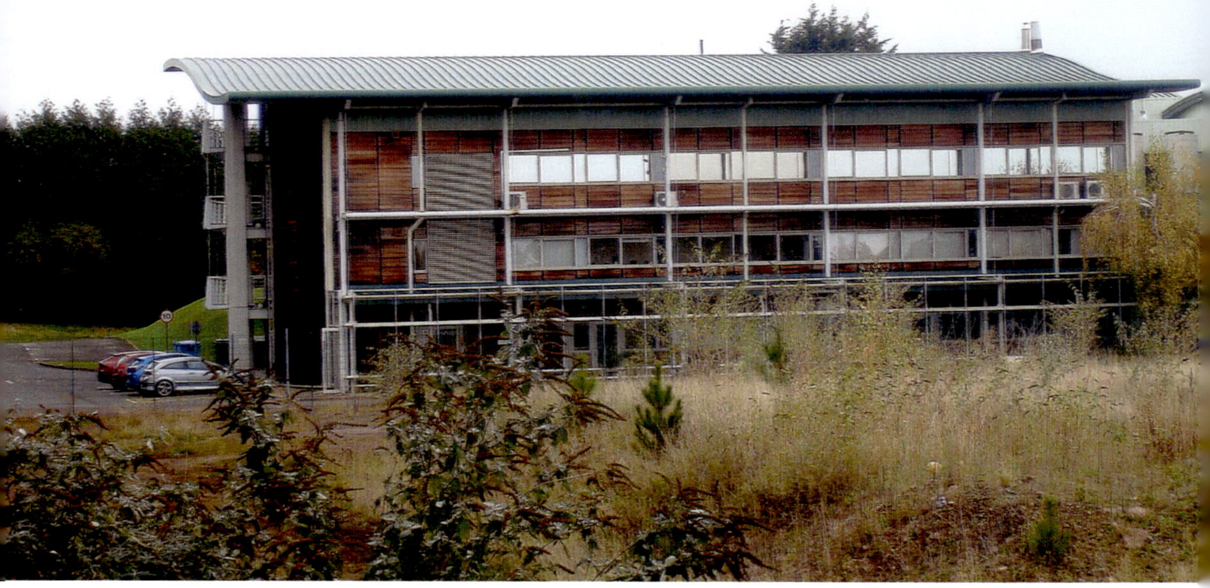

Malvern Science Park Phase Two building.

43. Malvern Hills Science Park/Phases One and Two (2000/01), Geraldine Road, Malvern, WR14 3SZ

Across the road from the highly secure Malvern Technology Centre/QinetiQ site a new Science Park has now been established. This now hosts some forty scientific and technology businesses and has developed in a number of stages.

Phase one of the Malvern Hills Science Park, named The Innovation Centre, offered twenty-three individual units ranging from 350 to 2,000 square feet in extent, with short-term leases available.

Phase Two, called The Regional Technology Exchange, provided further discrete units and laboratory facilities, increasing the range of premises available for businesses in this fast-expanding sector.

Malvern is definitely on the map in the sphere of scientific and technological innovation and development.

44. The Malvern (2006–08), Grovewood Road, Malvern, WR14 1GD

For the first time since the nineteenth century a new spa was opened in Malvern in 2008. The brainchild of local entrepreneur John Williams, the new spa has its own natural water supply from a borehole on site that accesses a deep underground aquifer.

The spa includes an eighty-room hotel with a separate health spa that includes a herb sauna, a salt grotto, crystal steam rooms and an ice fountain, as well as warm and cold pools that extend outdoors so you can swim inside or out as you choose, whilst being massaged by air and water jets.

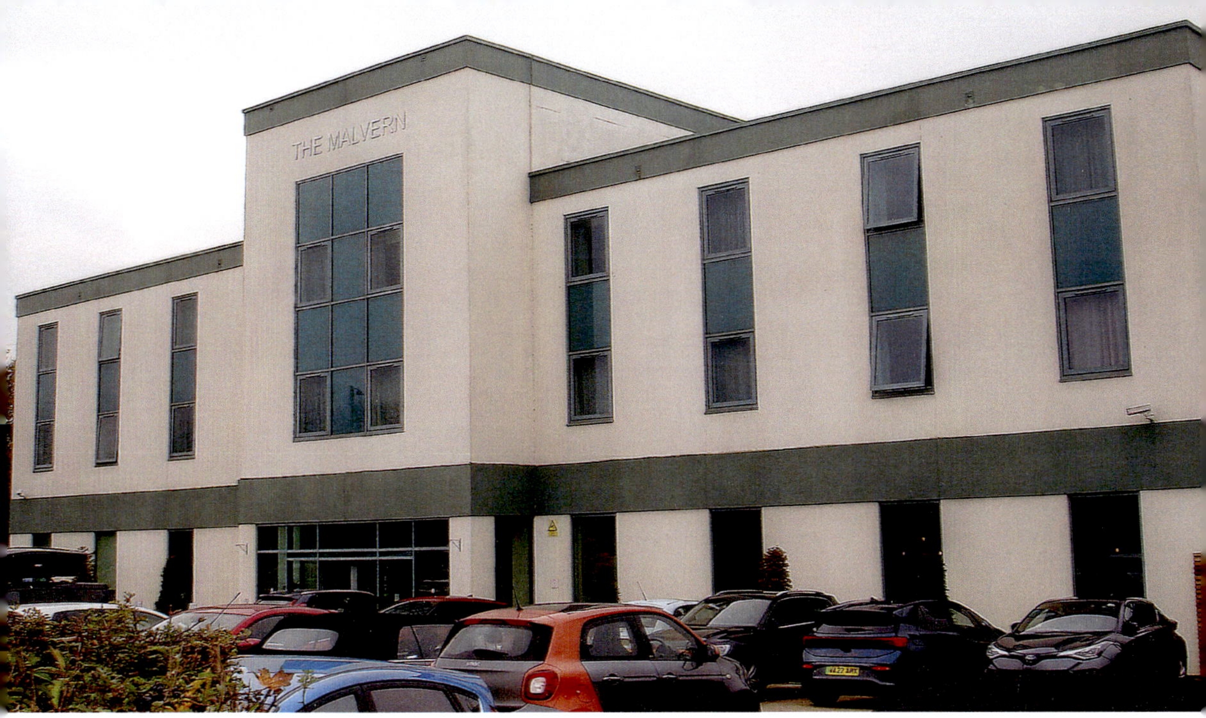

The Malvern Spa Hotel.

As part of the planning application process The Malvern spa has agreed to and completed cycle paths linking to the nearby Enigma Business Park.

The Malvern spa offers a much more pleasant experience than the old hydropathic establishments but hopefully just as healthy and beneficial.

45. Malvern Hills Science Park/Phase Three (2008), Geraldine Road, Malvern, WR14 3SZ

Phase three of the Malvern Hills Science Park has taken the form of this interesting and, I think, rather attractive and quirky award-winning building. The light green

Malvern Hills Science Park Phase Three building.

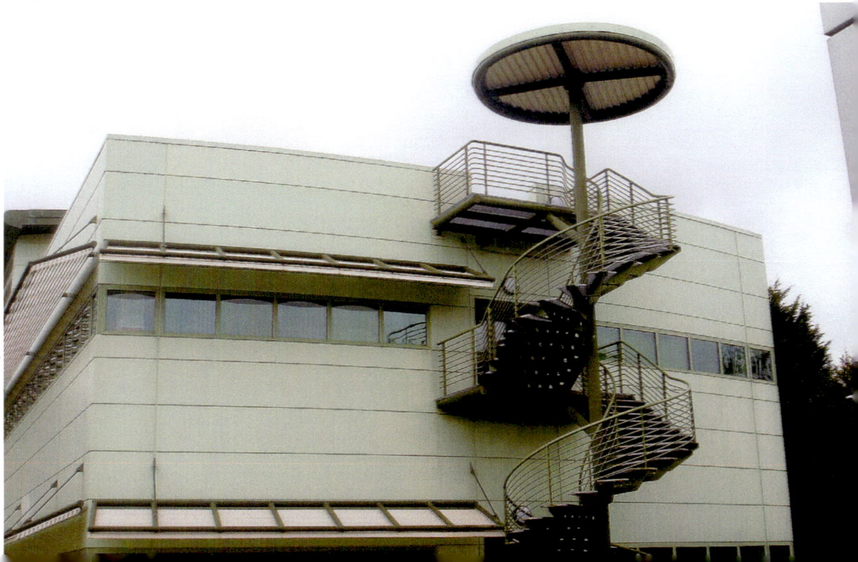

colour is immediately eye-catching, as is what I assume to be the outside fire escape stairs with a thoughtfully sited 'umbrella disc' above.

The new building has some 35,000 square feet of available space for business units composed of offices, laboratories, meeting room facilities, conferencing suites and the onside Beacon Café for those working in the Science Park and their guests. The building is heated and cooled with ground source heat pumps. Perhaps these 'green' credentials are the reason the building is coloured as it is!

The Malvern Hills Science Park Phase Three building is by Hunter Douglas Architectural and Rubicon Design Ltd.

46. Malvern Community Hospital (2010), No. 185 Worcester Road, Malvern, WR14 1EX

A cottage hospital in Malvern was originally set up in Lansdowne Crescent in 1909. Funded by benefactor Charles William Dyson, this has since been demolished and replaced by a new modern community hospital.

The new building, designed by DSA Environment and Design with Design Buro Architects, offers a range of National Health Service facilities including a minor injury unit, mental health care units, and in-patient and out-patient services

Malvern Community Hospital.

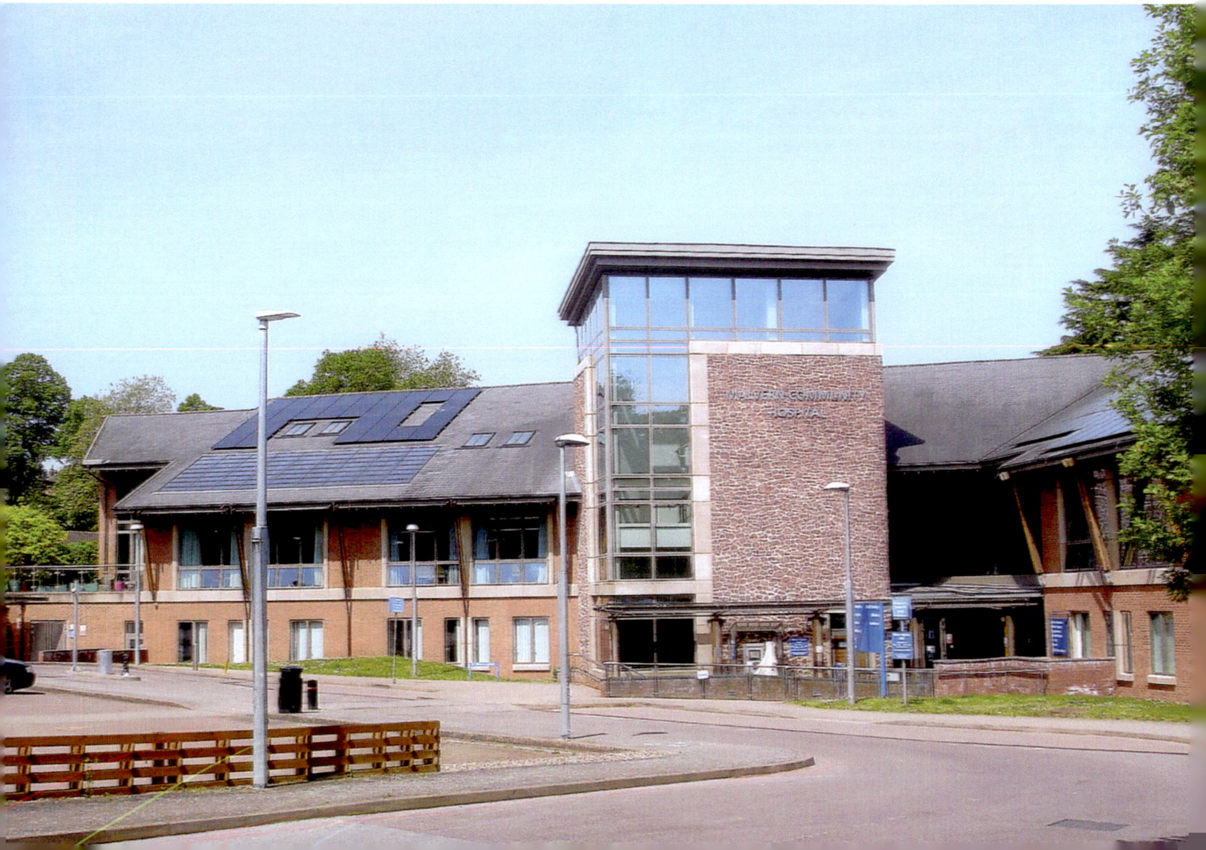

supporting people after surgery or illness when they don't require acute care but can't be treated at home. This is one of seven community hospitals/rehabilitation units across Worcestershire.

The new Community Hospital looks a fairly standard modern building but has some interesting exterior stonework on the outside of the prominent tower. The entrance is enhanced by an unusual sculpture by Peter Yarwood, carved from Portland stone and inspired by the structural patterning of cells in our central nervous system. As with many such stone sculptures people are encouraged to touch and feel the stone's surface.

A fountain once situated in the earlier hospital has been moved to and installed on the first floor of the new building.

Considerable effort has been put into landscaping the surrounds of the hospital including the creation of a Physio Trail that enables physiotherapy staff to carry out rehabilitation work with patients. Since 2011 a horticultural learning area has allowed children from nearby St Matthias Primary School to have lessons in growing fruit and vegetables using a greenhouse and outside beds. The grounds of the hospital are maintained by a Friends group.

Below left: Exterior stonework on Community Hospital Tower.

Below right: Portland stone sculpture by Peter Yarwood at the entrance to Community Hospital.

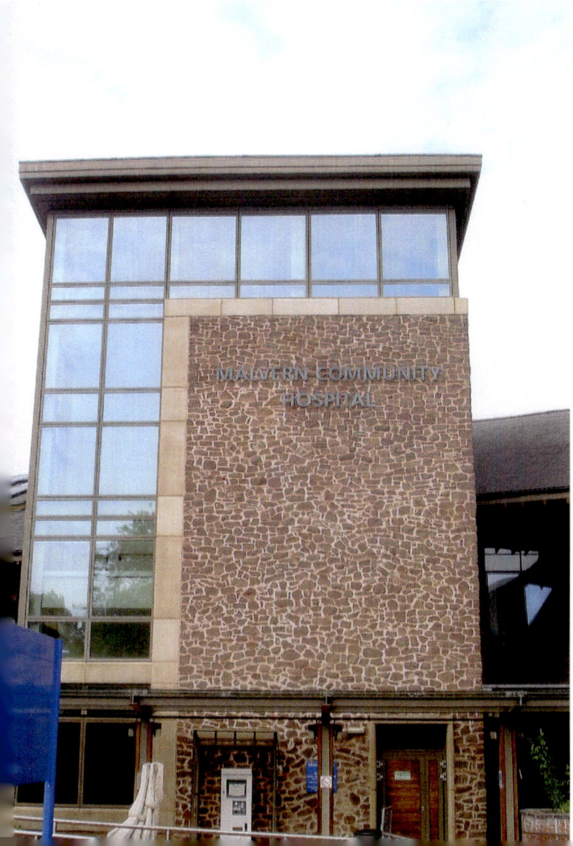

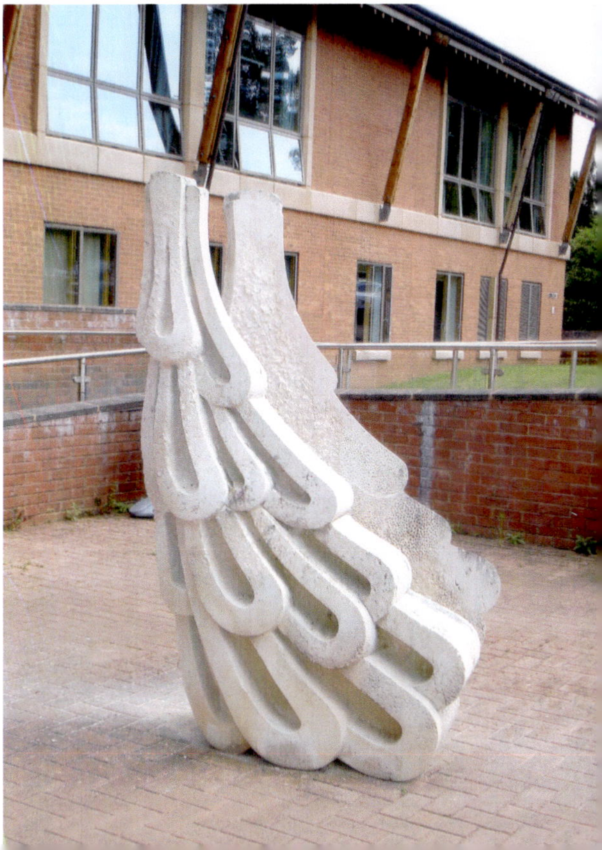

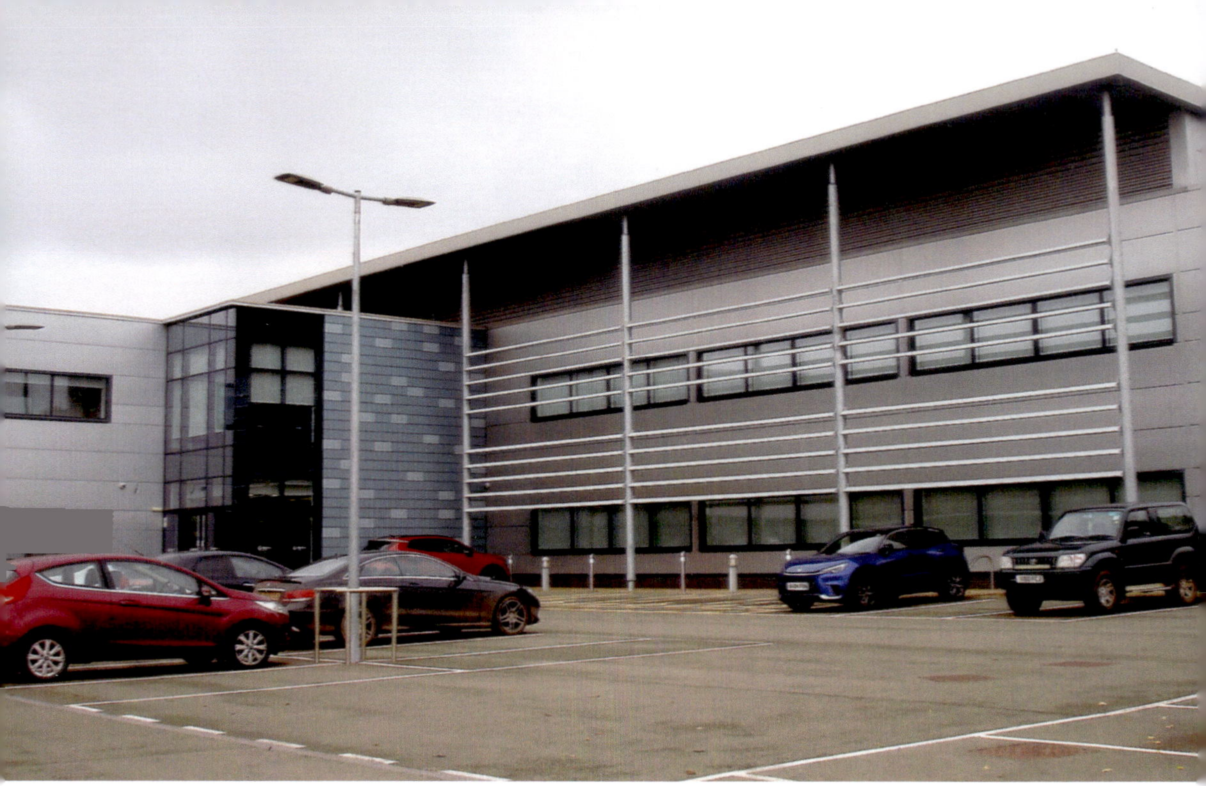

Malvern Hills Science Park Phase Four.

47. Malvern Hills Science Park/Phase Four (2016), Geraldine Road, Malvern, WR14 3SZ

A large unit intended for use by one corporate entity rather than a number of individual businesses by Trebor Developments and Corstophine and Wright, this large grey and silver building has over 25,000 square feet of space and is occupied by a major aerospace and surveillance company of international standing, one of the world's largest suppliers of aerospace and defence products.

48. Malvern Hills Science Park/Phase Five (2019), Geraldine Road, Malvern, WR14 3SZ

The 10 acres of the Malvern Hills Science Park have been gradually filling up with space for more expansion. The most recent addition at the time of writing is known as Phase Five and was established in 2019.

The latest phase contains another 16,000 square feet of space for new companies or existing tenants wanting to expand their operations. Businesses taking up these opportunities are mainly in the tech sector, IT, cyber security, etc. Together the Malvern Technology Centre with the Science Park is creating a technology hub of European-scale importance.

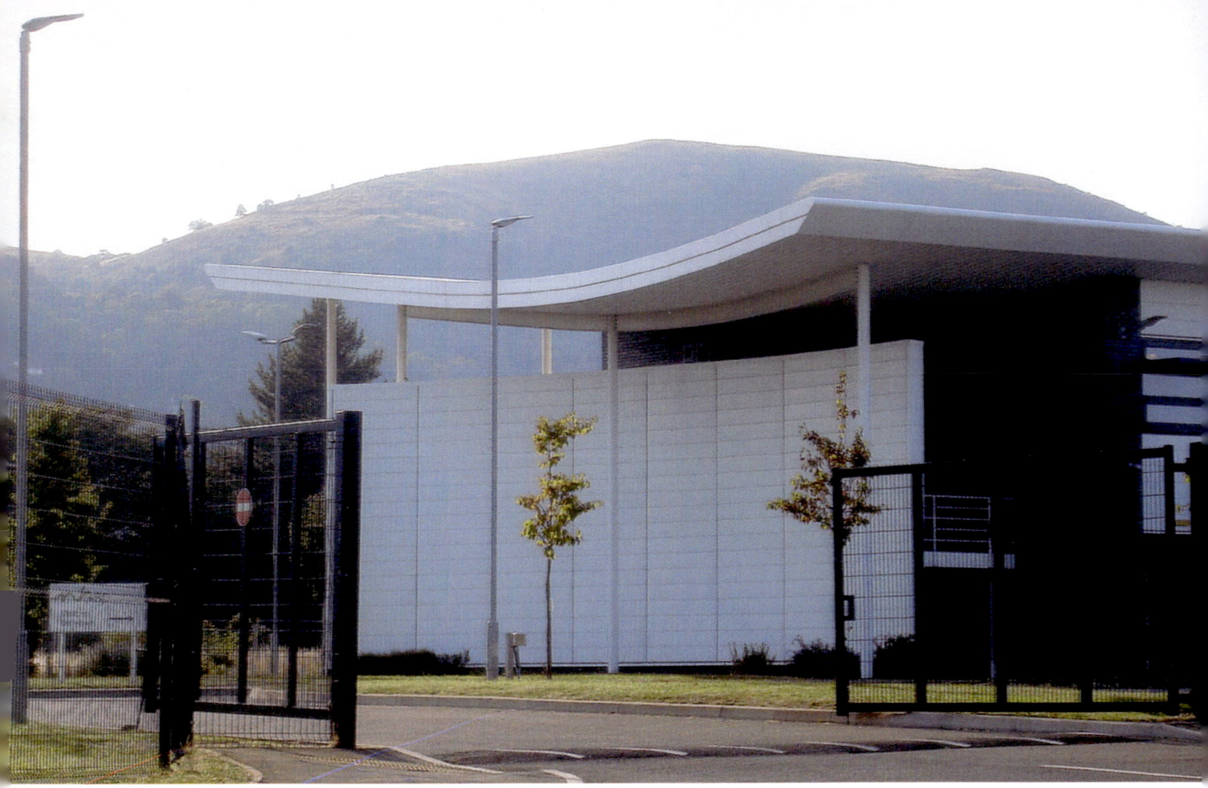

Above: Malvern Hills Science Park's main gate, with Phase Five and the Malvern Hills in the background.

Below: Malvern Hills Science Park Phase Five.

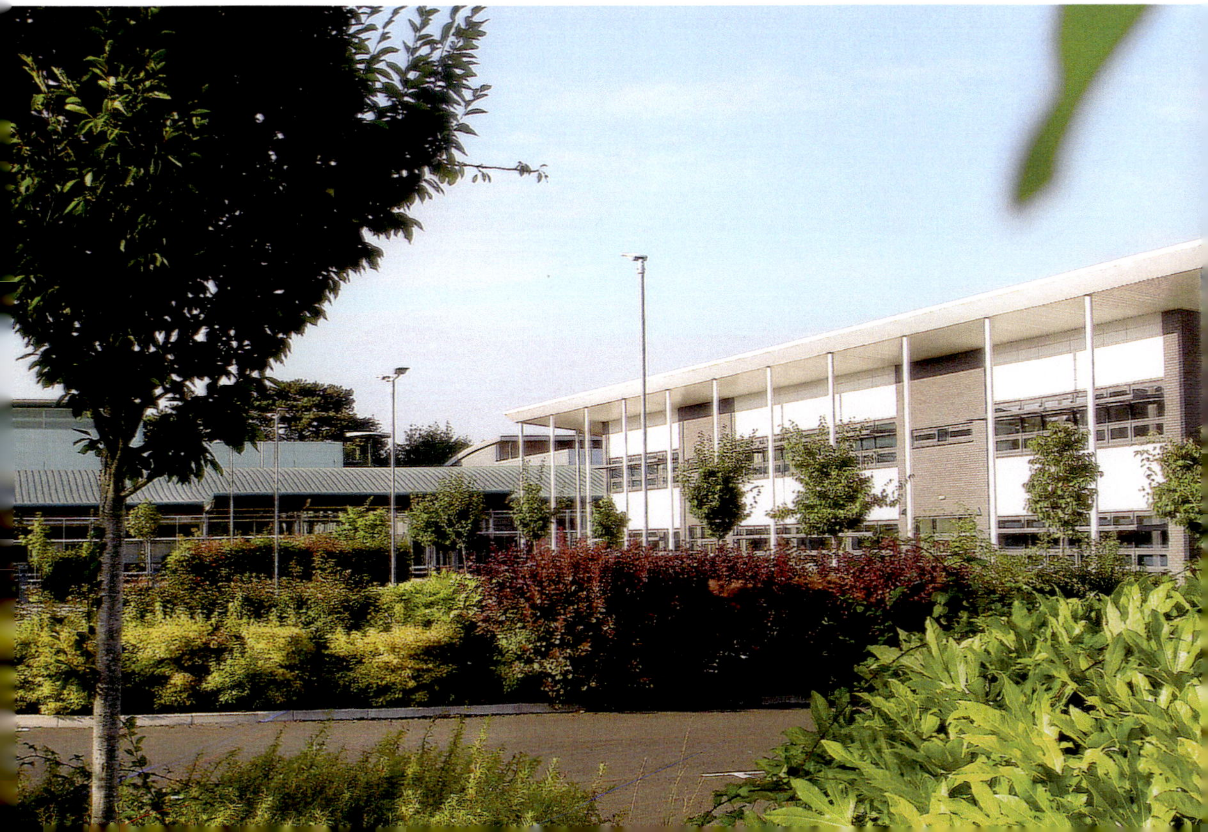

49. Morgan Experience Centre (2020), Spring Lane, Malvern Link, WR14 2LS

For those interested in knowing more about one of Malvern's most iconic creations this is the place to come to. Here you can not only wander around the centre looking at the beautiful cars within the showroom and outside displays, but also shop within the Morgan-themed retail outlet, discuss the cars with staff, use the café or do something more exciting.

How about an 'Experience Drive' in a Morgan car around the Malvern Hills, delivered by an experienced and knowledgeable guide. These usually last for about an hour. You can also hire a Morgan to drive yourself – perhaps the ultimate 'carrot' to encourage you to invest in one. Within the centre itself there are regular tours of the nearby Morgan factory so you can learn about the unique manufacturing process on the production line. Also, over your coffee or snack in the café you can watch a constantly running film of the Morgan story including detailed images of work on the production line. All Morgan vehicles are based around an ash wood frame crafted by hand using traditional woodworking tools. The supply of ash wood comes from a substantial ash forest owned by the Morgan Motor Company that is free from the dreaded 'ash die back' disease that has

The Morgan Experience Centre.

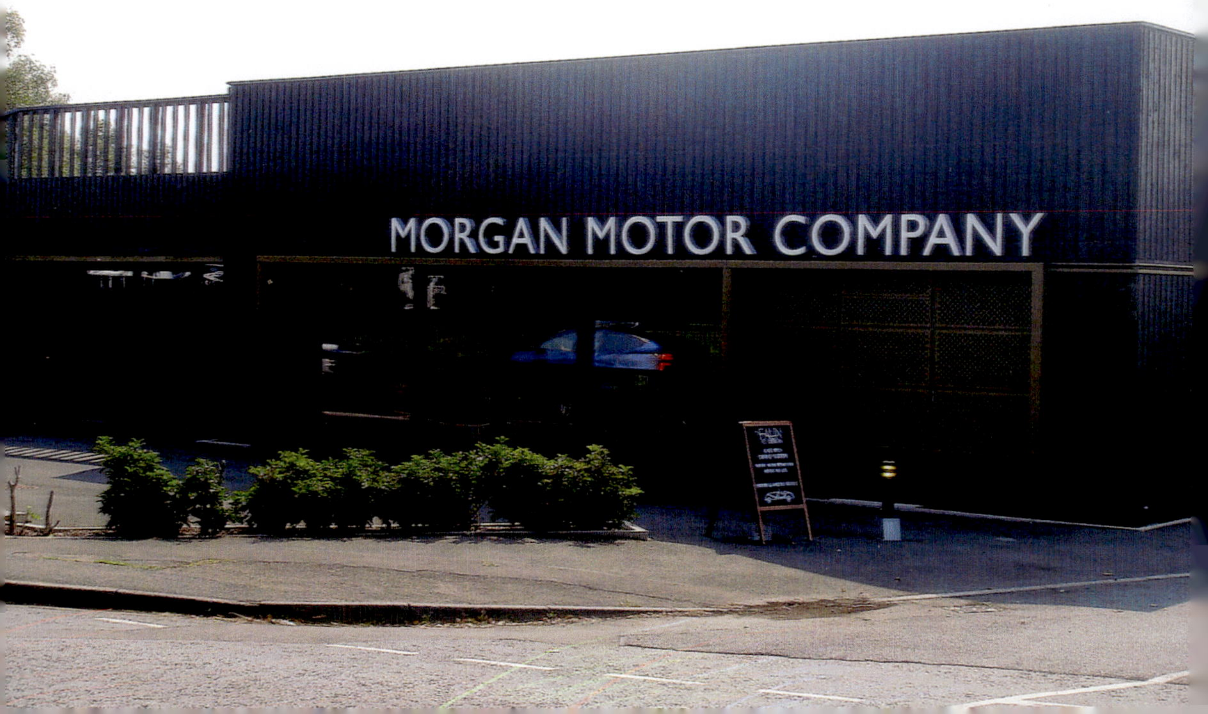

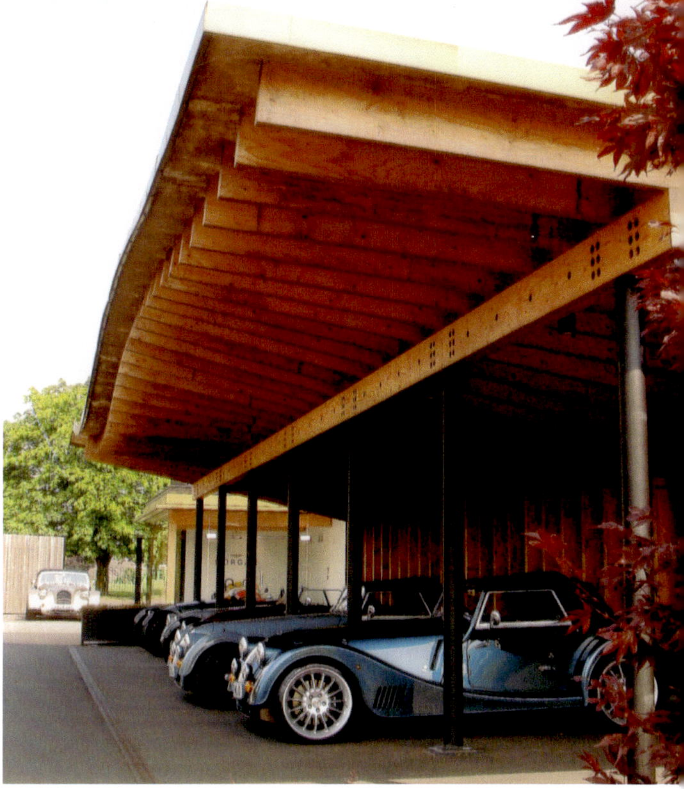

Right: An outside display at the Morgan Experience Centre.

Below: Outside display at the Morgan Experience Centre.

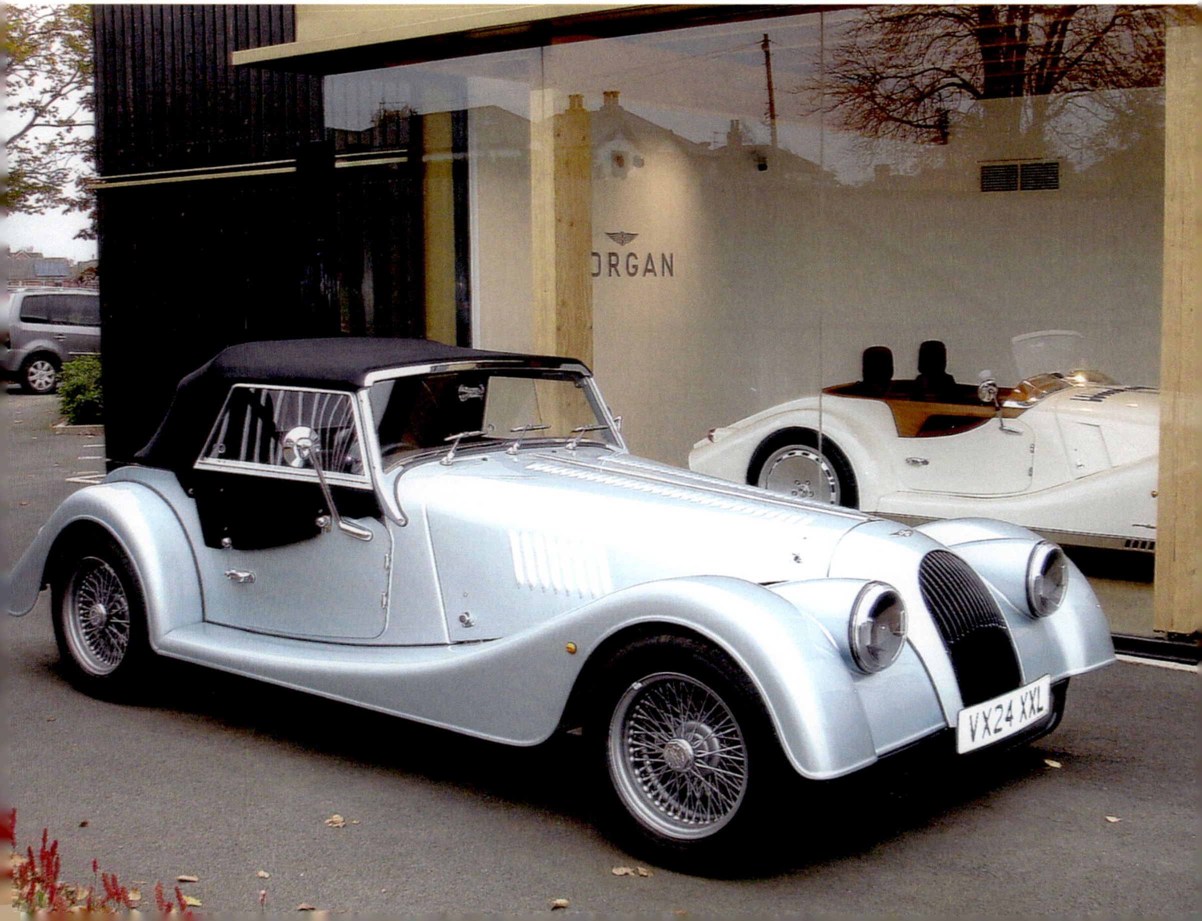

afflicted this tree species. There are enough trees here to keep Morgan production going for many years to come. Around the wooden frame the aluminium car body is hand beaten into shape, a long process to achieve perfection. New models are coming on stream every two years or so, the latest, in 2024, being the Morgan Midsummer.

The complete details on Morgan cars, their manufacture and the Morgan Experience Centre can be found on their website: www.morgan-motor.com.

50. The Community Hub (2024), Victoria Park, Malvern Link, WR14 2JY

Completed in January 2024 and officially opened in August by councillor David Watkins and Mayor Marilyn Birks, the new Community Hub provides a welcome new vibrant space for the people of Malvern Link. This pleasing, green-coloured, single-storey building next to the children's play area in Victoria Park is not

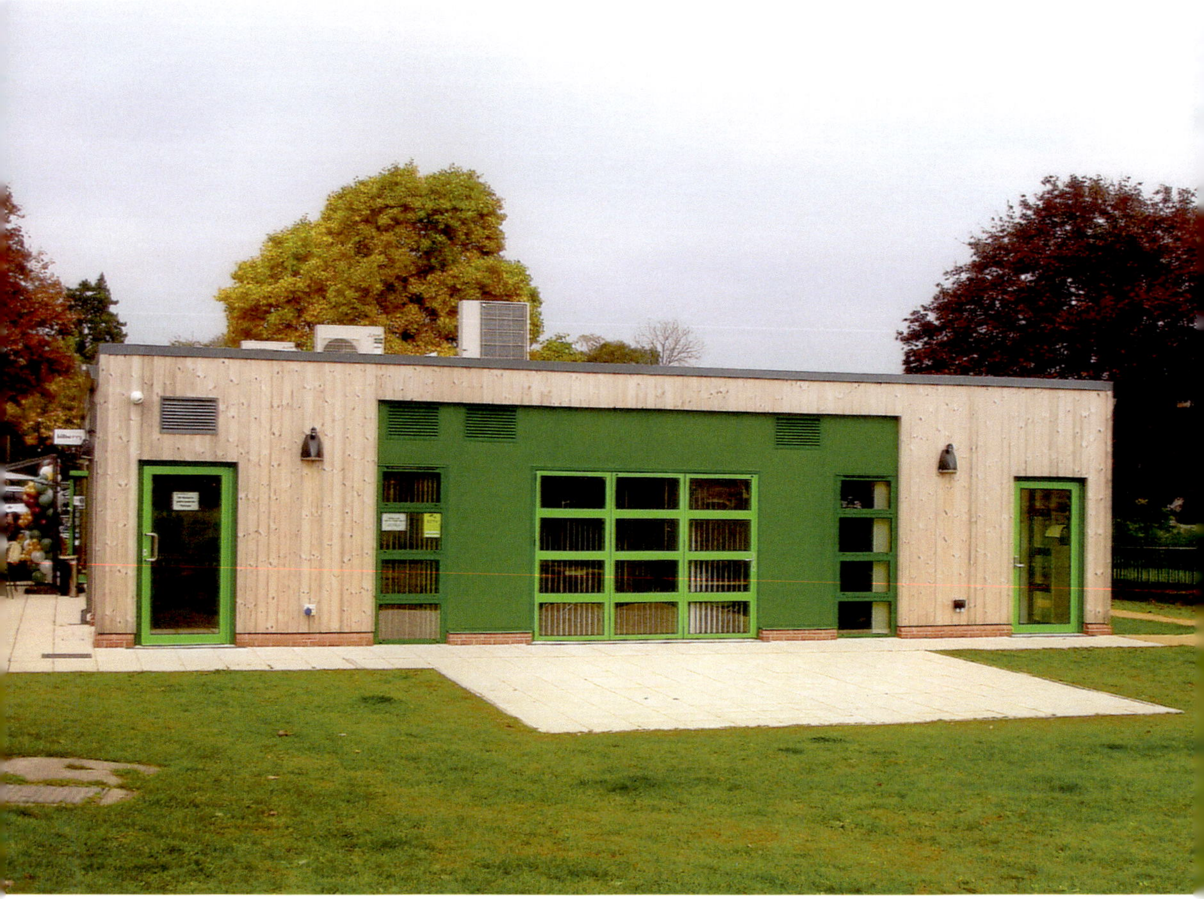

The Community Hub, Malvern Link.

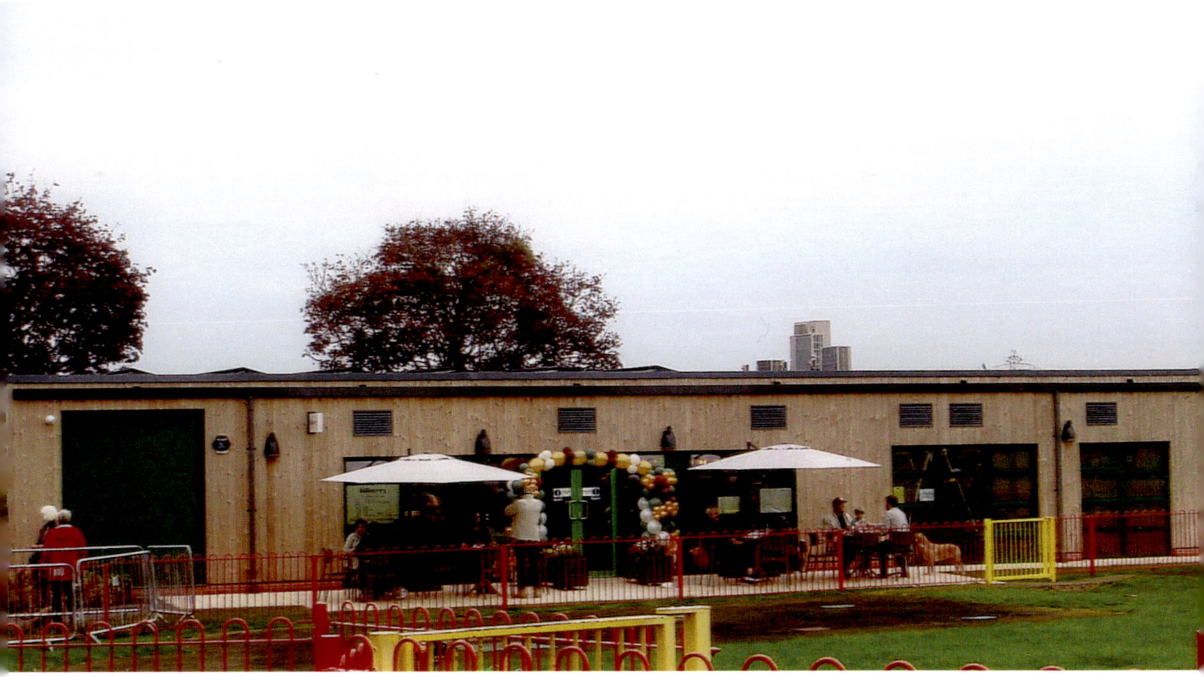

Bilberry Café opening, The Community Hub, Malvern Link.

only the home of Malvern Link Town Council with a staffed reception point on weekdays, but also a range of facilities open all week as well. These include the New Bilberry Café that opened in October 2024 and spaces for hire for meetings, conferences, parties, low-level exercise, or for use by town council-organised events and functions.

Not a grandiose building of architectural or historical importance but one serving a need which in other places and times has been served by the church, the town or village hall or even the local pub, a place that serves the community and what more important role has any building than that?

Bibliography

Brooks, Alan, and Pevsner, Nickolaus, *The Buildings of England: Worcestershire* (New Haven and London: Yale University Press, 2018)

Cockayne, Steve, *Lansdowne Crescent, A History* (Malvern: privately published, 2021)

Condon, Jan, *Malvern in a Day* (Malvern: Aspect Design, 2023)

Goodbury, Valerie, *Malvern Gas Lamps* (Malvern: leaflet privately published, 2010)

Jenkins, Simon, *Discover Britain's Historic Houses Western England* (London: The Readers Digest Association, 2007)

Langland, William, *The Vision of Piers Plowman* (London: Everyman, 1995)

Leech, J., *Three Weeks in Wet Sheets* (Malvern: Hamilton, Adams and Co., 1851)

Little, Katherine, *Tour of Great Malvern Priory* (Malvern: Friends of Great Malvern Priory, 2023)

Osbourne, Bruce, and Weaver, Cora, *Celebrated Springs of the Malvern Hills* (Andover: Phillimore and Co. Ltd, 2012)

Owens, Susan, *Spirit of Place: Artists, Writers and the British Landscape* (London: Thames and Hudson, 2020)

Putley, Ernest, *Science Comes to Malvern: TRE, A Story of Radar 1942–53* (Malvern: Aspect Design, 2009)

Redfern, Roger, *A Boot Up the Malvern Hills* (Wellington, Somerset: PIXYZ, 2014)

Simons, Amanda, *British Camp Herefordshire Beacon* (Birtsmorton, Malvern: Wisteria Books, 2011)

Smith, Peter, *C. S. Lewis, J. R. R. Tolkien and George Sayer: A Memoir by Peter Smith* (Malvern: Aspect Design, 2022)

Stanford, S. C., B.A. PhD. FSA, *The Malvern Hillforts: Midsummer Hill and British Camp* (Malvern: Archaeological Committee of the Malvern Hills Conservators, 1981)

Weaver, Cora, *A Short Guide to Charles Darwin and Evelyn Waugh in Malvern (Life and Death)* (Malvern: Cora Weaver, 2009)

Weaver, Cora, *A Short Guide to Malvern as a Spa Town (The Water Cure)* (Malvern: Cora Weaver, 2016)
Wells, Katherine, *A Tour of the Stained Glass at Great Malvern Priory* (Malvern: Friends of Malvern Priory, 2013)
Whatley, Heather, *Laura Knight in the Malverns* (Malvern: Aspect Design, 2020)
Yorke, Trevor, *Gothic Revival Architecture,* (Oxford: Shire Publications, 2017)

Acknowledgements

Thanks to all who helped me with the preparation of this book with supply of and permission to use images, the provision of information, loan or supply of written materials and general help and advice.

Particular thanks to Paul Bingham, Jan Sedlacek, Katherine Little and the Friends of Great Malvern Priory, Alison Hunka and Sue Johnson of Little Malvern Priory, staff at Malvern Museum of Local History, staff at the Abbey Hotel, Nathan Adams of the Malvern Tourist Information Centre at Lyttelton Well, David Adams, volunteers at The Technology Station, Helen Vose and the Family and Trustees at Madresfield Court, staff at The Morgan Experience Centre, Father Patrick of St Wulstan's Church, Candida Wright for helping to select photographs and Judith Hemmings for typing and helping to prepare the manuscript.

All picture credits appear in the book with the images, and all other photos are by the author.